I0455382

The Singularity and Socialism

Marx, Mises, Complexity Theory, Techno-Optimism
and the Way to the Age of Abundance

C. James Townsend

Email: Center4FutureStudies@live.com
www.TheSingularityandSocialism.com
Facebook: www.facebook.com/TheSingularityandSocialism

ISBN-13: 978-1503034730
ISBN-10: 1503034739

Cover Art

Dedication

I dedicate this work to Gene Roddenberry, creator of *Star Trek*, who inspired so many of us growing up in the 1960's to dream great dreams of humanity's possible technological future and to yearn "To boldly to go where no Man has gone before!" We are on the cusp technologically of the twenty-third century, two centuries early, and we are just beginning to glimpse beyond the coming economic event horizon at the approaching singularity. How you intuited and foresaw so much of it Gene, we will never know.

Acknowledgements

I wish to thank the following individuals for the great help they have offered me on the completion of this project: To Lizzette Rivera for her constant support and encouragement. To Matt Ridley, whose books and videos inspired me greatly. To Kevin Kelly, your ideas on the Technium (in your blog, books and videos) are magnificent. To Peter Diamandis, your new book *Abundance* was truly revolutionary reframing the evidence for the law of increasing returns for a new generation and to Ray Kurzweil, whose championing the visionary ideal of the Singularity is changing the world. I also wish to thank the great minds and intellects who have greatly influenced me throughout my life by my reading their great thoughts: Sir Isaac Newton, F. Bastiat, Thomas Payne, J. B. Say, K. Marx, F. Engels, Roger Garaudy, J.J. Nock, Ludwig von Mises, F.A. Hayek, J. Schumpeter, H. Hazlitt, A. Einstein, Jean F. Revel, Oriana Fallaci, Chantal Delsol, A.J. Galambos, J. Simon, I. Goklany, B. Shaffer, Brian Arthur, Francis Heylighen, Robert Zubrin and the many others whom space will not allow me to mention. I myself realized a long time ago that, "In order to have great thoughts you must read the great minds," and I have had the greatest pleasure throughout my life to read so many of them.

I wish to give a special thank you to Roberta Scarlett and Lee Welter for reading the finished manuscript, and giving me their input, advice and encouragement and editing suggestions. Also to Meghnad Desai and his excellent work *Marx's Revenge* whose book serendipitously fell into my lap during an Amazon search when I was 90 percent done with this book, as well as David Ramsay Steele and his book *From Marx to Mises* which I also stumbled upon when I was near completion. Throughout the writing of this book I had been receiving a hard time from my acquaintances and friends on the progressive as well as the libertarian side who all thought I was crazy. The Libertarian's thought I was crazy being supportive of socialism's humanistic vision and the criticism I received from my left leaning friends about classical liberal economics made me briefly question whether or not my reading of the Marxist controversy from the Austrian School of Economics had possibly influenced my perspective. Both Desai's and Steele's books cured me of those doubts. If an internationally acclaimed Marxian economist of Dr. Desai's stature could support, supplement and uphold my own discoveries, as well as the Austrians in so many places, I knew I was on solid ground. Steele's handling of the Misesean *socialism calculation* debate also further shored up my confidence allowing me to finish this book. I especially also wish to thank my greatest boyhood hero astronaut Neil Armstrong, whose "One Giant Leap for Mankind" will never be forgotten. Neil, may you rest in peace having gained the laurel wreath of the true adventurous hero.

"The challenges humanity sets for itself are those elements within humanity that measure our greatness of spirit. May we always set our sights on achieving the highest possible frontier!"

-C. James Townsend

A Letter of Explanation to My Readers

A majority of this work came from my Masters Project: *Karl Marx, Complexity Theory and the Eventual Convergence of Economic Ideology*, in which I had to get the entire work completed in less than 10 weeks in the fall semester of 2012. The Project ended up being over 180 pages long instead of the 50 pages it was supposed to be, which amounted to my having to write a staggering number of pages a week on average in order to complete it on time. This furious activity made the work read more like a stream of consciousness work than the planned and logically laid out and systematic treatise I had originally planned. In trying to get the Masters Project done I felt that I had left out over 10 chapters of material and hundreds of graphs that I felt needed to be included in order to create the comprehensive manuscript that I had conceived. When I returned to reorganizing and expanding the project into this book the task became a daunting one which would have basically required my rewriting the entire manuscript from scratch. Time, health and monetary concerns precluded that option. So the work you have in your hands, or in your e-reader, is not as organized and logically laid out or as comprehensive as I would have liked it to be. It still has many missing chapters that I feel it needs in order to flesh out its arguments and the issues that arise from them more fully. I have saved them for a forthcoming work.

This is one of those books within which everyone will find something they love within its pages as well as something they don't like as much. Whether you are a: Conservative, Libertarian, Progressive, Leftist, Marxist, Socialist, Techno-optimist, Transhumanist etc., there are things within that will both challenge and excite you. All that I ask of anyone who reads this work is to have an open mind and try to get beyond the baneful rigid psycho sclerosis of today's ideologies. My interest is only in where we can overcome our overly polarized and rigid arguments and come to a common cause where we can invent and create a much better almost "utopian" world for all of humanity. As Buckminster Fuller advised, *"You never change things by fighting the existing reality. To change something, build a new model that makes the existing model obsolete."* That is the goal that this book tries to undertake, to invent a new reality by changing our existing paradigms so that something better can be created that makes the present political and economic systems based on coercion and creating artificial scarcity obsolete.

TABLE OF CONTENTS

List of Tables

List of Figures

"Everything That Rises Must Converge."

Teilhard de Chardin

Foreword

The aim of parousiastic Gnosticism is to destroy the order of be-ing, which is experienced as defective and unjust, and through man's creative power to replace it with a perfect and just order.

-Eric Voegelin

Here at the beginning of the twenty-first century we stand upon a higher peak of scientific and technological discovery that heralds the coming of a new order of being. The world is gripped by two divergent visions of a utopian future for humankind. First: the environmental movement and much of the neo-left wishes to take humanity back to a Rousseauian paradise before the "original sin" of industrialization. The other vision shared by cornucopians, techno-optimists, Singularitans and complexity theorists who portend a futuristic utopia created by exponentially accelerating technologies that will not only transform society and economics, but (as the Transhumanist's theorize) humanity itself. This vision of human transformation coinciding with technological advancement is a heady one, but within it lies another equally compelling vision, a vision of what happens to economics and the means of production on our way to the Singularity's event horizon.

Complexity theory, the foundation of exponential thinking, is breaking apart hardened ideological ground using a new scientific plough; its discoveries are older than the nineteenth century and as fresh as today, with the forceful hurricane winds of a potential utopian futuristic tomorrow. It is a new discipline based on non-linear dynamics and systems proving an *a priori* praxeological science (economics) that had no mathematical mechanism to prove its theoretical assertions before complexity theory's arrival. Classical Liberalism and the Austrian School of Economics was much like the laser, it awaited the invention of fiber optic cable many decades later in order for it to have a practical application and to begin changing the world. Complexity theory and complexity economics is that "fiber optic cable" as it now gives the means by which both Classical Liberalism and the Austrian School can prove their theories. Complexity Economics presently is already well on the way of doing so, while the Austrian School quixotically remains on the sidelines awaiting further developments in the field. The cornucopians and techno-optimists have greatly supported the complexity theorists with their own discoveries. That this area of investigation also confirms and proves Karl Marx's later insight regarding the necessity for "the full evolution of capitalism in order for the revolution to come" (as the Marxist economist Meghnad Desai expounds in his book *Marx's Revenge)*, is one of the amazing coincidences of this emerging co-evolutionary process. That the proving of Marx's insights by the techno-optimists has been unfortunately missed by the neo-left today is one of the tragedies of the pointless battle between ideologies. What divides us is far less important and interesting then what actually unites us and it is in the evolutionary dynamic forces of the Technium that we are slowly coming to the verge of a new era in human development. To paraphrase Teilhard of Chardin's quote at the beginning of this book, "That which evolves eventually converges" is now beginning to happen in our time.

The idea of spontaneous, interrelated, complex, evolutionary systems is centuries old. It took a new field of science to transfer it out of the realm of mysticism into that of empiricism. As it evolves it is uniting together once disparate schools of thought, left, right and center into a new convergent whole. As Butler Shaffer so relevantly states "in a period of significant change, we must be prepared to engage in significant learning, rather than just reaffirming what we already know ... For an individual or a civilization to maintain its sense of vibrancy, a more fundamental kind of learning must be employed: *paradigm breaking.*"[1]

The arising economic data and discoveries from the techno-optimists and Singularitarians indicate that emerging technological advancements will dramatically and exponentially change our world. The emerging technological evolution also indicates that the underlying pattern and framework upon which previously divergent ideologies rested can eventually converge so that once fierce ideological opponents can be reconciled. The study that follows is paradigm breaking in that it presents a way of seeing old paradigms and oppositional economic ideologies in a new synergistic fashion in light of recent discoveries. The techno-optimist Kevin Kelly summarizes this convergent process in the last chapter of his book *What Technology Wants*:

> What I have shown in this book is that a single thread of self-generation ties the cosmos, the bios, and the technos together into one creation. ... Technology is stitching together all the minds of the living, wrapping the planet in a vibrating cloak of electronic nerves, entire continents of machines conversing with one another. ...Technology amplifies the mind's urge toward the unity of all thought, it accelerates the connections among all people, and it will populate the world with all conceivable ways of comprehending the infinite.[2]

Technology is not only tying together the minds of the living, but also of the dead. The great minds of the previous centuries are uniting with those now living, slowly merging into a holism as they converge to a point of transcendence.

It was believed by the Medieval Scholastics that "Truth" was an interrelated jewel in which each facet reflected and conditioned every other part; each element of truth coalesces without any errors and

---

1 Butler Shaffer, *Boundaries of Order: Private Property as a Social System* (Auburn, AL: Ludwig von Mises Institute Press, 2009), 302, 304.
2 Kevin Kelly, *What Technology Wants* (New York: Viking, 2010), 356-359.

contradictions, as any errors and contradictions are *prima fascia* evidence that we don't possess "The Truth." It should then be no surprise that here at the beginning of the twenty-first century we should begin to see the coalescing of various elements within divergent ideologies into a complex whole as the world begins to slowly unite. It is then only natural that our philosophies and ideologies are ripe for unification as well as they begin to burst out of their old defective skins. Teilhard de Chardin intuited this time of convergence now upon us and the new discoveries in science, technology and economics indicate strongly the potential way forward in an arising paradigm of an interrelated networked system. In the words of Teilhard himself:

> Evolution has been weaving its web around us. We believed that we did not change; but now, like infants whose eyes are opening to the light, we are becoming aware of a world in which neo-Time, organizing and conferring a dynamic upon Space, is endowing the totality of our knowledge and beliefs with a new structure and a new direction.[3]

A new structure and a new direction are self-assembling before our eyes as we travel the path toward the future economic event horizon. Buckminster Fuller's *accelerating acceleration* is pushing human civilization there at ever increasing speed as Kevin Kelly's Technium evolves and pushes society up the slope of Ray Kurzweil's exponential curve toward his concept of the coming Singularity, a reimagining of Teilhard de Chardin's *Omega Point.* That so many great minds and visionaries, both religious and secular, throughout the centuries intuited this eschaton, this "Third Age of Humanity," is more than an amazing coincidence. This study is at heart an analysis of this synergistic phenomenon; its intention is best captured by the immortal words of Fichte:

---

3 Pierre Teilhard de Chardin, *The Future of Man* [1959] (New York: Image Books/Doubleday, 2004), 77.

What man of noble mind is there who does not want to scatter, by action or thought, a grain of seed for the unending progress in the perfection of his race, to fling something new and unprecedented into time, that it may remain there and become the inexhaustible source of new creations?[4]

So I scatter the seed of this work onto the winds of our time, hoping that it will take root in many places giving rise to a new evolutionary paradigm which will eventually bring us to the *economic event horizon* of the Singularity. Not only is abundance our future but so is the transcendence of the present economic and political paradigms which keep us locked into old 19th century neo-Malthusian scarcity thought. The arising techno-optimist paradigm bursts this static penury of the mind caused by our old ways of perception and opens our spirits up to the fullness and abundance which the human imagination and spirit is capable of achieving. *Homo Futuris* is right around the corner and ready to embrace us, we have only to leave the cave of our old limited ways of thinking to embrace her, to become her, to walk with her as our Dantesque guide on a new exponential journey through the event horizon of the coming singularity to our incredible and almost unimaginable abundant future in the heavens.

---

4 Johann G. Fichte, "What is a People in the Higher Meaning of the Word, and What is Love of Fatherland," in *European Romanticism: A Brief History with Documents*, ed. Warren Breckman (New York: Bedford/St Martin's, 2008), 115.

Introduction

"A specter is haunting Europe-the specter of Communism."[5] So wrote Karl Marx in the opening page of the *Communist Manifesto*, a revolutionary literary work that went on to have a profound effect on the world. There is a similar specter haunting the world today. That new specter is the specter of *Complexity Theory*, which holds as much, if not more, societal, political and economic upheaval and change as communism ever did in its heyday. This theory has gone from a little known scientific fringe before the 1980's to an upstart and dangerous "heterodoxy" threatening the prevailing established political, economic and societal paradigms of our time. Like all new scientific discoveries this arising paradigm shift has been ignored for most of the twentieth century, but as its discoveries and theories begin to seep into mainstream science and slowly into public consciousness, a dramatic paradigm shift is beginning to take place. As the Chaos theorist James Gleick reminds us, "shallow ideas can be assimilated; ideas that require people to re-organize their picture of the world provoke hostility."[6] This book itself will be one of those instances where hostility may well be provoked, as it requires one to change one's thinking and picture of the world.

---

5 Karl Marx, *The Communist Manifesto*, ed. Frederic L. Bender (New York: W. W. Norton & Company, Inc., 1988), 54.
6 James Gleick, *Chaos: Making a New Science* (New York, NY: Penguin, 1987), 38.

The once firm citadels of our monolithic ideologies are beginning to crack and I predict many will eventually crumble to be replaced by a more holographic paradigm. Evolutionary forces are strongly working to dialectically break apart our petrified, overly static, steady state and equilibrium based concepts founded upon older Cartesian and Newtonian reductionist and mechanistic views of the universe, an outdated parochial world view. Systems theory is now forcing us to realize as the ancient Greek philosopher Heraclitus did centuries ago, "that we cannot step into the same river twice" and that everything is in constant flux. Systems theory has become a viral meme lacing together various paradigms in fascinating and interesting ways allowing Singularitarians, Techno-optimists, cornucopians, techno-libertarians, and even older Marxists to slowly converge in this arising paradigm. Complexity theory and especially *complexity economics* has now uncovered and unveiled for the entire world to see the force which we as a species have been trying to put a name to and come to understand for millennia. Karl Marx's older term for this underlying dynamo of historical development—*the productive material forces*—has given way to Kevin Kelly's new theory of the *Technium*.[7] In this synergistic milieu the works of Julian Simon, Bjorn Lomborg, and Indur Goklany have supported and merged with the research of Matt Ridley, Kevin Kelly, Peter Diamandis, Ramez Naam and Ray Kurzweil to meld and surprisingly and even shockingly to support and prove the evolutionary outlook to be found in the later works of Karl Marx.

It is finally with *complexity theory* and *complexity economics* that we can begin to discern a new phenomenon that is now emerging in the world as well, that process is the eventual convergence of many divergent

---

7 Kevin Kelly describes the Technium as: "a difference engine. It is a machine, so to speak, that is manufacturing more and more extreme versions of structures: artifacts that burn hotter than any life, or run faster than any life, or stretch further than any life. The technium is exploiting the sink of entropy to build persistent disequilibrial clumps of matter and energy that have never before been seen in the universe. New potentials and differences. Different differences. And as long as the universe keeps expanding, technology is ordained to keep differentiating. What the technium creates is difference." Kelly, Kevin, "The Cosmic Genesis of Technology," *The Technium* (blog), January 23, 2009, http://www.kk.org/thetechnium/archives/2009/01/the_cosmic_gene. php.

ideologies in an almost Teilhardian *omega point.* In the vision of Ray Kurzweil it is a Singularity where humanity and technology co-evolve and merge, transforming humanity into a new transhuman entity. The Promethean and Protean dream of humanity, once so prevalent among classical liberal, socialist and communist intellectuals, now seems to be on the cusp of being realized as envisioned by the Transhumanist's. It is theorized by these technological trailblazers that with the exponential rise of science and technology an incredible transformation in economics and society will also develop and the driving force of all this change is scientific and technologically advancing *exponential capitalism.* The ever "increasing acceleration of the rate of acceleration" intuited by Buckminster Fuller bodes that a time is near when the forces of production will split apart the present "capitalist" system and a new system will arise from it transcending the old.

1

A Very Very Brief History of Evolutionary Dynamic Thinking

There is nothing permanent except change.
-Heraclitus

The ancient Greeks intuited the concept of evolution. As mentioned above, Heraclitus was one of the first Greek Philosophers to ponder upon and write about evolutionary concepts in his philosophy. Aristotle, who came after Heraclitus, also expressed the idea that all animal species evolved from less evolved ancestors. Western Civilization in rediscovering the ancient Greek philosophers in the Renaissance did much to bring these ideas into Western Europe. An Eastern influx of philosophical ideas into Europe has now been recognized by historians in the latter half of the twentieth century. The Chinese Taoist and Confucian classics entered Europe via the Catholic Church's missionaries to China beginning in the 13th century and had a revolutionary effect as well on the intelligentsia of the late Medieval and early modern period.

The other fertile strain that was to dramatically shape European philosophy and scientific thought was the influx of the Corpus Hermeticum, rediscovered and retranslated, which entered Europe in the twelfth century and went on to influence three great fields of spiritual thought: Catholic Mysticism, Jewish Cabbalism, and Hermeticism. Few today want to discover that the teacher of the great scholastic Thomas Aquinas, Albertus Magnus, was a Hermetic Philosopher, or that Hermeticism and alchemy played a great role in influencing such notable thinkers as Roger Bacon, Leibnitz, Isaac Newton, Goethe and Hegel, or that magical and mystical theories influenced such movements as the Romantics, Socialists, Modernists and the Russian Cosmists which all went on to influence the more well-known Teilhard of Chardin. These mystical ideas became an integral part of the European philosophical tradition and the Enlightenment and even went on to influence the classical liberal economic and political philosophers.

All of the elements were now present in the Western and Eastern European intellectual alembic to produce the golden philosophical elixir which would ripen at the end of the eighteenth century and blossom forth in the Romantic Movement and German Ideal Philosophy with its inherent reaction to Cartesian and Newtonian mechanistic thinking and its adoption of a meliorist, evolutionary and dialectical conception of the universe (In the 19th century Marx and the Russian Cosmists carried on the gnostic Promethean tradition, which the Transhumanists are doing today). By the end of the 18th century these ideas had ripened sufficiently so that the stage was now set for the creation of one of the most influential books on economics and social organization to be written, Adam Smith's *The Wealth of Nations*, the first economic systems theorist's exposition on spontaneous order in the field of economics.[8]

---

8 Note: I would have loved to go more deeply into the rich history of the mystical tradition showing its influence on: philosophy, science, economics, socialism and Transhumanism, but time did not allow.

2

Adam Smith; Founder of All Economic Schools and His Great Value Blunder

Science is the great antidote to the poison of enthusiasm and superstition.

-ADAM SMITH

Murray Rothbard, the Austrian economist, in his *Economic Thought before Adam Smith*[9] cites Alexander Gray, a Scottish historian of economics, about Smith's universal influence on the schools of economic thought that came after him, "it is a tribute to the greatness of Smith that all schools of [economic] thought may trace to him their origin and interpretation."[10] Though Smith is commonly considered merely the promulgator of conservative economic ideas, insightful economic historians consider Adam Smith the grandfather of all modern economics: Conservative, classical liberal, libertarian and even socialist. As Murray Rothbard relates,

It is then from the Whiggish pages of the *Wealth of Nations* that the doctrines of the English socialists as well as the theoretical exposition

---

9 Murray Rothbard, *Economic Thought before Adam Smith, Vol. 1* (Auburn, AL: Edward Elgar Publishing, 2006).
10 Ibid., 460.

of Karl Marx, spring. The history of social thought furnishes many instances where theories elaborated by one writer have been taken over by others to justify social doctrines antagonistic to those to which the promulgator of the theory gave adherence. But had the gift of prevision been granted to those men, few would have been more startled than Adam Smith in seeing himself as the theoretical founder of the doctrines of nineteenth-century socialism.[11]

It is this forgotten fact that Adam Smith is the unrecognized foundation from which all economic systems arise that gives me a basis of much hope for a rapprochement of ideologies in the ever rising evolution of the present system. Karl Marx's entire system of economics as formulated in *Das Kapital* was highly influenced and founded upon one of Smith's later English adherents David Ricardo and his popular work *On the Principles of Political Economy and Taxation* printed in 1817.

All of the economic fallacies of later *neo-classical* economics were also founded upon Ricardo's and Smith's works, which according to Rothbard actually set economic theory back nearly two centuries and which unfortunately sent Karl Marx down the wrong path of value:

Paul Douglas properly with rare insight noted that Marx was ... simply a Smithian-Ricardian trying to work out the [labor] theory of his masters:

Marx has been berated by two generations of orthodox economists for his [labor] value theory. The most charitable of the critics have called him a fool and the most severe have called him a knave for what they deem to be transparent contradictions of his theory. Curiously enough these very critics generally commend Ricardo and Adam Smith very highly. Yet the sober facts are that Marx saw more clearly than any English economist the differences between the labor-cost and the labor-command theories and tried more earnestly

---

11   Ibid., 456.

than anyone else to solve the contradictions which the adoption of a labor-cost theory inevitably entailed. He failed of course: but with him Ricardo and Smith failed as well....The failure was a failure not of one man but of a philosophy of value, and the roots of the ultimate contradiction made manifest, in the third volume of *Das Kapital*, lie embedded in the first volume of the *Wealth of Nations*.[12]

The Marxist economist Meghnad Desai explains further the historical situation and the problem Marx was trying to solve based on the labor value fallacies of Smith and Ricardo:

Wages were determined by the subsistence cost of labour, and rent was pure surplus. But how are profits determined? Neither Smith nor Ricardo had much to say about this. All they could say was that profit rates were equalized across sectors. But regardless of that equality, it was unclear how the level of the profit rate was determined.

Marx saw this as the major unresolved problem of political economy. Classical political economy had proposed a theory of value: the labour theory of value. This had seemed to provide a satisfactory theory of price determination. So if price was determined by labor values and wages by the subsistence cost of producing labourers, could not profits be consistently explained in this framework?... Classical political economy had a labor theory of price, but not a labor theory of either wages or profits. If the labor content of a good explained its price (as all economists seemed to have agreed by then), why couldn't there be a labour theory of wages, why should profits be thought to be residual, and not integrated within a single theory of value?[13]

---

12 Ibid., 454.
13 Meghnad Desai, *Marx's Revenge*, (New York, NY: Verso, 2004), 55. N.B. This is a great book, I highly recommend it.

This is the task which Karl Marx set for himself, but his training in philosophy did not give him a strong enough foundation in the early discipline of economics when he:

> Used a well-known device in political economy to make his breakthrough. Every commodity had two kinds of value: value in use (use value) and value in exchange (exchange value). Price was a monetary expression of exchange value; thus the labor theory of value was a theory of exchange value. Things were sold at their exchange value, but bought by the buyer for their value in use... Labour-power as a commodity had its exchange value (wages) but it also had its use value... Marx had therefore cracked the basic issue of providing a single theory of prices, wages and profits. The separation of the exchange value and use value of labour-power, and their commensurate quantitative measurement, was central to his breakthrough.[14]

Marx, following his training in philosophy and the early economic philosophers, thought that profits arose from the difference between *use value* and *exchange value*, the same way philosophers used to think that there was a difference between essence and substance. By keeping the wage subsistence theory of Ricardo he extrapolated the idea that the difference between profits and wages was thus *surplus value*, a value that is expropriated from the laborer by the capitalist, making all profits then coming out of capitalist exploitation. There is one glaring problem in Marx's entire economic analysis though as products which have no use value also have no exchange value and thus no price. Marx himself mentions this situation in the first chapter of the first volume of *Capital* where he discusses commodities when he said:

---

14 Ibid, 56.

[L]astly, nothing can have value, without being an object of utility. If the thing is useless, so is the labour contained in it; the labour does not count as labour, and therefore creates no value."[15]

Marx now has an incredible problem in the very first chapter of his Magnum Opus as he himself opened the door to the subjective theory of value[16] later discovered by Carl Menger, as "how can that which has no utility, also have no value, once it has had labor infused into it?" As all utility, or use values are in the minds of human beings and every human being values things differently, all values are thus ultimately subjective and heterogeneous. So only the subjective theory of value then describes how value can "magically" vanish from objects which have no utility regardless of the amount of labor that was put into them. As the New Left author David Ramsay Steele states about this theory's trouble for Marx:

> The marginal productivity theory of distribution was developed by a number of writers around the end of the 19th century, notably Wicksteed and Clark.[17] This beautiful theory is empirically well corroborated as at least a good approximation to the truth in most instances, and definitively solves a swarm of theoretical niggles that beset earlier economists. The theory completely undermines the concerns that led Marx to develop his theory of surplus value. ... One of the many fateful consequences of marginal productivity is that it sweeps away such theories as Marx's which sees interest as consisting of 'unpaid labor'. Under competitive market conditions, a worker tends to be paid what his labor contributes to output, no more and no less. The same goes for the owner of the machine or a piece of real estate. The analysis demonstrates the symmetry of all types of inputs: there is as much sense as saying that capital exploits

---

15   Karl Marx, *Capital, A Critique of Political Economy*. Edited by Frederick Kautsky, (Chicago: Charles H. Kerr & Co., 1909). 32. http://oll.libertyfund.org/title/965.
16   More generally known as the marginal utility theory or marginal productive theory of value.
17   Carl Menger is credited with the original discovery.

labor as in saying that labor exploits capital, or that electricity exploits roofing tiles.[18]

And as F.A. Hayek cogently mentioned:

Marxian economics is still today attempting to explain highly complex orders of interaction in terms of single causal effects like mechanical phenomena rather than as prototypes of those self-ordering processes which give us access to the explanation of highly complex phenomena. It deserves mention however that, as Joachin Reig has pointed out (in his Introduction to the Spanish translation of E. von Bohm-Bawerk's essay on Marx's theory of exploitation (1976)), it would seem that after learning of the works of Jevons and Menger [on subjectivity theory], Karl Marx himself completely abandoned further work on *Capital*. If so, his followers were evidently not so wise as he.[19]

This contention is held by many economists and historians. Marx had volumes II and III of *Capital* basically ready to go to press but spent the last decade or more of his life sitting on them. He defended himself against bourgeois economists who "didn't understand his work" in private letters, but didn't bother to release the remaining volumes as he had promised he would. It was up to Engels to publish them posthumously.

The other major issue that this philosophically based bicameral theory of value has is that it violates Ockham's Razor. In simplest terms Ockham's Razor states that, "entities must not be multiplied beyond necessity," or translated more clearly, "It states that among competing hypotheses, the hypothesis with the fewest assumptions should be selected."[20] A theory of value that is overly complex and has too many parts to it thus must be rejected if a competing hypothesis has fewer as-

---

18 David Ramsay Steele, *From Marx to Mises* (La Salle, IL: Open Court Press, 1992), 141-43.
19 F.A. Hayek, *The Fatal Conceit: The Errors of Socialism*, (Chicago, IL: University of Chicago Press, 1988), 150.
20 Ockham's Razor, http://en.wikipedia.org/wiki/Occam%27s_razor.

sumptions and fits the facts, which the Subjective Theory of Value does. As Hayek succinctly stated:

> Classical political economy broke down mainly because it failed to base its explanation of the fundamental phenomenon of value on the same analysis of the springs of economic activity which it had so successfully applied to the analysis of the more complex phenomena of competition. The labor theory of value was the product of a search after some illusory substance of value rather than an analysis of the behavior of the economic subject. The decisive step in the progress of economics was taken when economists began to ask "what exactly were the circumstances which made individuals behave toward goods in a particular way."' To ask the question in this form led immediately to the recognition that to attach a definite significance or value to the units of different goods was a necessary step in the solution of the general problem which arises everywhere when a multiplicity of ends compete for a limited quantity of means.[21]

Once this truly unifying theory of subjective value was accepted the last hold outs for the labor theory of value of the classical economists came crashing down and along with it Marx's entire theoretical economic solution based on Hegelian alienation. All of which is based on the philosophical bifurcation of use values and exchange values. One value now accounted for all valuations, which is what science demands of a valid theory and hypothesis. This should have been apparent from the start as both classical liberal economics and Marx's thinking were praxeologically based. That economists missed the subjective basis of value for so long is a derivative of philosophy's continuing baneful influence over the natural sciences of the 19th century.

The labor theory of value created innumerable problems in economic theory for Classical Economics for which there was no way out, other than

---

21   F.A. Hayek, *Individualism and the Economic Order*, [1948] (Chicago, IL: University of Chicago Press, 1980), 136.

to eventually abandon it, which they did beginning in the late 1820's and by the 1870's it was finished. Marx's mighty struggle to correct the errors and gaps that arose from the labor value theory was laudable, but in the end futile as Marx's philosophical training led him to keep the bifurcation of values in classical economics while at the same time trying to come up with a unified theory of value which explained prices, wages and profits. He had a contradiction in his system from the very beginning which was irreconcilable, which he had inherited from Ricardo and Smith. The Subjective Theory of Value was staring him in the face all along, but like Ptolemy before him, he took as axiomatically proven the value theory of his economic progenitors, which made him overly complicate his system in order to explain the real world situations he saw before him. No matter how mightily he constructed his theories and how many gyrations he went through to make his "math" fit the observations of the heavens, while faithfully keeping to the false paradigm of those who came before him, in the end it was as futile for him as it was for Ptolemy.

In the play of economic history Carl Menger was to play Copernicus and Bohm-Bulwark Galileo and the Ptolemaic value system of the classical economists and Marx, was refuted for all time. Today only ardent "religious" Marxists still cling to the labor theory of value in a futile attempt to keep the "true faith" alive, yet in doing so they eventually betray Marxism, as Marx himself wanted a *scientific socialism* not a "true faith" filled with "true believers" with himself cast as the omnipotent infallible Old Testament prophet. Even such an incredibly intelligent and brilliant Marxian economist as Meghnad Desai, in writing a book that challenges the basic premises and revisionism of neo-Marxism, incomprehensibly keeps to the labor theory of value. We need to recognize that the labor theory of value is nothing but a totem fetish consciousness arising from humanity's primitive stage of seeing objects imbued with "magical and mythical forces." We cannot move forward into Futurity unless and until we also give up primitive ways of thinking. The ideological "burning in the bosom" of a true faith does not give us the vision necessary to see the way forward to the coming economic singularity. We must remember one of the most important things about Marxism, as the Marxist author John Molyneux himself stated:

> Marxism is, as Engels said, 'not a dogma, but a guide to action', that it must be a living, developing theory, capable of continuous growth, which has to analyze and respond to an ever changing reality–a reality which has in fact changed enormously since Marx's day. Even if, for historical reasons, naming the theory after the individual who did most to establish it, we cannot, at the price of total impotence, reduce or confine it to what that individual himself wrote. As Trotsky observed, 'Marxism is above all a method of analysis-not analysis of texts but analysis of social relations.'[22]

And as the French Communist and author Roger Garaudy stated:

> To be Marxist or Leninist is not to apply Marx's or Lenin's analysis to radically different circumstances in which they have ceased to be valid. Rather it is to make use of their method of research in order to find new historical initiatives."[23]

Marxism, to be like all scientific theories, must be open to evolution, change, refutation and new discoveries. It must never become a catechism set in stone at one extreme of the spectrum, or totally thrown out completely as nonsense and fantasy at the other extreme by postmodern neo-socialists and the neo-leftist catechetical thinking of today which is light years away from a scientific approach, especially where it agrees with other schools of thought.

My citing the problems and issues above is not to solely go into the foundational errors and problems with Classical and Marxian economics. It is instead to lay the foundations to eventually bring out the issues

---

22 John Molyneux, *What is the Real Marxist Tradition*, (Chicago, Haymarket Books, 2003), page 8.
23 Roger Garaudy, *The Crisis in Communism, The Turning Point of Socialism*, (New York, NY: Grove Press Inc.,1969), 68.

which lead to the inherent cross fertilization and co-foundational elements in today's economic ideologies as I believe that we are fast approaching, with the help of nonlinear complexity theory, a convergence of ideology's which will make the old battles between right and left meaningless and pointless. As Lew Rockwell stated from Ayn Rand so perceptively:

> The doctrine of liberty contains elements corresponding with both [the] contemporary left and right. This means in no sense that we are middle-of-the-roaders, eclectically trying to combine, or step between, both poles; but rather that a consistent view of liberty includes concepts that have also become part of the rhetoric or program of [the] right and of [the] left. Hence a creative approach to liberty must transcend the confines of contemporary political shibboleths.[24]

It is where the various ideologies agree and coalesce that they are the most fascinating and insightful, and not where they continually bicker and disagree, where we unfortunately spend too much of our time focusing on, that matters most. In the next chapter I shall enter upon the discussion of Adam Smith's works which I believe is relevant to complexity theory and its vision of evolutionary complex processes.

---

24 Llewellyn H. Rockwell, *The Left, The Right, & The State* (Auburn, AL: Ludwig von Mises Institute Press, 2008), 219.

3

Adam Smith and the Invisible Hand: Early Systems Thinking

Without the assistance and co-operation of many thousands, the very meanest person in a civilized country could not be provided, even according to, what we very falsely imagine, the easy and simple manner in which he is commonly accommodated.

-ADAM SMITH

Adam Smith's most famous passage from his *Wealth of Nations* has caused much debate and inspired a tremendous amount of research, when he wrote in 1776:

> He [the merchant] generally indeed neither intends to promote the public interest, nor knows how much he is promoting it. By preferring the support of domestic to that of foreign industry, he intends ... only his own gain, and he is in this, as in many other cases, led by an *invisible hand* to promote an end which was no part of his intention. Nor is it always the worse for the society that it was no part of it. By pursuing his own interest he frequently promotes that of the society more effectively than when he really intends to promote it. I have

never known much good done by those who affected to trade for the public good.[25]

Smith in many parts of his great work mentions the unintended results of individual's actions. Ralph Raico in his, "The Rise, Fall, and Renaissance of Classical Liberalism," sums up the milieu that the eighteenth century intellectuals were immersed in:

> In the 18th century, thinkers were discovering a momentous fact about social life: given a situation where men enjoyed their natural rights, society more or less ran itself. In Scotland, a succession of brilliant writers that included David Hume and Adam Smith outlined the theory of the spontaneous evolution of social institutions. They demonstrated how immensely complex and vitally useful institutions –language, morality, the common law, and above all the market– originate and develop not as the product of the designing minds of social engineers, but as the result of the interactions of all the members of society pursuing their individual goals.[26]

Norman Barry describes the theory of spontaneous order in more depth:

> Despite the complexity of the social world, which seems to preclude the existence of regularities which can be established by empirical observation, there is a hypothetical order which can be reconstructed out of the attitudes, actions, and opinions of individuals and which has considerable explanatory power. What is important about the theory of spontaneous order is that the institutions and practices it investigates reveal well-structured social patterns, which appear to be a product of some omniscient designing mind yet which are in reality the spontaneous coordinated outcomes of the actions of, possibly,

---

25 Adam Smith, *The Wealth of Nations: An Inquiry into the Nature and Causes of,* [1776] (Washington, DC: Regnery Publishing, 1998), 513.
26 Ralph Raico, "The Rise, Fall, and Renaissance of Classical Liberalism," Ludwig von Mises Institute (August 23, 2010), http://mises.org/daily/4600.

millions of individuals who had no intention of effecting such overall *aggregate* orders. The explanations of such social patterns have been, from Adam Smith onwards, commonly known as 'invisible hand' explanations since they refer to that process by which "man is led to promote an end which was no part of his intention." It is a major contention of the theory of spontaneous order that the aggregate structures it investigates are the outcomes of the actions of *individuals.* In this sense spontaneous order is firmly within the tradition of methodological individualism. ... The theory of spontaneous order, then, is concerned with those 'natural processes' which are not the product of reason or intention. The classic example is the free market economy in which the co-ordination of the aims and purposes of countless actors, who cannot know the aims and purposes of more than a handful of their fellow-citizens, is achieved by the mechanism of prices. A change in the price of a commodity is simply a signal which feeds back information into the system enabling actors to 'automatically' produce that spontaneous co-ordination which appears to be the product of an omniscient mind. The repeated crises in dirigiste[27] systems are in essence crises of information since the abolition of the market leaves the central planner bereft of that economic knowledge which is required for harmony. There is no greater example of the hubris of the constructivist than in this failure to envisage order in a natural process (which is not of a directly physical kind).

Hayek echoes this line of reasoning in his "*Principles of a Liberal Social Order*":

> Much of the opposition to a system of freedom under general laws arises from the inability to conceive of an effective co-ordination of human activities without deliberate organization by a commanding intelligence. One of the achievements of economic theory has been to explain how such a mutual adjustment of the

---

27 Dirigiste: economic planning and control by the state.

spontaneous activities of individuals is brought about by the market, provided that there is a known delimitation of the sphere of control of each individual. [28]

As Barry's work, "The Tradition of Spontaneous Order" shows the theory of spontaneous order predates modern complexity theory by centuries, it even predates evolutionary theory. What once was the subject of mystics and visionaries now burst forth into economic theory.

Long before Darwin penned his *Origin of Species,* evolutionary ideas were becoming common among late eighteenth and early nineteenth century thinkers. An interesting fact arises about Darwin and the origin of his ideas, as F.A. Hayek relates:

Not only is the idea of evolution older in the humanities and social sciences than in the natural sciences, I would even be prepared to argue that Darwin got the basic ideas of evolution from economics. As we learn from his notebooks, Darwin was reading Adam Smith just when, in 1838, he was formulating his own theory... In any case, Darwin's work was preceded by decades, indeed by a century, of research concerning the rise of highly complex spontaneous orders through a process of evolution.[29]

Systems thinking is centuries old and yet it has been discounted by many mainstream economic thinkers and economists for most of the last 100 years. Even Smith's notion of the *invisible hand* has been sneered at and denigrated by many as a throwback to the idea of the providence of God, and yet Edna Ullman-Margalit states a different origin than the religious foundation of this idea:

---

28 Norman Barry, "The Tradition of Spontaneous Order," *Library of Economics and Liberty,* 1982, Retrieved November 6, 2012: B.4, http://www.econlib.org/library/Essays/LtrLbrty/bryTSO1. html.

29 F.A. Hayek, *The Fatal Conceit: The Errors of Socialism* (Chicago: The University of Chicago Press, 1988), 24.

F. A. Hayek talks about the "shock caused by the discovery that [not only the kosmos of nature but] the moral and political kosmos was also the result of a process of evolution and not of design." What he alludes to here is the natural human response to the phenomenon of order. Upon encountering orderliness and patterned structures, people tend naturally to interpret these as the products of someone's intentional design… If complex order is exhibited by the physical world-say, the lunar period-The postulated designer would be a superhuman agent, God. The "argument from design" (or the cosmological argument, as it is sometimes called) is indeed a most powerful argument, psychologically, for the existence of God. The very core of religious sensibility is a conviction that the world is not just the product of divine creation, but that it is the manifestation of divine, cosmic design.

It is against this background that the idea that the kosmos can be seen as a result of a process of evolution rather than design is described by Hayek as "shocking" … Since a nineteenth-century notion of evolution, or spontaneous order, is itself rooted in the eighteenth-century notion of the invisible hand, there is a sense in which we may take the notion of the invisible hand as expressing a major anti-religious institution. This notion was meant to replace that of the "Finger of God," or "Divine Providence." It was to play a central role in forging modern secular sensibility.[30]

Ullman-Marglit goes on to link the invisible hand with the rational Enlightenment tradition:

Only when an invisible-hand mechanism can be pointed to, can the spell of an explanation that postulates a creator, a designer, or a conspiracy be effectively broken … the liberating role from the grip of this [theological] picture is assumed by an invisible-hand explanation

---

30 Edna Ullman-Margalit, "The Invisible Hand and the Cunning of Reason," *Social Research*, Vol. 64, No. 2 (Summer 1979): 181.

that succeeds in showing, through spelling out the workings of an appropriate mechanism (or process), how the social institution in question could have come about "as a result of human action but not of human design." This liberating role firmly establishes the notion of the invisible hand as a cornerstone in the secular, rationalist worldview that we associate with the Enlightenment.[31] [32]

The invisible hand explanation of cultural order became super-naturalized as Smith's insight was seen as being adopted from the newly arising Gothic genre where the invisible hand motif appeared for the first time in Walpole's *The Castle of Otranto* in 1764 and went on to influence many more Gothic novels, which may have influenced Smith's adopting the term as well as his *Wealth of Nations* did not appear until 1776, twelve years later. This led to Smith's systems thinking being erroneously linked either to the superstitions of the pagan past or to Protestant theology as many suspected Smith of smuggling in either his Calvinist beliefs under different terms or Gothic supernaturalism. Stephan Andriopolous in his work, "The Invisible Hand: Supernatural Agency in Political Economy and the Gothic Novel,"[33] makes the exact opposite point as Ullman-Marglit above and links Smith's invisible hand theory back to a supernatural agency. Both sides miss the fact that Smith was also greatly influenced by Sir Isaac Newton and the idea of gravity, an invisible force acting at a distance, may be another source for Smith's idea.

The argument of whether the invisible hand is a rational nonspiritual explanation of spontaneous order influenced by Newton's theory of the invisible force of gravity, or an immanentizing of old supernatural sensibilities, seems a puerile one today as complexity theory and *systems thinking* has actually proven the ideas of Smith's ideas of spontaneous

---

31 Ibid., 184.
32 Ms. Margalit misses the historical evidence that Adam Smith was very much influenced by Sir Isaac Newton and that his "invisible hand" theory may well have been influenced by Newton's ideas on gravity as "an invisible force acting upon objects at a distance." Smith used Newtonian language to describe many of his theories in *The Wealth of Nations*. See *The Science of Liberty* by Timothy Ferris, Harper Perennial Books, 2010.
33 Stefan Andriopolous, "The Invisible Hand: Supernatural Agency in Political Economy and the Gothic Novel," *ELH*, Vol. 66. No. 3 (Fall 1999): 739-758. www.jstor.org/stable/30032092.

order as being inherently correct. Andriopolous goes on later in his work to uncover amazing connections between Smith's *invisible hand* and Marx and Engels' writings.

> As a detailed outline the migration of these figures-from Smith's "invisible hand" via Hegel's List der Vernunft, [cunning of reason], which "operates in the background," to Marx-is beyond the scope of this paper, it may suffice to point at only one instance of this reproduction of Smith's tropes in Marx's and Engels's writings. In Ludwig Feuerbach Engels ascribes the unintended, seemingly accidental consequences of human actions to hidden interior laws operating in history:
>
>> The aims of actions are intended, but the results which really follow from those actions are unintended, or, in so far as they first seem to comply with the intended aim, they finally have consequences completely differing from the intended ones. Thus the historical events appear to be ruled by contingency. But while chance plays its game on the surface, it is always determined by interior, *hidden laws*.
>
> This ascription of seemingly contingent accidents to hidden laws operating history replicates Hegel's account of political economy as discovering "necessary laws" behind a "conglomerate of contingencies." [34]

Sprinkled throughout Marx and Engel's works are insights indicative to systems theory, which we can ascribe back to their adherence to the philosophy of Hegel and his dialectical conception of history in their youth. Hegel himself, along with Goethe were both strongly influenced by spiritual sources beyond Smith's *The Wealth of Nations*, most notably the mystical writings of Jacob Bohme and the Hermetic alchemical tradition.

---

34 Ibid., 750.

We cannot remove the underlying theme of "supernatural agency" from Smith, Marx and Engels nor any of the classical economic philosophers or socialist writers as Gnosticism was in the air in the Europe of the time and was highly influential on so many artistic, literary and intellectual movements, as Eric Voeglin illustrates:

> The more we come to know about the gnosis of antiquity, the more it becomes certain that modern movements of thought, such as progressivism, positivism, Hegelianism, and Marxism, are variants of Gnosticism ... [the] idea that one of the main currents of European, especially of German, thought is essentially Gnostic sound[s] strange today, but this is not [a] recent discovery. In 1835 appeared Ferdinand Christian Bauer's monumental work Die christliche Gnosis, order die Religionsphilosphie in ihrer geschichtlichen Entwicklung. Under the heading "ancient Gnosticism and modern philosophy of religion," the last part of this work discusses: (1) Bohme's theosophy, (2) Shelling's philosophy of nature, (3) Schleiermacher's doctrine of faith, and (4) Hegel's philosophy of religion. The speculation of German idealism [philosophy] is correctly placed in this context and the Gnostic movement since antiquity. [35]

Magee agrees with Voeglin:

> Hermeticism has influenced such mainstream rationalist thinkers as Bacon, Descartes, Spinoza, Leibnitz, and Newton and has played a hitherto unappreciated role in the formation of the central ideas and ambitions of modern philosophy and science, particularly the modern project of the progressive scientific investigation and technological mastery of nature. [36]

---

35 Eric Voeglin, *Science, Politics and Gnosticism*, [1968] (Wilmington, DE: ISI books, 2004), 3.
36 Glenn Alexander Magee, *Hegel and the Hermetic Tradition* (London: Cornell University Press, 2001), 7.

Intellectual and spiritual "heresies" underlie all genres of thought and revolutionary movements arising in the Europe of the middle and late modern period, one cannot ignore or deny this mystical undercurrent as a motivating factor for political, economic, societal, literary, scientific and technological change.

To denigrate Smith's supernaturalism of the *invisible hand* is like the *"pot calling the kettle black,"* so to speak, as to do so we must ignore socialism's own gnostic mystical influences and foundations which are detailed in such works as Igor Shafarevich's *The Socialist Phenomenon,*[37] Murray Rothbard's *Karl Marx: Communist as Religious Eschatologist,* [38] Robert C. Tucker 's *Philosophy and Myth in Karl Marx*[39] and Leonard P. Wessell Jr,'s *Karl Marx, Romantic Irony, and the Proletariat.*[40] Though these authors run the gamut on how they view socialism, with Shafarevish and Rothbard openly casting aspersions upon the entire philosophical tradition by associating it with irrational and heretical religious movements. Neither of these two authors truly succeeds in denigrating the essential evolutionary insights that came through the various mystical and gnostic movements into the philosophical and scientific thought of Europe, which eventually found their full expression in today's modern nonlinear systems theory and Transhumanism. Rothbard himself once denigrated F.A. Hayek for his systems approach to economics and his theory of *economic ignorance.*[41] In this instance he was trying to adhere too much to Enlightenment rationality and in doing so he was trying to out Mises, Ludwig von Mises and Complexity Theory has since cinched his failure to impugn Hayek on this matter. Tucker and Wessell on the other hand do an outstanding job of laying the foundations and framework for understanding Karl Marx's thought and the influences upon him from such sources as Hegel, Romanticism and German Ideal philosophy.

---

37 Igor Shafarevich, *The Socialist Phenomenon* (New York: Harper & Row, 1980).
38 Murray Rothbard, "Karl Marx: Communist as Religious Eschatologist," *The Review of Austrian Economics*, Vol. 4, (1990): 123-79.
39 Robert C. Tucker 's *Philosophy and Myth in Karl Marx* (New Brunswick, USA: 2001).
40 Leonard P. Wessell Jr,'s *Karl Marx, Romantic Irony, and the Proletariat* (Louisiana State University Press, USA: 1979).
41 Murray Rothbard, "Fallacies of Hayek and Kirzner," in *Economic Controversies* (Auburn, AL: Ludwig von Mises Institute Press, 2011), 845.

Indeed Complexity theory has given the win to Hayek over Rothbard. In his presidential address before the London Economic Club in 1936, Hayek stated the concept of *emergent intelligence* superbly, decades before Complexity Theory was discovered,

> Clearly there is here a problem of the division of knowledge, which is quite analogous to, and at least as important as, the problem of the division of labor. But, while the latter has been one of the main subjects of investigation ever since the beginning of our science, the former has been as completely neglected, although it seems to me to be the really central problem of economics as a social science. The problem which we pretend to solve is how the spontaneous interaction of a number of people, each possessing only bits of knowledge, brings about a state of affairs in which prices correspond to costs, etc., and which could be brought about by deliberate direction only by somebody who possessed the combined knowledge of all those individuals. Experience shows us that something of this sort does happen, since the empirical observation that prices do tend to correspond to costs was the beginning of our science. But in our analysis, instead of showing what bits of information the different persons must possess in order to bring about that result, we fall in effect back on the assumption that everybody knows everything and so evade any real solution of the problem.[42]

And later on in the same speech,

> I still believe that, by what is implicit in its reasoning, economics has come nearer than any other social science to an answer to that central question of all social sciences: How can the combination of fragments of knowledge existing in different minds bring about results which, if they were to be brought about deliberately, would require a knowledge on the part of the directing mind which no single person can possess? To show that in this sense the spontaneous actions of

---

42 F.A. Hayek, Economics and Knowledge, *Economica IV* (new ser., 1937), 33-54,

individuals will, under conditions which we can define, bring about a distribution of resources which can be understood as if it were made according to a single plan, although nobody has planned it, seems to me indeed an answer to the problem which has sometimes been metaphorically described as that of the "social mind." But we must not be surprised that such claims have usually been rejected, since we have not based them on the right grounds.

This process of the "social mind" that so concerns Hayek above is known in Complexity Theory as *Emergent Intelligence*. In the end, modern science through Complexity Theory has actually authenticated many of the intuitional and spiritual insights of the early mystical visionaries. Could it be that in our own over preoccupation with materialism in all of its various forms, hidden and expressed, we missed the fact that as we climb over the mountains of scientific discovery we find that mystical theology has been there waiting for us all along? Can it be that a dynamic phenomenology has been operating as an unconscious motif and driver of our evolutionary insights throughout the late medieval and early modern periods and is still motivating us today here in the era of Early Futurity? [43]

Whether it is Smith's "invisible hand," Hegel's "cunning of reason," Marx's "productive material forces," Teilhard's "Noosphere and Omega Point," Buckminster Fuller's "Ephemeralization," Hayek's "Social Mind," Kevin Kelly's "Technium," or Kurzweil's "Singularity," we are dealing with concepts and representations of nonlinear dynamic systems thinking trying to come to grips with spontaneous, emergent, complex, evolutionary forces at work in the universe and its almost "magical" multiplying of our loaves and fishes. "Our shock" in Hayek's words, is that our eighteenth and nineteenth century overly Cartesian and Newtonian reductionist and mechanistic views, which called for a central organizing planner for all of society and the universe, are being overthrown. We find ourselves locked out of the safety and petrified security of Plato's cave, naked and in a

---

43 Early Futurity is the name I have given to the times that we are living in here at the beginning of the Twenty-First Century.

new mostly unexplored, uncertain and complex world. The older political ideas of the Imperium, monarchy, oligarchy, aristocracy, representational democracy, communism, socialism, fascism, conservatism et al. are set to fade into the dust bin of history. We shiver existentially naked in a cold withering wind trying desperately to grasp onto old familiar static intellectual clothes being torn out of our grasp by an ever increasing dynamic evolutionary technologically-driven hurricane.

We seem to be moving as the centuries pass and as our science and technology evolves from a centralized system (A), to a decentralized system (B) and now as the idea of Omniarchy, the rule of all by all through an evolving technologically advanced complex interconnected distributed network such as the Internet to a new distributed system (C).

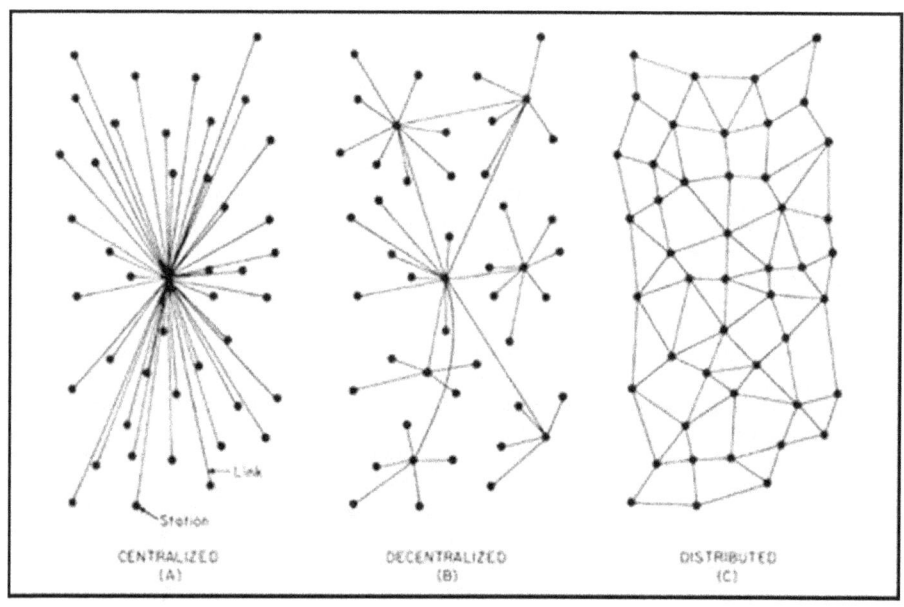

1 The Evolution of Social and Economic Systems 44

This new distributed system is slowly emerging from the bottom-up as many futurists are beginning to theorize like the futurist Marina Gorbis

44   Marina Gorbis, *The Nature of the Future* (New York, NY: Free Press, 2013), 23.

does in her book *The Nature of the Future*. One can see that our social and political systems have been evolving, as she states;

> John Culkin summed up his colleague Marshall McLuhan's perspective on technology as follows, "we shape our tools and thereafter they shape us." We've put in place a new technology infrastructure, and now this technology is reshaping the landscape of our lives. Like the invention of the steam engine, which ushered in the Industrial Revolution, the architecture of the Internet, with its unique distributed communication nodes, is revolutionizing our social and economic landscapes, reshaping how we live, produce, trade, and innovate.[45]

The concept stated by Culkin above is from the new discipline of Ontological design and is summed up by Anne-Marie Willis, "We design our world, while our world acts back on us and designs us," and is beautifully stated in the video "How Our Creations Change Us" by Jason Silva,[46] a beautiful example of convergence with the dialectical outlook.

The must see TED video[47] by Johann Gevers describes the four pillars of a decentralized system as containing: 1). Decentralized Communication, 2). Decentralized Law, 3). Decentralized Production, and 4). Decentralized Finance. In Adam Thierer's article titled "The Debate over the Sharing Economy,"[48] he goes into the essential features of the emerging collaborative economy's evolving features. His second paragraph is worth quoting in its entirety:

---

45 Ibid., 23.
46 Jason Silva, "How Our Creations Change Us," *Shots of Awe*, 3:16, www.youtube.com/watch?v=hHCo9U4jxzE&feature=youtu.be.
47 Johann Gevers, "The Four Pillars of a Decentralized Society," *Youtube:TEDxZug*, July 7, 2014, 16.12 minutes, https://www.youtube.com/watch?v=8oeiOeDq_Nc.
48 Adam Thierer, "The Debate Over the Sharing Economy: Talking Points and Recommended Reading," *Techliberation* (Blog), October 1, 2014, http://techliberation.com/2014/09/26/the-debate-over-the-sharing-economy-talking-points-recommended-reading/.

The Internet and information technology alleviates the need for top-down regulation & actually does a better job of serving consumers.

1. Ease of entry/innovation in online world means that new entrants can come in to provide better options and solve problems previously thought to be unsolvable in the absence of regulation.
2. Informational empowerment: The Internet and information technology solves old problem of lack of consumer access to information about products and services. This gives them monitoring tools to find more and better choices. (i.e., it lowers both search costs & transaction costs). ("To the extent that consumer protection regulation is based on the claim that consumers lack adequate information, the case for government intervention is weakened by the Internet's powerful and unprecedented ability to provide timely and pointed consumer information." – John C. Moorhouse)
3. Feedback mechanisms (product & service rating / review systems) create powerful reputational incentives for all parties involved in transactions to perform better.
4. Self-regulating markets: The combination of these three factors results in a powerful check on market power or abusive behavior. The result is reasonably well-functioning and self-regulating markets. Bad actors get weeded out.
5. Law should evolve: When circumstances change dramatically, regulation should as well. If traditional rationales for regulation evaporate, or new technology or competition alleviates need for it, then the law should adapt.[49]

The old social technology of a political and economic system based on a pyramidal structure with the power at the top: controlling, regulating and commanding all those below it is slowly being pushed into the tar

---

49 Ibid.

pit of history by the accelerating force of the technological evolution of the Technium. In a sense the old Imperium of the commands of heaven are giving way to the system of the Tao. A new circular shaped interrelated holographic social system as Butler Schaffer in *Boundaries of Order* mentions below seems to be in the process of being born:

> A holographic system of social organization, on the other hand, is one in which both the purpose and the authority for decision making is distributed throughout the social system through the principle of private ownership. Only as decision making is horizontally distributed can a peaceful and creative social order emerge from the boundless diversity and imaginations of free individuals and autonomous groups each seeking the full expression of their sense of being.[50]

Robert Klassen sums up this new paradigm destroying force inherent in the arising distributed system of the Internet:

> The Internet represents existential democracy and intellectual liberty undreamed of in all of [human] history. Even in its present chaotic condition it is a threat to all political governments on this planet. Our very first imperative must be to ensure that our American political government does not tax or restrain our use of the Internet in any way, shape or form, including attacks on hardware and software innovation. If we lose this battle [for Internet freedom], we lose the war.[51]

Max Border states clearly the dramatically changing political structure's situation today:

---

50 Butler Schaffer, *Boundaries of Order* (Auburn, AL: Ludwig von Mises Institute, 2009), 259.
51 Robert Klassen, *Economic Government* (Lincoln, NB, Writers Club Press, 2001), 99.

So many of the administrative functions of jurisdiction can increasingly be found in the cloud. It's early, yes. The network is fragile. But we will soon be able to pass in and out of legal systems, selecting those that benefit us, employing true self-government. It is time to follow Thoreau, who in Civil Disobedience asked, "Is a democracy, such as we know it, the last improvement possible in government?"... Peer-to-peer interaction means we're a nation of joiners again– on steroids. It seemed for a while we had lost the republic to special interests. But the hopeless calculus of cronyism — concentrated benefits and dispersed costs – is being flipped on its head. Internetworking makes it so we're enjoying the fruits of the sharing economy–quite rapidly, in fact. Cronies and officials are finding it hard to play catch up.

New constituencies are forming around these new benefits. Special interests that once squeaked to get oil are confronted by battalions bearing smart phones. Citizens are voting more with their dollars and their devices, fed up with leaving prayers in the voting booth. Free association is now ensured by design, not by statute.

Technology that changes the incentives can change the institutions. The rules and regulations we currently live under came out of our democratic operating system (DOS). It used to be that these institutions shaped our incentives to a great degree. Now we have ways of coordinating our activities that go right around state intermediaries, corporate parasites, and moribund laws...We're becoming cultural cosmopolitans, radical communitarians, and standard bearers for a right of exit. Most importantly, we're freer than ever before. As my colleague Jeffrey Tucker writes on the workers' revolution, "This whole approach might be considered a very advanced stage of capitalism in which third parties exercise ever less power over who can and cannot participate." In this infinite space, there will be little room for political progressives with big plans. They'll find it difficult to impose hierarchy on the new frontier folk who will run among network nodes. The progressive program, as such, will dwindle down to what Steven B. Johnson calls "peer progressivism."

The incentives for social change are strong, so strong that the gales of creative destruction can finally blow apart much of the state apparatus, which seemed impervious to reform. And that's a good thing for a self-governing people.[52]

As yet only those on the cutting edge of technological development seem to be aware of this startling new realization: that as capitalist production is evolving and becoming ever more exponential it is driving us toward the omega point of a new revolutionary distributed and collaborative: economic, social and political system at the event horizon of the coming Singularity. Our political systems of today are heavily leaning, being undermined from the bottom up by the forces unleashed by the Internet as it evolves and as Marx advised, "That which is leaning deserves to be pushed." Our greatest ally in the fight for a new and truly progressive evolutionary social and economic system is a free and open internet, untrammeled by any government regulation or intervention, as Klassen stated above, "If we lose this battle [for total Internet freedom], we lose the war."

---

52 Max Borders, "The New Frontier: Peer technologies are enabling self-government in the cloud," *The Freeman* (Blog), November 12, 2014, http://fee.org/the_freeman/detail/the-new-frontier.

4

Teilhard de Chardin:
The Noosphere Rising

Our duty, as men and women, is to proceed as if limits to our ability did not exist. We are collaborators in creation.

-TEILHARD DE CHARDIN

Teilhard de Chardin was a Jesuit priest and an amateur paleontologist whose mystical musings had a profound effect on several generations of theologians, sociologists, socialists and philosophers. His eclectic mystical philosophy combined elements of: Hegel, Neo-Platonism, socialism, various Romantic writers and scientists, Russian Cosmism and Darwinian evolution. As Carter Phipps in his book *Evolutionaries* quotes from Teilhard about the overall importance of evolution, "Is evolution a theory, a system, or a hypothesis? It is much more: it is a general condition to which all theories, all hypotheses, all systems must bow and which they must satisfy henceforth if they are to be thinkable and true. Evolution is a light which illuminates all facts, a curve that all lines must follow."[53]

Though what Teilhard propounded through his theories falls more in the realm of cosmist scientism, his unique outlook and take on human

---

53 Carter Phipps, *Evoluitionaries: Unlocking the Spiritual and Cultural Potential of Science's Greatest Idea* (New York, NY: HarperCollins, 2012), 11.

evolution inspired an entire genre of thinking that itself led to a more holographic evolutionary paradigm that is such a powerful undercurrent in many New Age, philosophical and Process theological circles today. From my own point of view two of his theories are the most relevant, his take on the theory of the *Noosphere* and the *Omega Point*. The Noosphere according to Teilhard de Chardin, is a spiritual envelope that is slowly forming and enveloping the world and will consciously and spiritually unite all humanity. It is a collective network of human knowledge and consciousness that evolves and interconnects humanity as a species as we evolve to a convergence point in the future, the Omega point. While this concept has a strong affinity to Hegel's *Geist*, Teilhard took great pains to try to ground his concept in more scientific Darwinian evolutionary terms, which ended up putting Teilhard in a middle position between Hegel's dialectical mysticism and Marx's dialectical materialism. This may account for his strong attraction among religious and theologically inclined left leaning intellectuals as he tried to reconcile both traditions with his Catholic faith. T.A. Goudge describes the noosphere thusly:

> What does the [noosphere] model amount to? Briefly, it is built on the classical representation in geology of the earth as a sequence of concentric, spherical shells or envelopes—barysphere, lithosphere, hydrosphere, atmosphere and biosphere. The last of these, introduced by the geologist Suess, was designed to represent the envelope of organic matter which originated and spread around the globe during the Pre-Cambrian era. What Teilhard proposes is that we regard the process of cultural evolution as having generated another planetary envelope, distinct from but superimposed on the biosphere, a "sheet of humanized and socialized matter" which he calls the "noosphere". The title seems reasonably apt since the noosphere is exclusively the product of Homo sapiens, and embraces not only technological but also intellectual and social creations. Viewed historically, the noosphere is the ensemble composed of evolving man and his various cultures.[54]

---

54 T.A. Goudge, "Salvaging the Noosphere," *Mind, New Series*, Vol. 71, No. 284 (Oct., 1962): 543, http://www.jstor.org/stable/2251897.

For our purposes Teilhard's intuition had a more profound impact on later complexity theorists as many have commented on the similarity between Teilhard's noosphere and the evolving internet, which has been described as the arising *global brain*. Teilhard's noosphere is in the emergentist tradition, as the complexity theorist Francis Heylighen discusses:

> The best known author to develop this [emergentist] argument is the French paleontologist and Jesuit priest Pierre Teilhard de Chardin, who combined his knowledge of evolution and theology into a mystical and poetic vision of future evolutionary integration. According to Teilhard's *law of complexity-consciousness*, evolution is accompanied by increases in both complexity and consciousness, characterized by a growing number of connections between components. Thus, the human brain with its billions of neurons and synapses is the most complex and most conscious biological system. But evolution in the biosphere is followed by the emergence of the *noosphere*, the global network of thoughts, information and communication, and it is here that spiritual union will be achieved:
>
> > No one can deny that ... a world network of economic and psychic affiliations is being woven at ever increasing speed which envelops and constantly penetrates more deeply within each of us. With every day that passes it becomes a little more impossible for us to act or think otherwise than collectively.
> >
> > We are faced with a harmonized collectivity of consciousness, the equivalent of a sort of super-consciousness. The idea is that of the earth becoming enclosed in a single thinking envelope, so as to form, functionally, no more than a single vast grain of thought on the cosmic scale.[55]

---

55 Francis Heylighen, "Conceptions of a Global Brain: An Historical Review," *Technological Forecasting and Social Change*, special issue on the Global Brain, (n.d.):8, http://www.academia.edu/1823746/Conceptions_of_a_Global_Brain_an_historical_review.

Heylighen describes this evolving super-organism from systems theory in more detail:

> New scientific developments have done away with rigid, mechanistic views of organisms. When studying living systems, biologists no longer focus on the static structures of their anatomy, but on the multitude of interacting processes that allow the organism to adapt to an ever changing environment. Most recently, the variety of ideas and methods that is commonly grouped under the header of "the sciences of complexity" has led to the understanding that organisms are self-organizing, adaptive systems. Most processes in such systems are decentralized, indeterministic and in constant flux. They thrive on "noise", chaos, and creativity. Their collective intelligence emerges out of the free interactions between individually autonomous components ... This development again opens up the possibility of modeling both organisms and societies as complex, adaptive systems. ... These scientific approaches, together with the more mystical vision of Teilhard de Chardin (1955), have inspired a number of authors in recent years to revive the organismic view. ... The main idea of this model is that global society can be understood as a superorganism, and that it becomes more like a superorganism as technology and globalization advance. A superorganism is a higher-order, "living" system, whose components (in this case, individual humans) are organisms themselves.[56]

He describes the global brain:

> The "Global Brain" (GB) is a metaphor for this emerging, collectively intelligent network that is formed by the people of this planet together with the computers, knowledge bases, and communication links that connect them together. This network is an immensely complex, self-organizing system. It not only processes information, but increasingly

---

56 Francis Heylighen, "The Global Superorganism: an Evolutionary-Cybernetic Model of the Emerging Network Society," *Journal of Social and Evolutionary Systems*, (n.d.): 2, http://pespmc1. vub.ac.be/Papers/Superorganism.pdf.

can be seen to play the role of a brain: making decisions, solving problems, learning new connections, and discovering new ideas. No individual, organization or computer is in control of this system: its knowledge and intelligence are distributed over all its components.[57]

This organismic view of human society and human biological and technological evolution united with accelerating technological development is a synergistic co-evolutionary force that humanity is intimately involved in both creating and being transformed by. The global brain is also closely aligned with Karl Marx's conception of the productive material forces. Teilhard wasn't the first person to propose this concept, but he was one of the few to see it in such an arising evolutionary organismic fashion. The science and technical writer Kevin Kelly updates this concept from Teilhard and as I have stated earlier renamed the noosphere as *The Technium*, he explains in evolutionary terms his vision of this impetus for technological becoming:

> *Homo sapiens* are a tendency, not an entity. Humanity is a process. Always was, always will be. Every living organism is on its way to becoming. And the human organism even more so, because among all living beings (that we know about) we are the most open-ended. We have just started our evolution as *Homo sapiens*. As both parent and child of the technium-evolution accelerated-we are nothing more and nothing less than an evolutionary ordained becoming. "I seem to be a verb," the inventor/philosopher Buckminster Fuller once said. We can likewise say: the technium and its constituent technologies are more like a grand process then a grand artifact. Nothing is complete, all is in flux, and the only thing that counts is the direction of movement.[58]

---

57 Heylighen, *Global Brain*, 2.
58 Kevin Kelly, *What Technology Wants*, (New York, Viking Press, 2010), 128.

The noosphere today has become a technologically based paradigm increasingly incorporated into the thoughts and philosophy of those on the cutting edge of technological development.

Teilhard's other great insight was the "omega point," the coming evolutionary unification of all humanity through the unification of consciousness. This collectivity would be the organic synthesis that arose out of the fully completed noosphere. As he described it:

> We have seen and admitted that evolution is an ascent towards consciousness ... and in the establishment now proceeding through science and the philosophies of a collective human *Weltanschauung*[59] in which every one of us cooperates and participates, are we not experiencing the first symptoms of an aggregation of a still higher-order, the birth of some single center from the convergent beams of millions of elementary centers over the surface of the thinking earth?... Because it contains and engenders consciousness, space-time is necessarily of a convergent nature. Accordingly its enormous layers, followed in the right direction, must somewhere ahead become involuted to a point which we might call Omega.[60]

All human consciousness and evolution for Teilhard is being pulled by a *forward attractor* ahead of us, the omega point, which is driving human evolutionary consciousness toward an eventual coalescence, a point at which we would become greatly interrelated without losing our own unique individuality. At this "eschaton," humanity would become spiritualized and merge with the divinized universe. Many Transhumanist's see in Teilhard's mystical vision the point at which humanity and technology will merge and all human limitations will be overcome. Complexity theorists go back and forth between these two poles and most take a wait and see attitude as to humanity's future, though the evolution of the

---

59 Weltanschauung: worldview, a comprehensive view or personal philosophy of human life and the universe.
60 Pierre Teilhard de Chardin, *The Phenomenon of Man*, [1955] (New York: Harper Perennial, 2008), 258.

global brain through the Internet does portend an almost Teilhardian evolutionary development. The Futurist, visionary and inventor Ray Kurzweil takes this view and imagines six great epochs of human evolution and in the last one humanity and technology evolve to a point of convergence where the universe itself wakes up. This closes the circle and reunites Kurzweil with Teilhard of Chardin and the Soviet scientist Vladimir Vernadsky[61] the inventor of the philosophy of evolutionary emergence who originally invented the concept of the noosphere.

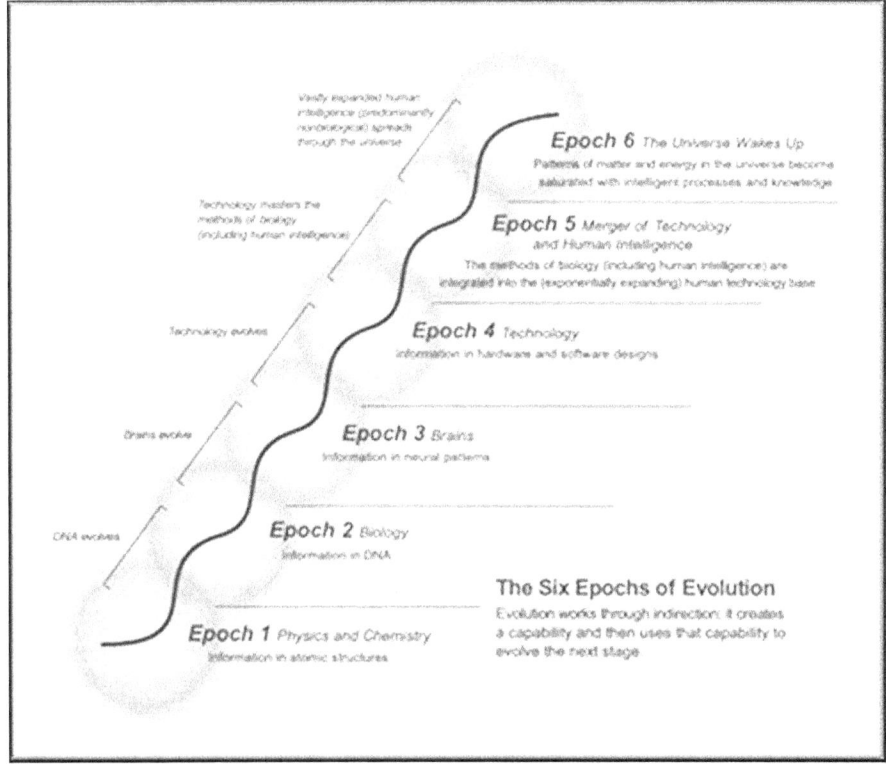

2. The Six Epochs of Evolution[62]

---

61 For more on Vladimir Vernadsky: http://en.wikipedia.org/wiki/Vladimir_Vernadsky

62 Kurzweil, "The Six Epochs of Evolution," *The Singularity is Near*, 15. Those with a comparative religions background readily see the gnostic elements of Kurzweil's Singularity paradigm and its strong affinity to such ideas as Joachim of Fiore's Three Ages of the Spirit, echoed in such science fiction works as Babylon 5's Third Age of Man. See Joachim of Fiore: http://en.wikipedia.org/wiki/Joachim_of_Fiore.

The question that now arises is where does Karl Marx fit in with the evolutionary view of things? Phipps definitively answers this question;

> Darwin and Marx were both driven by the same fundamental idea–evolution! For better or worse, evolution was the context of each of their life's work. Marx was a student of one of the first great evolutionary philosophers, Hegel. And while Darwin, a meticulous collector of data, was focused on biology and Marx on political theory and economic history, both drank liberally from the same philosophical insight–that the given categories of life as it exists today are not static or fixed or unchanging, the "way things are," but rather are a momentary snapshot in an ongoing developmental process. They both saw through the illusion of permanence created by the seeming solidity of the objects of their respective work–for Darwin, the living world; for Marx, economic structures and historical processes–and understood that these are part of the deeper underlying process of evolution over time.[63]

And as Engels states about Marx's work, "Marx treats the social movement as a process of natural history, governed by laws not only independent of human will, consciousness and intelligence, but rather, on the contrary, determining that will, consciousness and intelligence"[64]

In reviewing all of these ideas, especially those coming from complexity theory, an ideological omega point is now becoming a feasible possibility in the near future. A point at which, when these organimistic theories are more mature and readily accepted and the false pantomime battle between ideologies can finally be transcended, unification can happen. As Teilhard himself describes under the heading, *A New Soul for a New World: Faith Renewed in the Progress of Mankind*:

---

63 Phipps, 10.
64 Karl Marx, Capital, 18.

From this standpoint it is at once apparent that, to unify the living forces of humanity, at present so painfully at odds, the direct and effective method is simply to sound the call-to-arms and form a solid block of all those, whether of the right or the left, who believe that the principal business of present-day Mankind is to achieve a break-through straight ahead by forcing its way over the threshold of some higher-level of consciousness. Whether Christian or non-Christian, the people inspired by this particular conviction constitute a homogeneous category. Though they may be situated at the two extreme wings of Mankind on the march, they can advance unequivocally side-by-side because their attitudes, far from being mutually exclusive, are virtually an extension one of the other and ask only to be completed. What more do they need that they may know and love one another? The *union sacrée*,[65] the common front of all those who believe that the World is still advancing: what is this but the active minority, the solid core around which the unanimity of tomorrow must harden?[66]

This is the dynamist versus stasis, extropy versus entropy, argument and divide discussed by Virginia Postrel in her work *The Future and its Enemies*. Teilhard places himself directly and securely in the dynamist extropic camp. Extropy is driving humanity onward and upward to the stars and utopia. The *omega point* up ahead will transform all human life and society. Using Cosmist spiritual sympathies, the evolutionary theogonic ideas of the Kabbalah state that:

> The theory of evolution accords with the secrets of Kabbalah better than any other theory. Evolution follows a path of ascent and thus provides the world with a base for optimism. How can one despair, seeing that everything evolves and ascends? When we penetrate the inner nature of evolution, we find divinity illuminated in perfect

---

65 French, the Sacred Union.
66 Teilhard de Chardin, *The Future of Man* [1959] (New York: Image Books/Doubleday, 2004), 72.

clarity. Ein Sof generates, actualizes potential infinity[67]... An epiphany enables you to sense creation not as something completed, but as constantly becoming, evolving, ascending. This transports you from a place where there is nothing new to a place where there is nothing old, where everything renews itself, where heaven and earth rejoice as at the moment of Creation[68]

A view that infuses the vision of a universal economics by the Russian Cosmist Sergei Bulgakov:

The interrelatedness of everything in the universe, physical and spiritual, means that economic activity is cosmic in scope. "Every living organism, as a body, as organized material, is inextricably connected with the universe as a whole, for the universe is a system of mutually connected and mutually penetrating forces, and one cannot disturb so much as a grain of sand, destroy so much as an atom, without, to one or another degree, disturbing the entire universe." This inextricable connectedness, this holistic relationship, extends beyond the familiar world and beyond this present life. "There is a certain cosmological karma of essences. The unity of the universe, the physical communism of being, means that, physically, everything finds itself in everything else, every atom is connected with the entire universe; or if we compare the universe to an organism, we can say that everything enters into the makeup of the world body."[69]

Ideas in affinity and perfect accord with Teilhard de Chardin and many other philosophers throughout history as the Technium seems to be evolving to a point of transcendent harmonization in which a unified humanity in a unified world and universe emerges. Prescientific writers

---

67 Daniel C. Matt, *The Essential Kabbalah: The Heart of Jewish Mysticism* (New York: Harper Collins, 1996), 31.
68 Ibid., 99.
69 George M. Young, *The Russian Cosmists: The Esoteric Futurism of Nikolai Federov and His Followers* (Oxford: Oxford University Press, 2012), 111.

intuited this convergence mainly as a spiritual and mystical unity as many Russian Cosmists and Teilhard described, while techno-optimists like Ray Kurzweil sees it as a technological evolution. Kevin Kelly describes this evolutionary technological force in almost mythopoetic terms:

> It may seem like I am painting a picture of a supernatural force, akin to a pantheistic spirit roaming the universe. What I'm outlining is almost the opposite. Like gravity, this force is embedded in the fabric of matter and energy. It follows a path of physics and obeys the ultimate law of entropy. The force that is waiting to erupt into the technologies of the technium was first pushed by extropy, built up by self-organization, and gradually thrown from the inert world into life, and from life into minds, and from minds into the creation of our minds. It is an observable force found in the intersection of information, matter, and energy, and it can be repeated and measured, though it has only recently been surveyed.[70]

No matter how this force is intuited and seen, the important factor is that there is an underlying agreement that convergence is in the process of realization. How it will fully come about is as yet still hidden in the shadows of the future and is only now beginning to take shape on the event horizon of human consciousness. That this evolutionary paradigm and process is an essential and vital part of human evolution is the paramount recognition of both the spiritual and technological visionaries. Carter Phipps describes today's paradigm shift superbly:

> Today, we can see how the spell of solidity is being shattered in discipline after discipline. The result has been a long, slow revelation that the ground beneath our feet is moving forward in history. We are in the midst of an epochal shift from a world of stasis to one of constant movement, from a universe of settled being to one of

---

70 Kevin Kelly, *What Technology Wants* (New York, NY: Viking Press, 2010), 273.

creative becoming, from a cosmos composed of matter and stasis to one made of events in motion. As we add this new sense of temporality to our universe and it becomes more integrated into the patterns of our perception, informing our cultural worldview and restructuring our psychology and neurology, a new sense of the world will reveal itself.[71]

In examining all of the research and ideological musings, whether from the right or the left, and coming to confront the complexity paradigm, I cannot but agree with Teilhard de Chardin that we are slowly coming to the threshold of an exponentiality in which all of our paradigms are exploded and transcended and the potential for a harmonious convergence between our ideologies, right and left, finally becomes possible. When we view the past with the knowledge of the present illuminated by complexity and systems theories, this potentiality becomes even clearer: that we transcend the petty bickering and political battles of today is imperative to continuing human progress and evolution. As Teilhard said to Jean Houston as a little girl as recounted by Phipps, "I believe that I'm a pilgrim of the future, ... Jean the people of your time, toward the end of this century, will be taking the tiller of the world. Remain always true to yourself, but move ever-upward toward greater consciousness and greater love."[72]

---

71 Phipps, *Evolutionaries*, 308.
72 Ibid., 306.

5

Complexity: Theory and Economics

But in a turbulent environment the change is so widespread that it just routes around any kind of central authority. So it is best to manage the bottom-up change rather than try to institute it from the top down.

-**KEVIN KELLY**

C omplexity theory's history is a long involved and convoluted one that is outside the scope of this work. It is the outcome of complexity research and its subsequent findings that is so fascinating and directly relevant to this book. To give the reader a feel for complexity theory, I will let Melanie Mitchel describe complex systems herself:

> A definition of the term *complex system*: a system in which large networks of components with no central control and simple rules of operation give rise to complex collective behavior, sophisticated information processing, and adaptation via learning or evolution ... a system that exhibits nontrivial emergent and self-organizing behaviors.[73]

---

73   Melanie Mitchel, *Complexity a Guided Tour* (New York: Oxford University Press, 2009), 13.

These systems surround us, from the organization of ant colonies, the wiring of the human brain, ecosystems, climate, the decentralized network of the internet, and the structure of the entire universe. All of these systems are complex systems and they are emergent as Doyne Farmer describes:

> Organisms cooperate and compete in a dance of co-evolution, thereby becoming an exquisitely tuned ecosystem. Atoms search for a minimum energy state by forming chemical bonds with each other, thereby becoming the emergent structures known as molecules. Human beings try to satisfy their material needs by buying, selling, and trading with each other, thereby creating an emergent structure known as a market. Humans likewise interact with each other to satisfy less quantifiable goals, thereby forming families, religions, and cultures. Somehow, by constantly seeking mutual accommodation and self-consistency, groups of agents manage to transcend themselves and become something more.[74]

Evolution consists in individual organisms following simple and broad general rules to interrelate with one another and thus spontaneously give rise to emergent complex systems. After millions and even billions of years, these complex emergent systems can appear as if they were organized by a central controlling divine architect, but they are all structures that arose through the process of self-organization as the complexity theorist Stephen Wolfram discusses:

> Whenever you look at very complicated systems in physics or biology ... you generally find that the basic components and the basic laws are quite simple; the complexity arises because you have a great many of these simple components interacting simultaneously.

---

74 M. Mitchell Waldrop, *Complexity: The Emerging Science at the Edge of Chaos* (New York: Simon & Schuster, 1992), 288.

Complexity is actually in the organization–the myriad possible ways that the components of the system can interact.[75]

George Cowan, another complexity scientist, goes on to discuss this process further:

What [Emergent complex systems have] at [their] heart is a system composed of many, many "agents." These agents might be molecules or neurons or species or consumers or even corporations. But whatever their nature, the agents were constantly organizing and reorganizing themselves into larger structures through the clash of mutual accommodation and mutual rivalry. Thus, molecules would form cells, neurons would form brains, species would form ecosystems, consumers and corporations would form economies, and so on. At each level, new emergent structures would form and engage in new emergent behaviors. Complexity, in other words, was really a sign of emergence.[76]

The affinity and similarity with these new ideas and the earlier ideas of Adam Smith and other economic and political philosophers are self-evident. They have a fractal quality of self-similarity with the earlier ideas from the classical liberal economists as well as from Hermeticism, German Ideal Philosophy and the Romantics. David Colander states in his work *The Complexity Vision and the Teaching of Economics*, "In the complexity vision the key idea is that the individual creates the world simultaneously as he or she is influenced by the world. In such a world one cannot assume far-sighted deductive rationality; individual's rationality is shaped by the world they co-create,"[77] and the Chaos Theorist James Gleick states in a similar way, "Nonlinearity means that the act

---

75 Ibid., 86.
76 Ibid., 88.
77 David Colander, *The Complexity Vision and the Teaching of Economics* (Cheltenham, UK: Edward Elgar, 2000), 8.

of playing the game, has a way of changing the rules."[78] In both state-ments one finds an affinity with Marx's dialectical philosophy and his assertion that "society makes the man and in return man makes society."

Brian Arthur is the name most associated today with complexity eco-nomics. He was trained as a mathematician and then sought a higher degree in neoclassical economics, but became dissatisfied with the basic premises of that school of economics as they are all based on the as-sumption of a static economic system at full equilibrium, a state that does not describe the real dynamic economic world. It was while reading an article by the Belgian physicist, Ilya Prigogine, that Arthur had an epiphany, here related by Mitchell:

> In fact, wrote Prigogine in one article, it's conceivable that the economy is a self-organizing system, in which market structures are spontaneously organized by such things as demand for labor in the demand for goods and services.

> Arthur sat up immediately when he read those words. "The economy is a self-organizing system." That was it! That was precisely what he had been thinking ever since he'd read [Judson's] *The Eighth Day of Creation*, though he hadn't known how to articulate it. Prigogine's principal of self-organization, the spontaneous dynamics of living systems–now Arthur could finally see how to relate all of it to eco-nomic systems.[79]

Brian Arthur had made the reverse journey that Charles Darwin had; Arthur had started out reading Horace Judson's book on the history of microbiology in order to be introduced to complex systems

---

78 James Gleick, *Chaos: Making a New Science* (New York, NY: Penguin Books, 1987), 24.
79 Waldrop, *Complexity*, 34.

and that led him to economics. As Arthur's journey is related by Waldrop:

> One tiny accident can change everything.[80] Life develops. It has a history. Maybe, he thought, maybe that's why this biological world seems so spontaneous, organic, and-well, alive.

> Come to think of it, maybe that was also why the [neo-classical] economists' imaginary world of perfect equilibrium had always struck him as static, machinelike, and dead. Nothing much could ever happen there; tiny chance imbalances in the market were supposed to die away as quickly as they occurred. Arthur couldn't imagine anything less like the real economy, where new products, technologies, and markets were constantly arising and old ones were constantly dying off. The real economy was not a machine but a kind of living system, with all the spontaneity and complexity that Judson was showing him in the world of molecular biology.[81]

Arthur, possibly unbeknownst to himself, went on to validate the theories of the earlier classical liberal economic philosophers and todays Austrian School of Economics by displaying the great foundational differences between the old linear economics and the "new" non-linear economics in the following chart:

---

80 The *Butterfly Effect* from Chaos Theory. See The Butterfly Effect at http://en.wikipedia.org/wiki/Butterfly_effect.
81 Waldrop, Complexity, 31.

OLD ECONOMICS	NEW ECONOMICS
• Decreasing Returns.	• Increasing Returns.
• Based on 19th-century physics (equilibrium, stability, deterministic dynamics).	• Based on biology (structure, pattern, self-organization, lifecycle).
• People [are] identical.	• Focus on individual life; people [are] separate and different.
• If only there were no externalities and all had equal abilities, we'd reach Nirvana.	• Externalities and differences become [the] driving force. No Nirvana. System [is] constantly unfolding.
• Elements are quantities and prices.	• Elements are patterns and possibilities.
• No real dynamics in the sense that everything is at equilibrium.	• Economy is constantly on the edge of time. It rushes forward, structures consciously coalescing, decaying, [and] changing.
• Sees subject as structurally simple.	• Sees subject as inherently complex.
• Economics as soft physics.	• Economics as high-complexity science. [82]

As anyone well versed in political and economic philosophy and its history readily notices is that almost all of the premises under the *New Economics* are ideas originating in the Classical Liberal School of Economics.

In *The Economy as an Evolving System II*, the Santa Fe Institute details the basics of complexity economics:

Dispersed Interaction. What happens in the economy is determined by the interaction of many dispersed, possibly heterogeneous, agents acting in parallel. The action of any given agent depends upon the anticipated actions of the limited number of other agents and on the aggregate state these agents cocreate.

---

82 Ibid., 36.

No Global Controller. No global entity controls interactions. Instead, controls are provided by mechanisms of competition and coordination among agents. Economic actions are mediated by legal institutions, assigned roles, and shifting associations. Nor is there a universal competitor-a single agent that can exploit all opportunities in the economy.

Cross-cutting Hierarchical Organization. The economy has many levels of organization and interaction. Units at any given level-behaviors, actions, strategies, products-typically serve as "building blocks" for constructing units at the next higher level. The overall organization is more than hierarchical, with many sorts of tangled interactions ... across levels.

Continual Adaptation. Behaviors, actions, strategies, and products are revised continually as individual agents accumulate experience-the system constantly adapts.

Perpetual Novelty. Niches are continually created by new markets, new technologies, new behaviors, [and] new institutions. The very act of filling a niche may provide new niches. The result is ongoing, perpetual novelty.

Out-of-Equilibrium Dynamics. Because new niches, new potentials, new possibilities, are continually created, the economy operates far from any optimum or global equilibrium. Improvements are always possible and indeed occur regularly.

Systems with these properties have come to be called *adaptive nonlinear networks...* There are many such in nature and society: nervous systems, immune systems, ecologies, as well as economies. An essential element of adaptive nonlinear networks is that they do not act simply in terms of stimulus and response. Instead they anticipate.

In particular, economic agents form expectations–they build up models of the economy and act on the basis of predictions generated by these models. These anticipative models need neither be explicit, nor coherent, nor even mutually consistent.

Because of the difficulties outlined above, the mathematical tools economists customarily use, which exploit linearity, fixed points, and systems of differential equations, cannot provide a deep understanding of adaptive nonlinear networks.[83]

Complexity Economics challenges the older mathematical biases of the neoclassical school and argues against its notions of: *perfect competition, perfect knowledge,* static *equilibrium* states, *perfectly rational actors* and *perfect co-ordination* using the same language and many of the same arguments that the Austrian School of Economics has been using against econometrics since the early twentieth century. As Ludwig von Mises stated many decades earlier:

Now one of the main shortcomings of the mathematical economists is that they deal with this evenly rotating economy-they call it the static state-as if it were something really existing. Prepossessed by the fallacy that economics is to be treated with mathematical methods, they concentrate their efforts upon the analysis of static states which, of course, allow a description in sets of simultaneous differential equations. But this mathematical treatment virtually avoids any reference to the real problems of economics. It indulges in quite useless mathematical play without adding anything to the comprehension of the problems of human acting and producing. It creates the misunderstanding as if the analysis of static states were the main concern of economics. It confuses a merely ancillary tool of thinking with reality. The mathematical economist is so blinded by his

---

83 *The Economy as an Evolving System II,* W. Brian Arthur, Steven N. Durlauf, David A. Lane, Ed. (Westview Press, 1997) 3.

epistemological prejudice that he simply fails to see what the tasks of economics are.[84]

And as Murray Rothbard explains:

[N]eoclassical economic theory clearly rests on absurdly unrealistic assumptions, such as perfect knowledge, the continuing existence of a general equilibrium with no profits, no losses, and no uncertainty, and human action being encompassed by the use of calculus that assumes infinitesimally tiny changes in our perceptions and choices.[85]

Brian Arthur takes Mises and Rothbard's position himself decades later when he states:

"Neoclassical" economics, as the fundamental theory was known, had reduced the rich complexity of the world to a narrow set of abstract principles that could be written on a few pages. Whole textbooks were practically solid with equations. ... The mathematical economists had been so successful at turning their discipline into ersatz physics that they had leeched their theories of all human frailty and passion. Their theories described the human animal as a kind of elementary particle: "economic man," a godlike being whose reasoning is always perfect, whose goals are always pursued with serenely predictable self-interest. ... Neoclassical economics likewise described a society where the economy is poised forever in perfect equilibrium, where supply always exactly equals demand, where the stock market is never jolted by surges and crashes, where no company ever gets big enough to dominate the market.[86]

Only a Marxist economist of Desai's stature could deliver the *coup de grace* to econometrics by putting the argument in its historical perspective

---

84 Ludwig von Mises, *Planning for Freedom* [1952] (Grove City, PA: Libertarian Press, 1980), 142.
85 Murray Rothbard, *Economic Controversies*, 133.
86 Waldrop, *Complexity*, 22.

about the immotile paradigm in the economics of the late 19th and early 20th centuries:

> Economics led social sciences in the statist direction. The state became a major–if not the crucial–agency for securing the welfare of its citizens. As a philosophical category, as a social institution and as a political reality, the state became an object of fascination for the social sciences–economics, political science, sociology. The earlier idea of civil society as being autonomous, as formulated by Adam Smith, was now abandoned. Society was also no longer seen as an organic entity but as a mechanical one. Lenin had described the developments in Russia as an organic process. For Marx as well, capitalism was a self-organizing organic process, as it was for Smith, Hegel or Menger. Now, even for Marxists, economies were machines or buildings to be constructed or regulated from an *a priori* design.[87]

Physics envy and nineteenth century reductionism derailed neoclassical economics (and neo-socialism) and shunted it into a fantasy world where impossible equilibrium economic states are described as real world market conditions. This was essentially taking Newton's Second Law of thermodynamics and smuggling it in to economics, where it doesn't belong, as a long run equilibrium state is essentially heat death–full entropy. This led the entire discipline in the direction of an overly mechanistic unreality. Economics which once gave Darwin his crucial insight on evolution, now in trying to become more like Newtonian mechanics (physics), squared the circle and readopted the static anti-evolutionary Tory conservative views which had preceded them.

The Austrian school of economics' aversion to mathematics is seen as somehow anti-intellectual and being anti-science and even today many of their detractors bring this issue up as a major issue with this school. Yet their opponents miss the fact that they rightly understood that linear dynamics, which only work in static steady state equilibrium

---

87 Desai, *Marx's Revenge*, 221.

conditions, does not describe real world non-linear and dynamic complex systems. With the advent of nonlinear dynamics, a mathematical system was finally discovered that can give this "marginalized" school a valuable tool by which to reengage the neoclassical school and other modern schools of economics. Complexity economics has validated this "heterodox" economic school in many fundamental and dramatic ways and challenges all of our old static mechanistic world views. It is of no comfort or benefit for the ideology and movement that once based itself firmly on dialectics to be championing irrationality, illogic and a static Cartesian linear top-down nonorganic mechanistic paradigm.

The main feature of *complex adaptive systems* is that they are to be found everywhere throughout nature and seem to be the norm even throughout the universe. The Complexity theorist John Holland, as related by Waldrop, describes these adaptive systems:

> In the natural world such systems included brains, immune systems, ecologies, cells, developing embryos, and ant colonies. In the human world they included cultural and social systems such as political parties or scientific communities. Once you learned how to recognize them, in fact, these systems were everywhere. ... Each of these systems is a network of many "agents" acting in parallel. In the brain the agents are nerve cells, in an ecology the agents are species, in a cell the agents are organelles such as the nucleus and the mitochondria, in an embryo the agents are cells, and so on. In an economy the agents might be individuals or households. ... Each agent finds itself in an environment produced by its interactions with the other agents in the system. It is constantly acting and reacting to what the other agents are doing. Because of that, essentially nothing in its environment is fixed. [88]

He goes on to describe the one feature that they all have in common:

---

[88] M. Mitchell Waldrop, *Complexity: The Emerging Science at the Edge of Chaos* (New York: Simon & Schuster, 1992), 145.

[T]he control of a complex adaptive system tends to be highly dispersed. There is no master neuron in the brain, for example, nor is there any master cell within a developing embryo. If there is to be any coherent behavior in the system, it has to arise from competition and cooperation among the agents themselves. This is true even in an economy.[89]

Complex systems do not need a central controller since the controlling function is highly dispersed throughout the system, just like in the Internet or the human brain. Complexity economics destroys the old neoclassical paradigm of economic equilibrium and stasis, using modern scientific discoveries, and shows it up to be the intellectual error that it is. Waldrop expounds this element from Holland's interview further:

Finally, said Holland, complex adaptive systems typically have many *niches,* each one of which can be exploited by an agent adapted to fill that niche. Thus, the economic world has a place for computer programmers, plumbers, steel mills, and pet stores, just as the rain forest has a place for tree sloths and butterflies. Moreover, the very act of filling one niche opens up more niches-for new parasites and prey, for new symbiotic partners. So new opportunities are always being created by the [complex] system. And that, in turn, means that it's essentially meaningless to talk about a complex adaptive system being in equilibrium: the system can never get there. It is always unfolding, always in transition. In fact, if the system ever does reach equilibrium, it isn't just stable. It's dead. And by the same token, said Holland, there's no point in imagining that the agents in the system can ever "optimize" their fitness, or their utility, or whatever. The space of possibilities is too vast; they have no practical way of finding the optimum. The most they can ever do is to change and improve

---

89   Ibid., 145.

themselves relative to what the other agents are doing. In short, complex adaptive systems are characterized by perpetual novelty.[90]

The real world is spontaneous, emergent, complex and adaptive and does not represent or mirror our unnatural overly rational and reductionist ideas of it founded upon the intellectual errors of the eighteenth and nineteenth century's mechanistic, constructivist and determinist Cartesian and Newtonian reductionism. Evolution is an extropic force always creating greater and greater complexity and forming larger and larger complex structures, which defeats entropy.

While many of the paradigms in progressive and conservative circles are still adhering to the static, equilibrium based neoclassical Walrasian models, the neo-Austrian School of Economics is continuing to evolve. With the publishing of Butler Shaffer's truly monumental book *The Boundaries of Order*,[91] a convergence of classical liberalism/libertarianism with chaos and complexity theory has happened in a dramatic and truly exciting way. In many ways, the dialectical nature of the theories of Chaos and Complexity reconnect us with the systems and dialectical thinking that underlies Karl Marx's own philosophy. As Shaffer so adeptly puts it:

> The holographic model provides a fitting metaphor for ending the institution-serving division between our *individual* and *social* natures, allowing us to see that they are complementary aspects of the same dynamic of self-interested behavior. The boundary lines in our dualistic thinking that help to separate us from one another, begin to dissolve once we see them as fabrications of our minds. In their place, perhaps, may arise the vision of ourselves and our neighbors as interconnected individuals. Each of us is a biologically and experientially unique person who, at the same time, needs the companionship, support, and cooperation of others in order to survive. We

---

90 Ibid., 147.
91 Butler Shaffer, *Boundaries of Order: Private Property as a Social System* (Auburn, Al: Ludwig von Mises Institute Press, 2009).

are neither isolated hermits nor fungible cells in some monstrous, six-billion headed leviathan that moves about the earth in response to an imagined collective will. The *individual* and the *numerous* are manifestations of the *wholeness* that lies hidden beneath our dualistic divisions of reality.[92]

A sentiment echoed by Karl Marx himself in so many ways throughout his works as he never attacked individualism and always expounded a Promethean individual ideal. As Kevin Kelly rightfully says, "the image of the economy as something alive is powerful. And it is hardly new age hokum. And Smith himself alluded to aliveness with his unseen "hand." Karl Marx often referred to the organic nature of the economy. Even the legendary no-nonsense economist Alfred Marshall wrote in 1948 that 'the Mecca of the economist lies in economic biology.'"[93] The economic system is now coming alive in a new way and being seen as an extropic evolving complex ecosystem. Complexity is breaking down the barriers between once bitter ideological enemies and showing us the holographic interrelatedness of all social and economic reality. Complexity economics is now helping to remove the ideological errors of our older paradigms so that we can readily comprehend real world complex systems without the rigid ideological blinders we once strenuously clung on to, and which we unfortunately inherited from earlier less scientifically evolved eras.

---

92 Ibid., 258.
93 Kevin Kelly, *New Rules for the New Economy* (New York, NY: Penguin Press, 1998), 116.

6

The Techno-Optimist Revolution: Ridley, Kelly, Diamandis, Kurzweil & Naam

Humanity is now entering a period of radical transformation in which technology has the potential to significantly raise the basic standards of living for every man, woman, and child on the planet. Within a generation, we will be able to provide goods and services, once reserved for the wealthy few, to any and all who need them. Or desire them. Abundance for all is actually within our grasp.

-PETER DIAMANDIS

Within a few years of each other, five books went into print from 2005 onward that are the harbingers of a tremendous new shift in the prevailing pessimistic and neo-Malthusian paradigm of our age. The first of these works was Ray Kurzweil's *The Singularity is Near*,[94] detailing the transforming power that Moore's Law is having on technology and the world. The other four books were: Kevin Kelly's *What Technology Wants*,[95] Matt Ridley's The *Rational Optimist: How Prosperity Evolves*[96] and

---

94   Ray Kurzweil, *The Singularity is Near: When Humans Transcend Biology* (New York: Penguin Books, 2005).
95   Kevin Kelly, *What Technology Wants* (New York: Viking, 2010).
96   Matt Ridley, *The Rational Optimist* (New York: Harper Perennial, 2010).

Peter Diamandis'[97] book, coauthored with Steven Kotler, *Abundance: The Future is Better Than You Think*[98]soon followed by Ramez Naam's *The Infinite Resource*. All five works are strong supporters of what has become known as Techno-optimism and those who hold this optimistic viewpoint have also even been termed *Techno-libertarians* because many hold free market ideas and the belief that technological innovations will solve today's pressing problems. Coupled with these works is the rising popularity of both complexity theory and complexity economics which give strong support to the techno-optimist position as well as upholding to a significant degree the ideas and beliefs held by the classical liberal economic philosophers of the eighteenth and nineteenth centuries.

What is techno-optimism and what is so radical about the techno-optimist position? Techno-optimism disproves the prevailing pessimistic neo-Malthusian wisdom that the world is getting progressively worse; that a dystopian world of ecological, economic, and environmental disaster with resource depletion will be our future and that overpopulation will drown us in a sea of humanity. Techno-optimism turns these views on their head and it does so using valid historical statistics and evidence going back over 200 years to the start of the Knowledge and Scientific Revolution that made the Industrial Revolution possible. Matt Ridley's TED[99] talk on *When Ideas Have Sex*[100] is a mind-expanding romp through the last 100,000 years of human development reminiscent of the mid 1980's PBS show done by the late science historian James Burke entitled *The Day The Universe Changed*.[101] Kevin Kelly's *How Technology Evolves*,[102] Peter Diamandis' *Abundance is our Future*[103] and Ray Kurzweil's

---

97   One of the major cofounders of the X Prize.

98   Peter Diamandis and Steven Kotler, *Abundance: The Future is Better than You Think* (New York: Free Press, 2012).

99   TED: Technology, Education and Design Conference, http://www.ted.com.

100   Matt Ridley, *When Ideas Have Sex*, TED.com, video, 16.27 min, 2010, http://www.ted.com/talks/lang/en/matt_ridley_when_ideas_have_sex.html.

101   James Burke, *The Day The Universe Changed*, film, Produced by Richard Reisz, 1985: United Kingdom: BBC: RKO Pictures.), TV.

102   Kevin Kelly, *How Technology Evolves*, TED.com, video, 19.58 min, 2005, http://www.ted.com/talks/lang/en/kevin_kelly_on_how_technology_evolves.html

103   Peter Diamandis, *Abundance is Our Future*, TED.com, video, 16.14 min, 2012, http://www.ted.com/talks/lang/en/peter_diamandis_abundance_is_our_future.html

The Accelerating Power of Technology,[104] also found on the TED website, are dramatic paradigm changers. One cannot view these talks and not have an epiphany and say to oneself, "If this is true then Utopia is possible for all humanity in the near future without the need to restrict, redistribute, or ration any of the world's resources," a truly dramatic paradigm changer that goes against the reigning neo-Malthusian orthodoxy of the ideological position of today's world.

Though vehemently resisted and fought against in the vast majority of today's neo-left and Green circles. This new scientific paradigm is rising and gaining strength, and it is doing so by using empirical and scientific research based not on the older linear scientific and mathematical processes but on the new and rising discipline of nonlinear dynamics discovered in the mid-twentieth century and gaining momentum since the founding of the Sante Fe Institute in the 1980s. Where complexity theory arose out of the questions that chaos theory left unanswered, (questions such as, "How is it that order arises spontaneously out of chaos?") Techno-optimism is arising out of this new field. It is doing so based upon foundational discoveries, economic evidence and ideas which will eventually drive a dramatic paradigm shift for all of humanity. What is truly revolutionary about this new dynamic field and view of the universe is that it upholds the older classical liberal political and economic philosophers insights while at the same time surprisingly vindicating Karl Marx's evolutionary vision of the capitalist system. First a little historical background might be in order to flesh out this shocking convergent ideological phenomenon and how it applies to my argument of eventual economic ideological convergence and a coming economic singularity.

---

104 Ray Kurzweil, *The Accelerating Power of Technology*, TED.com, video, 23 min, 2005, http://www.ted.com/talks/lang/en/ray_kurzweil_on_how_technology_will_transform_us.html

7

The Two Teachings in Karl Marx: Revolution or Evolution?

There is an interrelated quality apparent to opposites which, when closely examined, provides intuitive glimpses of a more holistic universe.[105]

-BUTLER SHAFFER

When two schools of thought collide, their dialectical interaction changes both. Each conditions the other, perfecting the other and correcting each other so that a space is opened up where new understanding and insights can arise. This is the course and the process by which the argument between the older Marxists and the Austrian School of Economics has dialectically progressed for the last one hundred and twenty years. Beyond the homage paid by Oskar Lange, the socialist economist, to Mises' *socialism calculation* debate, a greater degree of thanks is owed to the Austrian's further in-depth analysis of Marx's doctrines and their winnowing of his system of thought separating the classical economic chaff from the golden wheat of evolutionary insight. For only the Austrians, especially Ludwig von Mises, clearly saw the

---

105 Butler Shaffer, *Boundaries of Order: Private Property as a Social System* (Auburn, Al: Ludwig von Mises Institute Press, 2009).

contradictions in Marx's thinking separating the earlier, younger, po-
lemical Marx from the later more mature Marx of *Das Kapital.*[106] Mises
stated this clearly in his chapter against interventionism in his book
Planning for Freedom:

> In later years Marx and Engels change their minds [from the
> Communist Manifesto]. In his main treatise, Das Capital, first pub-
> lished in 1867, Marx saw things in a different way. Socialism is bound
> to come "with the inexorability of a law of nature." But it cannot ap-
> pear before capitalism has reached its full maturity. There is but one
> road to the collapse of capitalism, namely the progressive evolution
> of capitalism itself. Only then will the great final revolt of the work-
> ing class give it the finishing stroke and inaugurate the everlasting
> age of abundance.

> From the point of view of this later doctrine Marx and the school of
> orthodox Marxism reject all policies that pretend to restrain, to reg-
> ulate and to improve capitalism. Such policies, they declare, are not
> only futile, but outright harmful. For they rather delay the coming
> of age of capitalism, its maturity, and therefore also its collapse.[107]

Further on in the book, Mises states this evolutionary ideal of Marx
more thoroughly:

> There are in the writings of Marx two distinct sets of theorems in-
> compatible with each other: the line of the integral revolution, as

---

106 It is a highly contested subject in Marxist Studies as to whether or not there are in fact two
separate and distinct theories in Marx's works between his earlier and later thought. Tucker
surmises that Marx's underlying idea of alienation is the glue that combines both halves of his
thinking together. Marx postpones the revolution until after the full and complete evolution
of capitalism in his later works and his opposition to all interventionism and revolutions prior
to this "omega point" becomes clear when one realizes that it is only at this point that material
abundance becomes so increased as to make the elimination of all alienation possible. This superabundance makes possible the end of all alienation and the realization of both Marx's and
older Marxists, as well as Libertarians like A. J. Galambos and Klassen's dream of a utopia where
the individual has complete control over their creative "property."
107 Ibid., 28.

upheld in earlier days by Kautsky and later by Lenin, and the "reformist" line of revolution by installments as indicated by Somebart in Germany and the Fabians in England. ... It is obvious that all the "reformers" of the last 100 years were dedicated to the execution of the scheme drafted by the authors of the *Communist Manifesto* in 1848. ... But on the other hand Marx also conceived a doctrine radically different from that expounded in the [Communist] Manifesto and absolutely incompatible with it. According to this second doctrine "no social formation ever disappears before all the productive forces are developed for the development of which it is broad enough, and new higher methods of production never appear before the material conditions of their existence have been hatched out in the womb of the previous society." [i.e.] **Full maturity of capitalism is the indispensable prerequisite for the appearance of socialism. There is but one road toward the realization of socialism, namely, the progressive evolution of capitalism itself which, through the incurable contradictions of the capitalist mode of production, causes its own collapse.** Independently of the wills of men this process "executes itself through the operation of the inherent laws of capitalist production."[108]

We leave it to none other than Karl Marx himself to state his evolutionary idea succinctly:

They [the proletariat] are not to hinder the evolution of capitalism as the narrow-minded petty bourgeois want to [do through interventionism]. The proletarians, on the contrary, should hail every step of progress in the Capitalist System of production. For socialism will not replace capitalism until capitalism has reached its full maturity, the highest stage of its own evolution. **"No social system ever disappears before all the productive forces are developed for the development of which it is broad enough, and new higher**

---

108 Mises, *Planning*, 91. Bold mine.

methods of production never appear before the material conditions of their existence have been hatched out in the womb of the
previous society." Therefore there is but one road toward the collapse of capitalism—i.e., the progressive evolution of capitalism
itself. Socialization through the expropriation of capitalists is a process "which executes itself through the operation of the inherent
laws of capitalist production." Then "the knell of capitalistic private
property sounds." Socialism dawns and "ends . . . the primeval history of human society." From this viewpoint it is not only the endeavors of social reformers eager to restrain, to regulate, and to
improve capitalism that must be deemed [in] vain.[109]

This passage is so important that I wanted to reiterate it from a modern
Marxist economist's viewpoint that uses a different quotation:

No social order ever disappears before all the productive forces for
which there is room in it have been developed; and new higher relations of production never appear before the material conditions of
their existence have matured in the womb of the old society itself.
Therefore, mankind always sets itself only such tasks as it can solve;
since looking at the matter more closely, you'll always find that the
task itself arises only when the material conditions necessary for its
solution already exist, or at least in the process of formation.

And Desai's comments directly after this quotation in his book are most
telling;

Practically all the commentary on Marx since his death, but especially since 1917, has been an attempt to deny this. This statement,
denounced as a crude–indeed, naïve-'theory', was vindicated at
the end of the twentieth century. Socialism was premature, since

---

109 Karl Marx, *Capital: A Critique of Political Economy*, ed. Frederick Kautsky (Chicago: Charles H.
Kerr & Co., 1909), xii. Bold mine.

capitalism had not as yet exhausted its capacity for development. We lost sight of this simple truth only because of the contingent factors–now, fortunately, removed–that characterized the short twentieth century: 1914-89.[110]

A quite telling indictment of the wrong step socialist theory and exegesis embarked upon after 1914. Let me return to my previous train of analysis from the Austrian School of Economics. Ludwig von Mises goes on to unequivocally state Marx's anti-interventionist premises:

> Karl Marx, in the second part of his career, was not an interventionist; he was in favor of laissez-faire. Because he expected the breakdown of capitalism and the substitution of socialism to come from the full maturity of capitalism, he was in favor of letting capitalism develop. In this regard he was, in his writings and in his books, a supporter of economic freedom. Marx believed that interventionist measures were unfavorable **because they delayed the coming of socialism**.[111]

Which is a point that can be confirmed throughout Marx's writings, here he himself confirms that:

> The stronger capital is, so much the stronger will the wage-earning class be; and hence so much closer will we be to the end of capitalist domination. Hence for us Germans, among whom I include the Viennese, I want to see a nice healthy growth of the capitalist economy, certainly not any swamping stagnation.[112]

---

110 Meghnad Desai, *Marx's Revenge* (London, UK: Verso, 2004), 44.
N.B. Desai in stating the date 1914-89 he is making an allusion to life span of the Soviet Union.
111 Ludwig von Mises, *Marxism Unmasked: From Delusion to Destruction* (New York: Foundation for Economic Education, 2006), 24. Bold mine.
112 Miranda, *Marx Against*, 63.

The old line Marxists were as determined against economic interventionism and for the growth of capitalism as the classical liberals were and libertarians are today, as Mises further elucidates:

> When economics was yet unknown, and man was unaware that goods prices cannot be "set" arbitrarily but are narrowly determined by the market situation, government commands sought to regulate economic life. Only classical economics revealed that all such interventions in the functioning of the market can never achieve the objectives which the authorities aim to achieve. The old liberalism which built its economic policies on the teachings of classical economics therefore categorically rejected all such interventions. Laissez-faire et laissez passer! Even Marxian socialists have not judged interventionism any differently from the classical liberals.

> They sought to demonstrate the absurdity of all interventionist proposals and labeled them contemptuously as "bourgeois." **The ideology that is swaying the world today [interventionism] is recommending the very system of economic policy that is rejected equally by classical liberalism and older Marxism.**[113]

Boris Brutzkus, an economist who lived under the Soviet regime from its inception until his expulsion in the 1930's, states this evolutionary ideal in Marxism as well:

> The utopian socialists believe that the socialist order would come into being through the initiative of small social groups which, convinced as to the benefits to be derived from socialism, would carry the rest of society with them in the fervency of their belief. In contradiction to this conception of the evolution of social phenomena, Marx maintained that social economic events must result from the

---

113 Ludwig von Mises, *Critique of Interventionism* [1929] (New York: The Foundation for Economic Education, 1996), 2. Bold mine.

action of the elemental processes of nature. The objective investigation of capitalist evolution leads, according to Marx, to the irrefutable conclusion that capitalism is marching inexorably towards its own fall, and that in its womb the elements of a new social order-the socialist order-are ripening. Thus Marx held that the immediate task of his age was not the establishing of small social groups on a socialist foundation, but in the consolidation and organization of the proletariat as a class; a class whose task should be, at a given point in social economic evolution-i.e. at the moment when the final crisis was upon capitalism-to take upon itself the reconstruction of society as a whole, and to rebuild it on a socialist foundation.[114]

Author A. James Gregor weighs in on this evolutionary theme:

Neo-Marxism rejected some of the central tenants of Marx's interpretation of world developments. For Marx and Engels "the bourgeois mode of production" is the first productive system in history driven by its own impetus to extend itself over all humankind. **In doing this capitalism would provide the material conditions for its own transcendence. The worldwide maturation of industrial capitalism would produce the economic abundance upon which socialism would be erected**.

In 1848, the first Marxists maintained that modern industry would be compelled by its intrinsic needs not only to establish a "world market," but to supervise an "immense development [in] commerce … navigation, [and] communication," which would accompany the global "extension of industry." Driven by the necessities of the system itself, capitalist production would "nestle everywhere, settle everywhere, establish connections everywhere," drawing "even the most barbarian nations into civilization." Industrial capitalism would

---

114 Boris Brutzkus, *Economic Planning in Soviet Russia* (Westport, CN: Hyperion Press, Inc., reprinted. 1993), 2.

"compel all nations, on pain of extinction, to adopt the bourgeois modes of production. ... In one word, it [would] create a world after its own image." The expansion of industrial capitalism was for Marx and Engels the necessary condition for the ultimate victory of social-ism. **It was the "infinite" productive potential of machine industry that capitalism brought with it that held the promise of socialism. Without universal industrialization, the entire tragic conflict of classes, the curse of poverty, and the exploitation of man by man, could not be overcome.**[115]

This constant evolutionary theme in Marx's philosophy is a consistent feature and focus of Marx's critics and detractors much more than from his admirers and adherents. Desai is the only modern Marxist econo-mist of note today that I know of who has rediscovered this "millennial-perspective", that capitalism was just one link in the chain of modes of production. "Like Smith, Marx had his stadial theory of history, but as with Hegel, there was yet another higher stage or two to come, which would eventually transcend capitalism."[116]

This evolutionary understanding within Marx's thought, along with his adamant rejection of all interventionism, is almost completely miss-ing in socialist circles today as they pursue the Second International's interventionism and Lassalle's and Hegel's love affair with the omnipo-tent state. Jose Miranda states this clearly in his book *Marx Against the Marxists*, "one of Marx's classic theses-that it is necessary to pass through capitalism and arrive at socialism-has been totally misunderstood and hence rejected."[117] He goes on later quoting Marx about the necessity of the Industrial Revolution:

It is through this Industrial Revolution that the productivity of hu-man labor has reached the point where, for the first time in the

---

115 A. James Gregor, *The Faces of Janus: Marxism and Fascism in the Twentieth Century* (New Haven, CT: Yale University Press, 2000), 65. Bold mine.
116 Desai, *Marx's Revenge*, 41.
117 Miranda, *Marx*, 242.

existence of humanity, through the ongoing division of labor among all, it is possible not only to produce enough for the abundant consumption of all the members of society and for an ample reserve-fund, but also to provide each and every individual with the leisure required, not only to preserve what deserves to be preserved of the culture transmitted to us by history-science, art, urbanity, etc.-but also to transform it from a monopoly of the ruling classes to a common good of society as a whole and perfect it even more. *And this is the decisive point.*[118]

Without the revolution caused by the evolution of the productive material forces the step off point to socialism could never come. Thus, the conundrum and crisis in Marxism of why the world revolution didn't arise in 1914 at the start of WWI and why the proletariat of the European nations all put on uniforms and marched and died fighting for the jingoist Western Imperialist capitalist powers is solved.[119] Capitalism was still too green and not technologically ripe enough yet to burst forth and for the revolution as it had not evolved sufficiently. It had yet to reach its exponential stage, which it is only now on the threshold of doing. So what some socialists see today as the "cancer stage of capitalism," are only the symptoms of its suffering a case of interventionist toxemia in its third trimester of pregnancy.

The revolutionary and interventionist Marx of the *Communist Manifesto* is expounded in socialist circles everywhere, while the more mature Marx, the Marx who was changed by his banishment to England where he spent his time voraciously reading the classical economic philosophers, which greatly influenced his later writings especially *Das Kapital,* is lost down a memory hole. This fact has been almost totally forgotten or relegated to obscurity over the last one hundred years by many critics and pundits alike. One can read Paul D'amato's *The Meaning*

---

118 Ibid., 252.
119 Note: Also what caused the collapse of the Soviet Union and why China has taken up freer market reforms is also solved.

of Marxism[120] and hardly find this evolutionary ideal of Marx anywhere within its covers. It is a work almost entirely influenced by Marx's earlier works and by revisionist Marxism-Leninism and Trotskyism, but even he recognizes the importance of material abundance for socialism to exist when he quotes from Marx:

> Socialism must be based upon material abundance. This is, Marx and Engels wrote, "an absolute practical premise [of communism], because without it, privation, *want* is merely made general, and with want the struggle for necessities would begin again, all the old filthy business would necessarily be restored."[121]

The need for material abundance through increased production was foundational in Marx's thought and works and among the older Marxists. It went hand in hand with his insight for the need for the full and complete evolution of capitalism.

The later classical liberal economists shared this incredible evolutionary insight with Marx and put it center stage in their works, once having refuted all of the errors he picked up from Adam Smith and David Ricardo, which has made such a difference today. Joseph Schumpeter, a former member of the Austrian school later lured away to the neoclassical school by Walrasian econometrics, and an admirer of socialism states Marx's insight definitively:

> The problem that has divided the disciples [of Marx is]: Revolution or evolution? If I have caught Marx's meaning, the answer is not hard to give. Evolution was for him the parent of socialism. He was much too strongly imbued with a sense of the inherent logic of things social to believe that revolution can replace any part of the work of evolution. The revolution comes in nevertheless. But it only comes in order to write the conclusion under a complete set of premises.

---

120 Paul D'Amato, *The Meaning of Marxism* (Chicago: Haymarket Books, 2006).
121 Ibid., 130.

The Marxian revolution therefore differs entirely, in nature and in function, from the revolutions both of the bourgeois radical and of the socialist conspirator. It is essentially revolution in the fullness of time.[122]

The famous philosopher of science Karl Popper, no friend of Marxism, goes on to illuminate this point further:

In Marx's view, it is vain to expect that any important change can be achieved by the use of legal or political means; a *political revolution* can only lead to one set of rulers giving way to another set-a mere exchange of the persons who act as rulers. **Only the evolution of the underlying essence, the economic reality, can produce any essential or real change-a s*ocial revolution*.** And only when such a social revolution has become a reality, only then can political revolution be of any significance. But even in this case, the political revolution is only the outward expression of the essential or real change that has occurred before. In accordance with this theory, Marx asserts that every social revolution develops in the following way. The material conditions of production grow and mature until they begin the conflict with the social and legal relations, out growing them like clothes, until they burst. 'Then an epic of social revolution opens', Marx writes. 'With the change in the economic foundation, the whole vast superstructure is more or less rapidly transformed ... New, more highly productive relationships' (within the superstructure) 'never come into being before the material conditions for their existence have been brought to maturity within the womb of the old society itself.'[123]

Marx's almost libertarian analysis of the need for capitalism to evolve fully and freely with little or no interference from revolutionaries,

---

122 Joseph A. Schumpeter, *Capitalism, Socialism and Democracy* [1942] (New York: Harper Perennial, 2008), 58. Bold mine.
123 Karl R. Popper, *The Open Society and Its Enemies: Marx & Hegel*, Vol. II (Princeton, NJ: Princeton University Press, 1962), 108.

conspirators or the interfering welfare-warfare state is of course avoided by almost all doctrinaire neo-socialists today. In fact, this is the main point of contention between the faithful Older Marxists that still exist and today's revisionist neo: Marxian's, Leninists, or Maoists.

Much of Marx's thinking (having been influenced by classical liberalism and classical economics) has many of the same foundational ideals as the heirs of classical liberalism today, the Austrian School of economics and libertarians. Marx's incredible insight was his applying Hegel's and the Romantic Movement's dialectical and evolutionary ideas to his economic studies so that he intuited one of his greatest discoveries of all time, that the true revolution would only come about through the full evolution of the productive material forces brought about by the full and complete evolution of capitalism itself. Marx himself said:

> Frantically bent on making value expand itself [the capitalists], ruthlessly forces the human race to produce for productions sake: he thus forces the development of the productive powers of society, and creates those material conditions that alone can form the real basis of a higher form of society based on the full and free development of every individual."[124]

The full and free evolution of capitalism would bring about the revolution in time as capitalism is the one and only real and major *change agent* whose processes Schumpeter described as "creative destructionism." Capitalism is a destructive transformative agent that is constantly rooting up, destroying, revolutionizing and changing the structure of production and with it economics, society, politics, and the legal structure. In the end capitalism's evolution as it becomes ever more exponential and rushes toward an economic singularity, will end up doing to itself what it has done before to all of the previous economic and social

---

124 Marx, *Capital*, Vol. 1, Ch XXII, 4.

systems that preceded it, "as Bertolt Brecht was one day to remark, as a Soviet supporter: 'Communism is not radical, capitalism is radical.'[125]

This idea is of tremendous and incredible significance, which the classical economists–Ludwig von Mises and the Austrian School–fully realized, as Mises stated so eloquently:

> The inherent tendency of capitalist evolution is to raise real wage rates steadily. This outcome is the effect of the progressive accumulation of capital by means of which technological methods of production are improved. Whenever the accumulation of additional capital stops, this tendency comes to a standstill. If capital consumption is substituted for an increase of capital available, real wage rates must drop temporarily until the checks to a further increase in capital are removed. The malinvestment, i.e., the squandering of capital that is the most characteristic feature of credit expansion and the orgy of the fictitious boom it produces, the confiscation of profits and fortunes, wars and revolutions, are such checks. It is a sad fact that they temporarily lower the masses' standard of living. But these sad facts cannot be brushed away by wishful thinking. There are no other means to remove them than those recommended by the orthodox economists: a sound money policy, thrift in public expenditures, international cooperation for safeguarding durable peace, economic freedom.[126]

The adherence of Mises and other intellectuals of his time to the ethos of the Enlightenment made them averse to making any future predictions as to where capitalism might be heading. They avoided overt prognostications as they felt that doing so would put them into the utopian tradition which they themselves thought was a tradition fraught with errors. Which is quixotic since F. A. Hayek himself "deplored the fact that

---

125 George Watson, *The Lost Literature of Socialism* (Cambridge: The Lutterworth Press, 1998), 44.

126 Mises, *Planning*, 10.

(genuine) liberalism never had its utopia," [127] as he himself succinctly expressed classical liberalism's failure to think in Utopian terms:

> [S]ocialist thought owes its appeal to the young largely to its visionary character; the very courage to indulge in Utopian thought is in this respect a source of strength to the socialists which traditional liberalism sadly lacks. This difference operates in favor of socialism, not only because speculation about general principles provides an opportunity for the play of the imagination of those who are unencumbered by much knowledge of the facts of present-day life, but also because it satisfies a legitimate desire for the understanding of the rational basis of any social order and gives scope for the exercise of that constructive urge for which [classical] liberalism, after it had won its great victories, left few outlets. The intellectual, by his whole disposition, is uninterested in technical details or practical difficulties. What appeal to him are the broad visions, the spacious comprehension of the social order as a whole which a planned system promises.

This fact that the tastes of the intellectual were better satisfied by the speculations of the socialists proved fatal to the influence of the liberal tradition. Once the basic demands of the liberal programs seemed satisfied, the liberal thinkers turned to problems of detail and tended to neglect the development of the general philosophy of liberalism, which in consequence ceased to be a live issue offering scope for general speculation. Thus for something over half a century it has been only the socialists who have offered anything like an explicit program of social development, a picture of the future society at which they were aiming, and a set of general principles to guide decisions on particular issues. Even though, if I am right, their ideals suffer from inherent contradictions, and any attempt to put them into practice must produce something utterly different from

---

127 Erik von Kuehnelt-Leddihn, *Leftism Revisited: From de Sade to Marx to Hitler and Pol Pot* (Washington, DC: Regnery Gateway, 1990), 321.

what they expect, this does not alter the fact that their program for change is the only one which has actually influenced the development of social institutions. It is because theirs has become the only explicit general philosophy of social policy held by a large group, the only system or theory which raises new problems and opens new horizons, that they have succeeded in inspiring the imagination of the intellectuals.... Paradoxically enough, one of the main handicaps which deprives the [classical] liberal thinker of popular influence is closely connected with the fact that, until socialism has actually arrived, he has more opportunity of directly influencing decisions on current policy and that in consequence he is not only not tempted into that long-run speculation which is the strength of the socialists, but is actually discouraged from it because any effort of this kind is likely to reduce the immediate good he can do. Whatever power he has to influence practical decisions he owes to his standing with the representatives of the existing order, and this standing he would endanger if he devoted himself to the kind of speculation which would appeal to the intellectuals and which through them could influence developments over longer periods. In order to carry weight with the powers that be, he has to be "practical," "sensible," and "realistic." So long as he concerns himself with the immediate issues, he is rewarded with influence, material success, and popularity with those who up to a point share his general outlook. But these men have little respect for those speculations on general principles which shape the intellectual climate. Indeed, if he seriously indulges in such long-run speculation, he is apt to acquire the reputation of being "unsound" or even half a socialist, because he is unwilling to identify the existing order with the free system at which he aims. ... While no socialist theorist has ever been known to discredit himself with his fellows even by the silliest of proposals, the old-fashioned liberal will damn himself by an impracticable suggestion. Yet for the intellectuals he will still not be speculative or adventurous enough, and the changes and improvements in the social structure he will have to offer will seem limited in comparison with what their less restrained imagination conceives…. The main lesson which the true liberal must learn from the success of the socialists is that it was their courage to be Utopian which gained them the support of the intellectuals and therefore an influence on public opinion.[128]

So sadly the heirs of classical liberal philosophy were distinctly allergic to any and all historicism–the stadial view of history. Though they distantly hinted about the possibility that the entire capitalist system may in fact actually be tending toward an omega point, to borrow the term once again from Teilhard de Chardin. A point where the system itself changes dramatically, where it is transcended and a new economic, political, legal and social system comes into being based on the *superabundance* of products produced and by their prices falling down the slope of an asymptote toward zero as the current economic system evolves toward exponentiality. Thus the classical liberals failed to capture the imaginations of the intellectuals as they never clearly fleshed out their ideas only making vague allusions to capitalism as an evolutionary system heading somewhere possibly utopian.

If Marx and Engels agree with the techno-optimists, classical liberals, and the Austrian School of economics on the necessity of the full evolution of capitalism and the inadvisability of interventionism, this naturally raises the pertinent question about *distributive justice*. What if anything remains of the desire to fairly redistribute the wealth of society in progressive and socialist thought? For it is here that a major disagreement in ideology between conservatives and libertarians, and progressives and socialists of today greatly diverge. Progressives and socialists today would be perplexed to learn what Marx and Engels had to say about distributive justice, as Robert E. Tucker "strikingly" relates:

---

128 F.A. Hayek, The Intellectuals and Socialism, Reprinted from *The University of Chicago Law Review* (Spring 1949), pp. 417-420, 421-423, 425-433, The University of Chicago Press; George B. de Huszar ed., *The Intellectuals: A Controversial Portrait* (Glencoe, Illinois: the Free Press, 1960) pp. 371-84., pg 380. Found on the web at: https://mises.org/etexts/hayekintellectuals.pdf.

'Social justice or injustice', writes Engels, 'is decided by one science alone-the science which deals with the material facts of production and exchange, the science of political economy.' 'Right', says Marx in his *Critique of the Gotha Program*, 'can never be higher than the economic structure of society and its cultural development conditioned thereby.'

The later work, consisting of marginal notes that Marx penned in 1875 on a draft program for a united German workers' party and published posthumously, contains a furious diatribe against the whole idea that fair distribution is a socialist goal. Marx points out sarcastically that socialists cannot agree on any criterion of distributive justice: 'and have not the socialistic sectarians the most varied notions about "fair" distribution?' He speaks of 'ideological nonsense about "right" and other trash so common among the democrats and French socialists.' He dismisses the notions of 'undiminished proceeds of labor', 'equal right' and 'fair distribution' as 'obsolete verbal rubbish' which it would be a 'crime' to adopt as a party programme. It is here that Marx quotes...the old French socialist slogan, 'From each according to his ability, to each according to his needs.' But in the very next breath he declares that 'it was in general incorrect to make a fuss about so-called *distribution* and to put the principal stress upon it.' To present socialism as turning principally on distribution was characteristic of 'vulgar socialism', Marx says, and he concludes by asking: 'Why go back again?' It should be clear in the light of all this that a fair distribution of the proceeds of labor is not the moral goal for Marx. The ideal of distributive justice is a complete stranger in the mental universe of Marxism.[129]

Many today would call these views of Marx and Engels conservative or libertarian in ethos, in doing so they miss the fact that Marx and

---

129 Robert C. Tucker, *Philosophy & Myth in Karl Marx*, 3rd ed. [1961] (New Brunswick, NJ: Transaction Publishers, 2001).

Engels' entire argument is based upon material and technological evolutionary processes and not on revolutionary interventionism. To equally distribute the income, profits or products of production before the eschaton, would keep the end of capitalism from ever coming, and in light of the new scientific and economic evidence arising from the techno-optimists distributive justice is actually taken care of naturally and organically as the system evolves and as products become progressively cheaper and more abundant over time, which is something the older Marxists knew and understood (Remember, in the realm of super-abundance prices drop to almost nothing and the entire world is transformed).

All of these similarities in thought are where Marxism and classical liberal–libertarianism–can be seen to ideologically converge with techno-optimism and complexity economics. As the insights and economic evidence of all these various authors, thinkers, scientists, and the arising new scientific discipline of *systems theory* point to a future convergence point, an omega point, where all of the old contradictions and errors are negated and a new paradigm stands free like a Promethean Titan from the suffocating old linear ideological chains that once bound it. The new messianic economic system destined to transform the world is being carried in the womb of the present capitalist economic system just awaiting the fullness of time to burst forth, as Marx so ingeniously intuited. It was left to the cornucopians, techno-optimists, techno-libertarians, Singularitarians, and the intellectual champions of the Technium to see it more clearly as they stand at the end of the twentieth century and the beginning of the twenty-first with more economic data, statistics and increasing technological development from which to draw their analysis from.

As Ray Kurzweil so ingeniously recognized, and I paraphrase him, "when you are travelling on the lower slope of an exponential curve it seems as if you are undergoing only linear development, until you reach the upward curve and then it becomes glaringly obvious that you are travelling on an exponential curve."

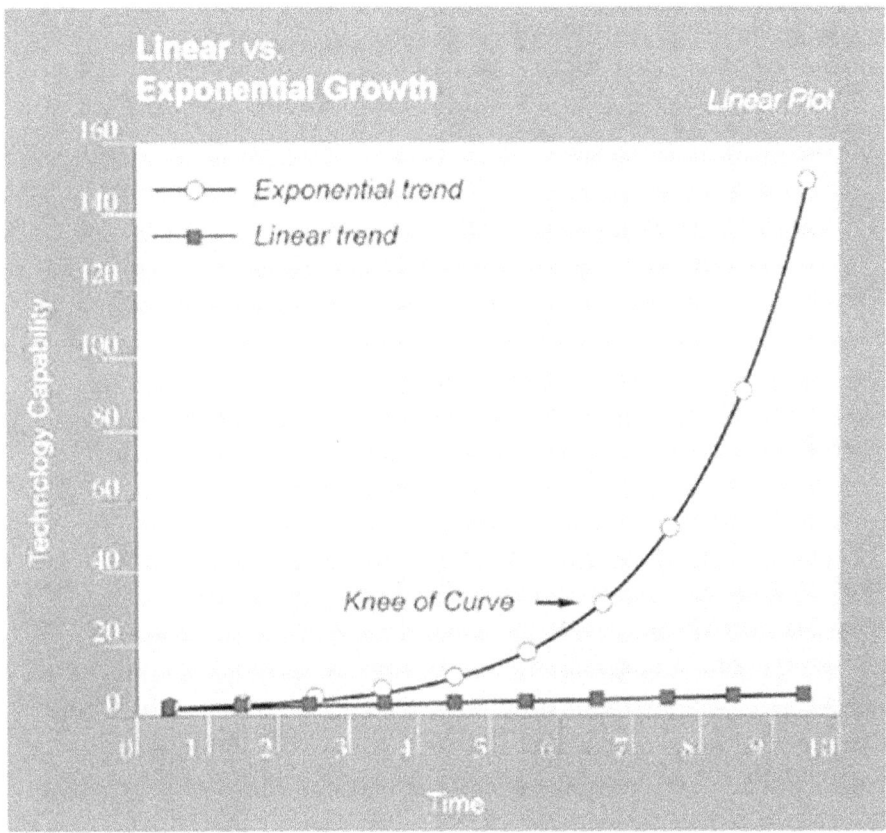

3 Linear vs. Exponential Growth.[130]

Previous generations of economists missed the fact that we were on an exponential curve as they lived on the lower end of a function that seemed as if we had only linear growth. Kurzweil describes this linear thinking versus exponential thinking:

> Most long-range forecasts of what is technically feasible in future time periods dramatically underestimate the power of future developments because they are based on what I call the "intuitive linear"

---

130   Ray Kurzweil, "Linear vs Exponential Growth," *The Singularity*, 10.

view of history rather than the "historical exponential" view. My models show that we are doubling the paradigm-shift rate every decade... Thus the 20th century was gradually speeding up to today's rate of progress; its achievements, therefore, were equivalent to about twenty years of progress at the rate in 2000. We'll make another twenty years of progress in just fourteen years (by 2014), and then do the same again in only seven years. To express this another way, we won't experience one hundred years of technological advance in the twenty-first century; we will witness on the order of twenty thousand years of progress (again, when measured by today's rate of progress), or about one thousand times greater than what was achieved in the 20th century.[131]

Now, as we ascend the exponential curve here in the early twenty-first century, we see more clearly that we are actually living in exponential times. *Homo Futuris* is an exponential being in the process of being born as the new social order that will give her birth, support and co-create her, evolves and emerges spontaneously from the bottom-up around us. The coming technological and economic exponential wave will totally transform and revolutionize our world. As Glenn Reynolds in his book, *An Army of Davids*, perceives:

One of the most significant consequences of this shift ... toward more cottage industry, more small enterprises and ventures, and more empowerment for individuals willing to take advantage of the [technological] tools that become available. ... is that the empowerment of individuals may lead to an interesting twist on Karl Marx's goal: workers control the means of production, all right, but it's a far cry from communism. Marx's view was tied to an outdated technological paradigm, but his desired outcome, a world in which "capital" is in the hands of the masses, not just the few, may ironically

---

131 Kurzweil, *The Singularity*, 11.

come about through the technological capitalism that Marx's heirs (though not Marx himself, really) despised.

Technologies that are still on the horizon, like molecular nanotechnology (whose enthusiasts predict will lead to machines that can make anything out of "sunlight and dirt") and biotechnology, may bring this trend to complete fruition. But everyday technologies are already moving us a long way in that direction. The worker's paradise may turn out to be a capitalist creation after all.[132]

It is continually accelerating technological evolution that will surprisingly bring us to the paradise that Karl Marx, older Marxists, Romantics and even libertarians so ardently hope for. We are thus on the edge of a verge, which shall bring this new world into being and it is the evolution of the Technium, fueling exponential capitalism, that is the dynamic force propelling us to this new utopian world.

---

132 Glenn Reynolds, *An Army of Davids: How Markets and Technology Empower Ordinary People to Beat Big Media, Big Government and Other Goliaths* (Nashville, TN: Nelson Current, 2006), 9.

8

Julian Simon, Bjorn Lomborg, Indur Goklany and Complexity Theory: Marx's Evolutionary Insight Upheld and Proven!

Therefore society tends to think statically and is always being surprised, often uncomfortably, sometimes fatally. Lacking dynamic apprehension it is difficult for humanity to get out of its static fixations and specifically to see great trends evolving. [133]

-BUCKMINSTER FULLER.

There is the historical and economic evidence for Marx's evolutionary insight that only through the full evolution of capitalism would the *omega point* of its negation be reached? Where a new system would arise creating a revolution in the social, political, legal and economic matrix of civilization? Literally the evidence is everywhere all around us and being constantly rediscovered by economists, historians, the techno-libertarians and techno-progressives. This is where Marx's quip that "first history plays out as a tragedy and then as a farce" becomes so apropos, as the individuals that have put forward the economic and

---

133 R. Buckminster Fuller, *Utopia or Oblivion: the Prospects for Humanity,* ed. Jaime Snyder [1969] (New York: Lars Müller Publishers, 2008), 155.

historical statistics and reality showing Marx's evolutionary insight correct, are the economists and historians with strong links to the classical liberal tradition and are the very ones the neo-Malthusian International Left fight and argue against so vehemently today.

The environmental movement especially has a hand in vilifying anyone who promulgates any data that proves that things are actually getting better and, in constant dollars, commodities have actually been getting cheaper and more abundant overtime. Such contradictions cannot seem to go unchallenged by the reigning politically correct "ultra-conservative"[134] and Luddite Romanticist orthodoxy of our day and many writers and activists have excoriated the cornucopians for their "wildly optimistic" positions. However, the evidence is so substantial and firmly grounded, even by the United Nation's own statistics, that only a devout secular religionist clinging to the prevailing rigid revisionist neo-left catechism du jour refuses to recognize it.

The center of the firestorm erupted after an economist from the University of Maryland, Julian Simon, published a book entitled, *The Ultimate Resource*, in 1981. In it he destroyed the reigning doom and gloom shibboleths of our age, which go all the way back to Thomas Malthus' book on *Population*. What was so dramatic and revolutionary about Simon's thesis? Everything! As Simon states in his conclusion:

---

134 N.B. When I call todays neo-left conservative, many people think I am mad because their own education in political and economic philosophy has been shallow and ideologically driven. Many researchers comment on this "shocking conservative aspect" of purportedly progressive ideologies. I leave it to Leon Surette to explain this issue fully:

> The true conservative rejects current arrangements as degradations of some primal state, and seeks to restore that state-a risorgimento or rebirth of the old amidst the new. The difference between Poundian or Nietzschean and Romantic or aesthetic conservatives is that the latter looked only to a pre-industrial past, whereas the former looked to a pre-rational past in paganism or the pre-Socratics. One consequence of this difference is that there is a confusing overlap between Jacobins, Masons, liberals, utilitarians, aesthetes, occultists, Poundians, Nietzscheans, and Marxists.‡

‡Leon Surette, *The Birth of Modernism: Ezra Pound, T.S. Eliot, W.B. Yeats and the Occult* (London, UK: McGill-Queens University Press, 1994), 78.

In the short run, all resources are limited ... a greater use of any resource means pressure on supplies and a higher price in the market, or even rationing. Also in the short run there will always be shortage crises because of weather, war, politics, and population movements.... The longer run, however, is a different story. The standard of living has risen along with the size of the world's population since the beginning of recorded time. And with increases in income and population have come less severe shortages, lower costs, and an increased availability of resources, including a cleaner environment and greater access to natural recreation areas. And there is no convincing economic reason why these trends toward a better life, and toward lower prices for raw materials (including food and energy), should not continue indefinitely.

Contrary to common rhetoric, there are no meaningful limits to the continuation of this process. ... There is no physical or economic reason why human resourcefulness and enterprise cannot forever continue to respond to impending shortages and existing problems with new expedients that, after an adjustment period, leave us better off than before the problem arose.[135]

All of which is heresy to the present doomsayers who predict all manner of crisis for the world. The only solution ever proffered in their dystopian narrative is a draconian top-down command and control, overly centralized political and economic system in order to save the world, which is the eighteenth and nineteenth century's reductionist conservative linear thinking model on steroids.

Paul Ehrlich, writer of *The Population Bomb*, challenged Simon's entire work, which led to the famous bet between them such that Simon told Ehrlich to choose any five commodities and that they would be cheaper and more abundant in ten years than they are today. Ehrlich

---

135 Julian L. Simon, *The Ultimate Resource* (Princeton, New Jersey: Princeton University Press, 1981), 345.

took the bet and theorized that all five metals that he chose: copper, nickel, tin, chrome, and tungsten would be more expensive and scarcer in ten years' time. He summarily lost the bet as every commodity that he chose was cheaper and more abundant as Simon had predicted. Chris Anderson in his book *FREE* recounts the results of the bet:

> *Wired's* Ed Regis reported on the results: "between 1980 and 1990, the world's population grew by more than 800 million, the largest increase in one decade in all of history. But by September 1990, without a single exception, the price of each of Ehrlich's selected metals had fallen, and in some cases had dropped through the floor. Chrome, which had sold for $3.90 a pound in 1980 was down to $3.70 in 1990. Tin, which was $8.72 a pound in 1980, was down to $3.88 a decade later."

> Why did Simon win the bet? Partly because he was a good economist and understood the substitution effect: if a resource becomes too scarce and expensive, it provides an incentive to look for an abundant replacement, which shifts demand away from the scarce resource ... Simon believed–rightly so–that human ingenuity and the learning curve of science and technology would tend to create new resources faster than we use them.[136]

As Simon himself states in his book *The Ultimate Resource II*:

> I do not say that "Infinite substitutability" is possible now or at any future moment. What I do say is that sustainability is increasing with the passage of time; there have been more and cheaper substitutes for each raw material with the passage of time. Finiteness by itself is not testable, except in so far as the fact that no one is able to state the absolute size of the relevant system (our cosmos) demonstrates the

---

136 Chris Anderson, *FREE: How Today's Smartest Businesses Profit by Giving Something for Nothing* (New York: Hyperion Books, 2009), 49.

absence of finiteness in its dictionary sense. But the relevant evidence we have available–decreasing prices and increasing substitutability–is not what one would expect from a finite system. (Hence the critics are reduced to saying that all the evidence of history is merely "temporary" and must reverse "sometime," which is the sort of statement that is outside the canon of ordinary science.) There is no doubt that my assertion of nonfiniteness is anti-commonsensical and, indeed, mind-boggling; regrettably… It is not explicit in standard economics, though it is not incompatible with standard received economics. But the critics simply do not come to grips with the matter that the available data are not consistent with the assumption of finiteness.[137]

The substitution effect was not the only phenomenon involved as the data for commodity production show. As the price of any commodity goes up, other resources are found to substitute for it, but another phenomenon also happens. A higher price generates more effort to find more of the resource, as well as generating inventions and scientific discoveries to more efficiently recover more ore from the previous mine tailings or ore-bearing materials that contain it. Aluminum is a perfect example of this process of an expansion of a resource as its purer ore deposits run out, as Peter Diamandis expounds in his book *Abundance*. Aluminum was once more valuable than platinum. All of the purer ore containing aluminum was exhausted by the turn of the twentieth century. The use of electrolysis allowed more ore to be obtained from increasingly less pure mineral deposits containing aluminum and it allowed more aluminum to be produced causing its price to steadily fall while its production took on an exponential curve. In a recent article on the new and quite substantial petroleum discoveries in North America in *Smart Money Magazine* entitled "The Return of Fossil Fuels," Kapadaia et al. stated:

---

137 Julian Simon, *The Ultimate Resource II*, 597.

It may sound contradictory, but investors say it's true: you can thank high oil prices for breakthroughs that might someday make prices lower. When prices are high, energy companies have the incentive (and cash) to figure out how to tap hard-to-reach reserves. The past decade proves the point. Fueled by demand from the developing world, oil prices have risen 265% in 10 years. The industry, in turn, put more resources into fracking and horizontal drilling–techniques that opened up huge North American finds like the Bakken and the oil sands of Alberta. Before the oil-price boom, says Brian Hicks, co[-]manager of the 500 million U.S. Global Investors Global Resources Fund, these reserves would have been unprofitable, now they're anchoring "a gold rush."[138]

High commodity prices acts as an attractor that brings in more competition and innovation, which in turn brings about more discoveries and more efficient production methods so that in the long run all commodity prices drop while their availability continually increases.

Simon went on to publish *The State of Humanity*,[139] a compendium of studies by ten economists, researchers and scientists in 1995, followed a year later by *The Ultimate Resource II*[140]in which he updated his statistics and argument from his earlier work. Throughout all of his works, Simon never wavered from his argument which he states noncategorically, "This is my long-run forecast in brief: the material conditions of life will continue to get better for most people, in most countries, most of the time, indefinitely. Within a century or two, all nations and most of humanity will be at or above today's Western living standards. I also speculate, however, that many people will continue to think and say that the conditions of life are getting worse.[141]" To date, Julian Simon has been prescient.

---

138 Reshma Kapadaia, Alyssa Abkowitz, Ian Salisbury and Missy Sullivan, "The Return of Fossil Fuels," *Smart Money Magazine*, August 2012, 54.

139 Julian L. Simon, *The State of Humanity* (Malden, MA: Blackwell Publishers, 1997).

140 Julian L. Simon, *The Ultimate Resource II* (Princeton, NJ: Princeton University Press, 1996).

141 From the cover page of *The Skeptical Environmentalist*.

A younger statistician and environmentalist, Bjorn Lomborg, discovered Julian Simon's work as he recounts in the preface to his book *The Skeptical Environmentalist*:

The idea for this book was born in a bookstore in Los Angeles in February 1997. I was standing leafing through *Wired* magazine and read an interview with the American economist Julian Simon, from the University of Maryland. He maintained that much of our traditional knowledge about the environment is quite simply based on preconceptions and poor statistics. Our doomsday conceptions of the environment are not correct. Simon stressed that he only used official statistics, which everyone has access to and use to check his claims.

I was provoked. I'm an old left-wing Greenpeace member and had for a long time been concerned about environmental questions. At the same time I teach statistics, and it should therefore be easy for me to check Simon's sources. Moreover, I always tell my students how statistics is one of science's best ways to check whether our venerable social beliefs stand up to scrutiny or turn out to be myths. Yet, I had never really questioned my own belief in an ever deteriorating environment–and here was Simon, telling me to put my beliefs under the statistical microscope.

In the fall [of] 1997 I held a study group with 10 of my sharpest students, where we tried to examine Simon thoroughly. Honestly, we expected to show that most of Simon's talk was simple, American right-wing propaganda. And yes, not everything he said was correct, but-contrary to our expectations–it turned out that a surprisingly large amount of his points stood up to scrutiny and conflicted with what we believed ourselves to know. The air in the developed world is becoming less, not more, polluted; people in developing countries are not starving more, but less, and so on.[142]

---

142 Bjorn Lomborg, *The Skeptical Environmentalist: Measuring the Real State of the World* (New York: Cambridge University Press, 2001), xix.

Lomborg's assumption that the techno-optimist data was nothing but right-wing propaganda is one unfortunately shared by far too many people today, but this data was even being examined by socialists in the 1970's. Jean-François Revel recognized that the capitalist system is making resources more abundant while at the same time it is raising real wage rates and lowering overall costs, as he mentioned in his magnificent book, *The Totalitarian Temptation*:

> Marx had predicted the lengthening of the workday and greater exploitation of the workers, these being necessary to the profiteers of an ever more technologically backward capitalism as they engaged in the final fratricidal struggle in which they would destroy each other. But on the contrary real incomes have risen steadily over the last one hundred years. Since 1870 average real per-capita income of the United States has risen by more than 2 [percent] a year. What caused this increase? If we assume that labor and the number of hours worked remained constant, the classical economists would say that increased productivity could only be explained by greater capital investment. They calculate that a 3 [percent] increase in capital results in a 1 [percent] increase in productivity. Between 1909 and 1949, capital investment in the private non-agricultural sector of the American economy increased by 31.5 [percent] per hour of work. Thus per-capita production should have increased by about 10 [percent]. In fact, it increased by 104.6 [percent]. The Neo-Marxist explanation of this phenomenon is that, granted that enormous difference is due to greater productivity, but that productivity was achieved only by harsher exploitations of labor, mostly by means of the "infernal" speed up. But that is not the case, for the productivity of manual labor is not the essential factor. The role of technological progress has been carefully measured and is known to be by far the most important factor in the rise in productivity.[143]

---

143 Jean-Francois Revel, *The Totalitarian Temptation* (New York: Penguin Books, 1978), 189.

And he goes on a few pages later to add:

Jean Fourastié has conducted a great deal of research on changing purchasing power in capitalist societies. In order to calculate the increase or decrease of the standard of living, he determines how many hours a laborer receiving base pay must work in order to earn enough to buy a given product. For example, a 2 CV Citroen car cost 3,456 hours of work in 1957 and 2,747 hours in 1967. In 1906 the cheapest French car, a Clement-Bayard two-seater, cost 10,000 wage-hours. In the mid-1970s the cheapest cars cost from 1,500 to 2,000 wage-hours, they're much more comfortable, faster, more capacious and more reliable. According to Fourastié, here is what has happened to the price in wage-hours of a ten-trip book of tickets for the Paris Metro:

> 1900:5 hours
> 1913:4 hours and 20 min.
> 1925:2 hours and 10 min.
> 1935:2 hours and 15 min.
> 1939:2 hours and 15 min.
> 1950:1 hour and 30 min.
> 1960:1 hour and 36 min.
> 1971:1 hour and 40 min.

Despite an occasional small rise, the general curve is strongly downward. One can also calculate earnings in kilograms of bread: in 1850 the miner at base pay earned in a month the equivalent of 80 kilograms of bread; in 1939 the laborer earned 300; and at the Renault plant in 1973 he earned 1,600 kilograms of bread. Of course, the numbers of hours worked was much less in 1973 than in 1850. Today, we must also add to the direct wages used in that calculation some 40 [percent] more for fringe and social benefits. Purchasing power has increased the most in those sectors where rising productivity has most reduced the cost of production: in wage-hours, a radio in 1975 cost one thirtieth of its 1925 price. Thus capitalist profit does not derive only from the exploitation of labor, but primarily from investment, research and innovation. *Labor is most exploited in the societies that have the lowest productivity.*[144]

Lower productivity means higher prices, lower technological development, fewer resources and less capital to reinvest in the lines of production and thus the slowing down or the ending of the evolution of the productive material forces, which means greater poverty for humanity.

Lomborg was mugged by statistical reality, but we needn't be too surprised by this, as he is just another person among many throughout recent history, who having stumbled upon the technological "invisible elephant" in the living room is stunned by what he discovers. The "force with many names" can be ignored but its power to transform human production, culture, life and civilization cannot be. He becomes just one more person in a long chain stretching back to Adam Smith and running forward through Karl Marx, Buckminster Fuller, Brian Arthur, Kevin Kelly, Peter Diamandis, Ramez Naam and Ray Kurzweil, discovering the same phenomenon. We are slowly coming to realize that this force, The Law of Increasing/Exponential Returns is what is feeding the evolution of the Technium, a force that seems to have a life of its own as Kevin Kelley theorized in his book *What Does Technology Want?* Lomborg does a superlative job of research and statistical analysis in his book. He goes on to present it in a more favorable fashion than even Julian Simon did in his works. For the purposes of this book, I wish to focus on only the vast deflationary effect on commodity prices over the last 150 years, as Lomborg states:

> Prices of the vast majority of industrial products have been dropping over the past 150 years. ... [figure 4] ... shows how the prices of industrial items have fallen by almost 80% since 1845. Equally, the World Bank has made an index for the world's 24 top-selling nonenergy products (such as aluminum, bananas and wool). Over the

---

144 Ibid., 196.

past century prices have been reduced to a third. The same picture repeats itself for metals. The IMF index ... shows how prices since 1957 have dropped approximately 50 percent.[145]

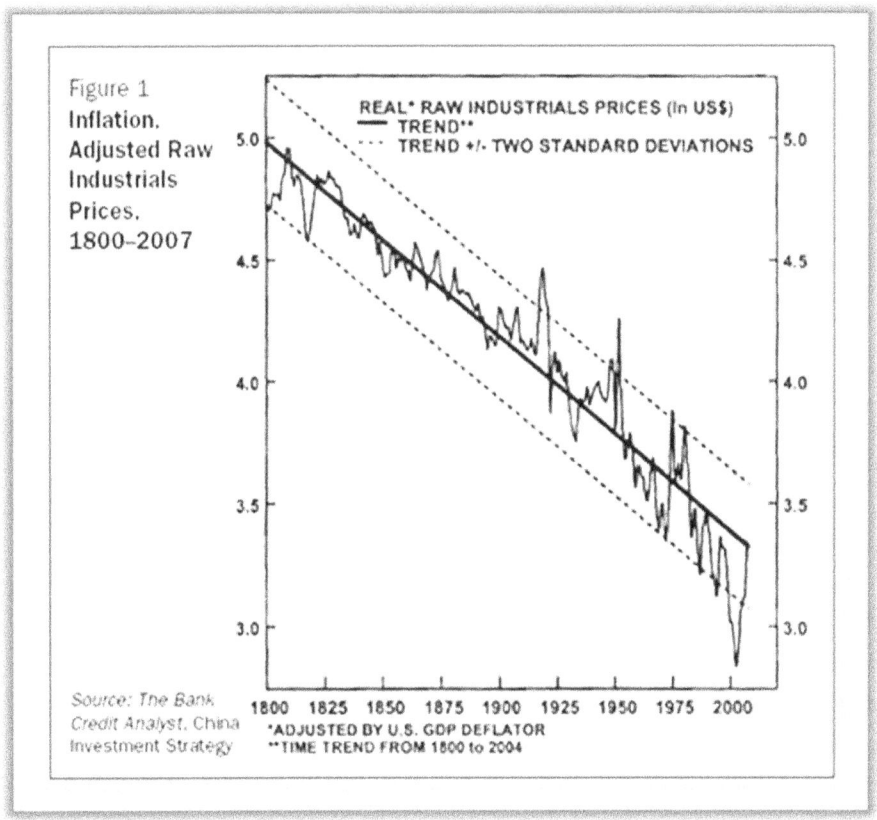

Figure 1
Inflation.
Adjusted Raw
Industrials
Prices.
1800–2007

REAL* RAW INDUSTRIALS PRICES (In US$)
— TREND**
··· TREND +/- TWO STANDARD DEVIATIONS

Source: The Bank Credit Analyst, China Investment Strategy
*ADJUSTED BY U.S. GDP DEFLATOR
**TIME TREND FROM 1800 to 2004

4 Inflation Adjusted Raw Industrial Prices.[146]

This phenomenon of continually declining cost with resource expansion can be found in almost every product, material or commodity produced since the rise of the Industrial Revolution. Even with price jumps and

---

145 Lomborg, 137.
146 Dan Denning, "The End of Abundance," *The Dailey Reckoning* (blog), April 27, 2011, http://www.dailyreckoning.com.au/the-end-of-abundance/2011/04/27/.

relative market scarcities in one time period the overall long term trend is still downward. Lomborg ends this chapter with the following remark:

> If we continue to use resources with no change in technology, we would eventually run out. The fact that this chapter can conclude that significant scarcities are unlikely is because we continually find new resources, use them more efficiently, and are able to recycle them, or substitute them.[147]

Which agrees with Simon's analysis completely:

> In effect, technology keeps creating new resources. The major constraint upon the human capacity to enjoy unlimited minerals, energy, and other raw materials at acceptable prices is knowledge. The source of knowledge is the human mind. Ultimately, then, the key constraint is human imagination acting together with educated skills. This is why an increase of human beings, along with causing an additional consumption of resources, constitutes a crucial addition to the stock of natural resources.[148]

The evolution of knowledge, science and technology revolutionizes the ability of humanity to search for and discover new pockets of known resources, create new resources, recycle the old ones, and/or to more efficiently use the resources we use presently and this process has been going on since human beings began using tools. As one well known quip goes, "We didn't leave the stone age because we ran out of stones." We also won't leave the petroleum age because we will have run out of oil. The discovery of a new more efficient and far more abundant and cheaper energy source will do to the petroleum age what the discovery of distilling kerosene and petroleum did to the whale oil industry, it shoved it into the tar pit of history forever, thus saving the whales. With the price of solar panel production dropping every year as its efficiency

---

147 Ibid., 148.
148 Simon, *The Ultimate Resource*, 408.

increases and with a new fusion generator being worked on by Skunk Works, it is only a matter of time before the oil age is over.

Indur M. Goklany entered the fray with the publication of his work, *The Improving State of the World*, in 2007.[149] His book furthers Simon's and Bjorn Lomborg's works and the techno-optimist argument and the economic evidence of their complex evolutionary expansion. His work goes over the same statistical evidence covered earlier by Simon and Lomborg using current data, but it has one major contribution that had to be made. The entire book is a refutation of Paul Ehrlich et al. IPAT equation. This equation is written as I=PAT—where I is the environmental impact, P is population, A is Affluence and T is technology. The untested and emotive foundation of this presumptive algebraic equation states that: as Population, Affluence and Technological advancement increase, the environmental Impact on the Earth increases in direct proportion dramatically and eventually destroying our ecosystem entirely. What is the evidence that this pseudo equation is correct? There is none; there never has been any. Goklany shows in case after case throughout his work using numerous tables that as technology and affluence have advanced environmental impacts have increasingly dropped in severity. As he has proven using statistical facts this controversial equation should be rewritten as $I=PA/T$. As technology increasingly advances and evolves the environmental impacts of both affluence and population begin to diminish down a negative slope. With the promise of nanotechnology, meta-materials, 3D and 4D printing the equation should now be rewritten as $I=PA/T^2$ where a higher powered exponential function dramatically causes all of the negative impacts of population and affluence to fall down an asymptote toward zero even faster.

I feel that one of Goklany's greatest contributions to the argument though is shown in his incredible image of the *Cycle of Progress*,[150] which makes the concept of the idea of the interrelatedness of the law of Increasing Returns incredibly easy to comprehend at a glance, which he presents in the following chart:

---

149 Indur M. Goklany, *The Improving State of the World: Why We're Living Longer, Healthier, More Comfortable Lives on a Cleaner Planet* (Washington, DC: Cato Institute Press, 2007).
150 Ibid., 91.

Box 4.1

Interlinkages in the Cycle of Progress

The figure in this box is a depiction of the cycle of progress, indicating the various links and the paths connecting those links.

Because this is a cycle, it has no definitive beginning or end. Here I will arbitrarily begin its description with economic growth (which leads to wealth) on the right-hand side.

Wealth harnesses human capital to create new or improved technologies (paths A and B). It also makes those new or improved, as well as existing-but-underemployed, technologies affordable (path C), which, among other things, enhances crop yields (path D). Crop yields help increase available food supplies (path E), boosting health (path F), as well as reducing mortality and increasing life expectancy. Better health then leads to greater wealth (path G).

If a nation cannot grow sufficient food, it can use wealth to trade (path H) in order to augment food supplies (path I).

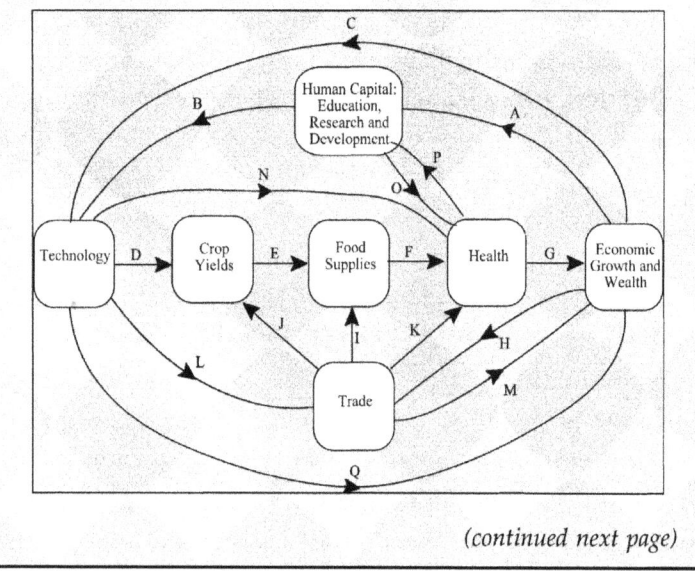

(continued next page)

5 Cycle of Progress [151]

---

151   Indur Goklany, "The Cycle of Progress," *The Improving State of the World*, Cato Institute Press, © 2007, page 91. Used with the permission of Cato Institute Press.

(continued)

Trade (in ideas as well as products) can also help improve a country's crop yield through obtaining technologies or inputs produced elsewhere (path J). Similarly, trade can be used to help improve a country's health status (path K).

This trade is facilitated by technology (path L), which enables rapid movement of large quantities of inputs and outputs from one location to another. Also, trade, by allowing specialization and economies of scale where they are useful, accelerates economic growth (path M).

Technology also improves health independent of food supplies and trade (path N), as does education, particularly of women (path O). In turn, better health enables fuller development of human capital (path P; see text), which, among other things, helps countries to develop, absorb, and diffuse new technologies (path B), which further enhances economic growth (path Q).

Thus, technological change and economic growth (supplemented by trade) are mutually reinforcing, coevolving mechanisms that drive the cycle of progress.

One may well ask which—technological change or economic growth—came first. This, in fact, is the chicken-and-egg question. Although the answer is historically important and intrinsically interesting, it is not all that relevant to today's world. We know that regardless of which may have come first, today we need both chicken and egg to have a sustainable population of chickens (although technology might change that in the future).

The interconnection shown in the diagram provides one explanation for the associations seen between per capita income and the levels of tertiary education, crop yields, available food supplies, infant mortality, and life expectancies, as well as the progress in those measures over time.

6 cycle of Progress cont. [152]

---

152 Indur Goklany, "The Cycle of Progress," *The Improving State of the World*, Cato Institute Press, © 2007, page 92. Used with the permission of Cato Institute Press.

Goklany summarizes this *cycle of progress*:

> The progress in human well-being in the past two centuries was sustained, if not put into motion, by a cycle consisting of the mutually reinforcing, co-evolving forces of economic growth, technological change, and free trade ... It is important to recognize that the cycle of progress evolved and was not the result of a conscious design. It fell into place as a result of self-organization. And the principle behind this self-organization was the desire on the part of every individual, family, and other social and economic unit to improve their well-being, and the political and economic system was necessary that would let them pursue that goal or was too weak to prevent them from doing so. This entire process took place in the context of Western societies' attitudes toward change, risk and reward, commerce, education, knowledge, and science and technology.[153]

Ray Kurzweil adds to this evolutionary insight on this exponential technological phenomenon:

> The 1990s and early 2000's have seen the most powerful deflationary forces in history, which explains why we're not seeing significant rates of inflation. Yes, it's true that historically low unemployment, high asset values, economic growth, and other such factors are inflationary, but these factors are offset by the exponential trends in the price-performance of all information-based technologies: computation, memory, communications, biotechnology, miniaturization, and even the overall rate of technological progress. These technologies deeply affect all industries. We are also undergoing massive disintermediation in the channels of distribution through the Web and other new communication technologies, as well as escalating efficiencies in operations and administration.

---

153 Ibid., 90 and 91.

Since the information industry is becoming increasingly influential in all sectors of the economy, we are seeing the increasing impact of the IT industry's extraordinary deflation rates. ... today's deflation is... caused by rapidly increasing productivity and the increasing pervasiveness in information in all its forms.

All of the technology trend charts... represent massive deflation. There are many examples of the impact of these escalating efficiencies. BP Amoco's cost for finding oil in 2000 was less than one dollar per barrel, down from nearly ten dollars in 1991. Processing an Internet transaction costs a bank one penny, compared to more than one dollar using a teller.

It is important to point out that a key implication of nanotechnology is that it will bring the economics of software to hardware-that is, to physical products.[154]

Once again, we are dealing with complexity theory, complexity economics, and the law of increasing returns as an emergent, spontaneous, self-organizing system that is constantly evolving and bringing down all costs of production and prices with it. That it took libertarians funded by such think tanks as the Cato Institute to rediscover an idea that once belonged solely to the domain of nineteenth century liberal, progressive and socialist thinkers is an ironic twist of fate. That they are fought against so vehemently by today's progressives and socialists is truly a consummate tragedy.

Ramez Naam's recent book weighs in on this extropic phenomenon as well while highlighting the failure of the neo-Malthusian predictions:

I highlight these past incorrect predictions [of the Club of Rome] for a slightly different reason. It's not that they were all wrong. It's that they were all wrong in the *same way*, and for the *same reason*.

---

154 Ray Kurzweil, *The Singularity*, 102.

They all ignored or underestimated the most critical human faculty that exists, and the most important source of our prosperity. Innovation. Malthus, Ehrlich, and the Club of Rome all dramatically underestimated the extent to which human ingenuity could lift the production of food. They made the mistake of looking at the physical resource–land–as the most important determiner of future output. They assumed that the invisible resource–our knowledge of how to maximize yields from that land–have only a small effect on overall productivity. The Club of Rome's predictions about energy and natural resources in the *Limits to Growth* made a similar mistake.

What we've seen is that the opposite is true. The physical resources matter. But the change in our knowledge resources–our science, our technology, our continual generation of new useful ideas–has made far more impact over the course of history. Knowledge acts as a multiplier of physical resources, allowing us to extract more value (whether it be food, steel, living space, health, longevity, or something else) from the same physical resource (land, energy, materials, etc.).

That's what has driven human history. And the continuation, willful direction, and acceleration of global innovation is our best hope of overcoming ... the whole panoply of resource limitations and environmental risks that we face.[155]

As Matt Ridley states in the same vein:

It is a common trick to forecast the future [based] on the assumption of no technological change, and find it dire. This is not wrong. The future would indeed be dire if invention and discovery ceased. As Paul Romer puts it: 'every generation has perceived the limits to

---

155 Ramez Naam, *The Infinite Resource: The Power of Ideas on a Finite Planet* (Lebanon, NH: University Press of New England), 105.

growth that finite resources and undesirable side effects would pose if no new recipes or ideas were discovered. And every generation has underestimated the potential for finding new recipes and ideas. We consistently fail to grasp how many ideas remain to be discovered.' By far the most dangerous indeed unsustainable thing the human race could do to itself would be to turn off the innovation tap. Not inventing, and not adopting new ideas, can itself be both dangerous and immoral.... [In the future] Technologies I cannot even conceive will be commonplace and habits I never knew human beings needed will be routine. Machines may have become sufficiently intelligent to design themselves, in which case the rate of economic growth may by then have changed as much as it did at the start of the Industrial Revolution - so that the world economy will be doubling in months or even weeks, and accelerating towards a technological 'singularity' where the rate of change is almost infinite... I forecast that the twenty-first century will show a continuing expansion of catallaxy–Hayek's word for spontaneous order created by exchange and specialization. Intelligence will become more and more collective; innovation and order will become more and more bottom-up; work will become more and more specialized, leisure more and more diversified. Large corporations, political parties and government bureaucracies will crumble and fragment as central planning agencies did before them.[156]

If Karl Marx were alive today, he would be squarely on the Cornucopians side and trumpeting their research as foundational proof of his theory that capitalism is evolving toward its own negation fueled by the law of ever falling prices through the expansion of the productive material forces–The Technium. What we are dealing with today is the clash of the inner contradiction that has been central in progressive ideology since the Romantic Movement, which Leszek Kolakowski states brilliantly:

---

156 Matt Ridley, *The Rational*, 354.

Romanticism in its classic form is a dream of attaining social unity by reviving some idealized feature of the past: the spiritual harmony of the Middle Ages, rural Arcadia or the happy life of the Savage, ignorant of laws and industry and contentedly identifying with the tribe. ... There is no suggestion in his [Marx's] work that mankind could or should revert to a primitive lifestyle. Unity will be recovered not by destroying modern technology or invoking primitivism and rural idiocy but by further technical progress and by obliging society to put forward its utmost efforts to perfect its control over natural forces. It is not by retreating into the past but by strengthening man's power over nature that we can salvage what was of value in primitive society: the process is a kind of spiral, involving the maximum negativity of the present [capitalist] system. The destructive effects of the machine cannot be cured by abolishing machines, but only by perfecting them. Technology itself, by its negative aspects as it were, makes it possible to revive what is destroyed. [157]

The socialist intellectual of the Radical Party of France Jean-Jacques Servan-Schreiber emphatically states the same idea:

Forget about the Golden Age, once and for all. It never existed. Our past, our entire past, is horrible. History books are still essentially fairy-tales about the powerful. The entire history of man including our father's generation–that of Hitler and Stalin–unfolded in the universe of penury and under the rule of the laws of scarcity.

If economic growth is erecting for us a disappointing and unharmonious city; if the political challenge of the end of this century is to assume power over the economy; if we are dissatisfied and, in solidarity with the weakest, resolved to propose real changes, then at least let us not make the mistake of so many intellectuals and young people who, following Proudhon ("poverty is good and we

---

157 Leszek Kolakowski, *Main Currents of Marxism* [1978] (New York: Norton Press, 2005), 337.

must consider it as the principle of our liveliness"), wish to believe that material austerity can constitute the basis of a social morality.

Let us look at actual history, not that which conquerors made their flatterers write and which schoolchildren are still learning, but that which the peoples of the world have written in silence, with their suffering, their ignorance, and their tears. This is the object lesson which can illuminate our proposals ... In any case, what is astonishing is not that two thirds of humanity is still hungry, but rather that one third is well fed.[158] This is the radically new phenomenon–the one which allows us to distinguish the two parts of history: the first characterized by fixity of techniques and the permanence of scarcity; the second, the one we are living in, marked by the accelerated progress of scientific techniques and, something which is entirely new, continuous economic growth.[159]

The irony today is that to be faithful to Marx, one would have to refute today's entire green neo-socialist Tory-Romantic Malthusians and take up once again the grand ideal that Marx and the classical liberals once held, and that the Transhumanists now hold, the ideal of Promethean humanity, which Kolakowski describes:

The Promethean idea which recurs constantly in Marx's work is that of faith in man's unlimited powers as self-creator, contempt for tradition and worship of the past, history is man's self-realization through labor, and the belief that the Man of tomorrow will derive his 'poetry' from the future ... Marx believed ... That the idea of 'production for production sake' meant developing the riches of human nature as an end in itself. ... Capitalism was the harbinger of socialism. By smashing the power of tradition, rudely rousing nations from their

---

158 This was written using the statistics available in 1971, today the number of people in the world defined as in absolute poverty has fallen to roughly 5% of the world's population while at the same time the world added more than 2 billion people.

159 Serban-Schreiber, *The Radical*, 33.

slumbers, revolutionizing production, and liberating fresh human forces, capitalism had made a civilization in which man for the first time was able to show what he could do, although as yet his prowess took nonhuman and anti-human forms. **It was pitifully sentimental to upbraid capitalism in the hope of stopping or diverting its victorious advance. The conquest of nature must go forward; in the next stage, men would achieve mastery over the social conditions of progress.**[160]

It is this convergence of ideology, here expressed in Marxism, techno-optimism and Transhumanism that we glimpse a way forward for all humanity. Progressives can no longer fight and agitate to bring capitalism down now, for if we understand Marx's evolutionary philosophy and economics thoroughly and accept the overwhelming evidence of the cornucopians who prove his ideas, the way forward to utopia is not to slow down or stop technological evolution as a way to end capitalism, rather it is to grease the skids of the free intellectual and scientific market system and allow it to evolve to the point of its own transcendence at which juncture the present economic system is negated and a new one arises. Post-Capitalism is a naturally occurring evolutionary process that is in the process of being spontaneously self-assembled from the ground up. I think Buckminster Fuller, the first real scientific complexity theorist said it best back in the 1960's, which was a heady time for futuristic ideals:

"The world has become too dangerous for anything less than utopia ..." Man's reflexes are conditioned to brush aside that statement on the grounds that "utopia" has become synonymous with the "unrealistic" or "impossible." This is because the many past attempts to establish utopias all failed. The fact is that all past attempts were unrealistic before they started. All the historical utopian attempts occurred when it was assumed that Malthus was right and that there

---

160 Kolakowski, *Main Currents of Marxism*, 338. Bold Mine.

never would be enough physical resources for more than 1% of humans to live out their potential four score and ten years in comfort; nor for more than one ten-thousandth of 1% to live it out in precarious luxury as well as comfort; nor for any to live out their full span in health, safety, comfort, luxury, good conscience, and happiness. The later would, of course, be the minimum requirements for everybody in the establishment of [a] utopia. That is why their attempts were "unrealistic" in the light of their working knowledge that those conditions could not then be met or even dreamed of ... No one thought in the terms of doing-more-with-less ... All of the would-be Utopians disdained all the early manifestations of industrialization as "unnatural, stereotyped, and obnoxiously sterile." The would-be Utopians, therefore attempted only metaphysical and ideological transformations of man's nature–unwitting any possible alternatives. It was then unthinkable that there might soon develop a full capability to satisfactorily transform the physical energy events and material structure of the environment–not by altering man, but by helping him to become literate and to use his innate cerebral capabilities, and thereby to at least achieve man's physical survival at a Utopianly successful level.[161]

We seem to be using nineteenth century linear thinking in trying to comprehend burgeoning twenty-third century "Star Trekian" exponential economic realities and so far mainstream thinkers and ideologists have taken the conservative Malthusian side of things.

That progressives today should be on the side of such conservative linear thinkers as the Right Reverend Thomas Malthus and have adopted a pessimistic, dour and reified consciousness so common of early nineteenth century Tory conservatives and Romantics is perplexing. That it is modern conservatives and neoclassical liberals that have taken the side of real extropic[162] progress, non-linear systems complexity

---

161 Fuller, *Utopia*, 357.
162 Extropy, an antonym of entropy. Reverse entropy. See Extropy: http://en.wiktionary.org/wiki/extropy.

thinking and new scientific discoveries in line with a dialectical outlook is quite astonishing! We have switched places and the movement that once fought for progress, change and scientific and technological evolution and societal transformation through more efficient production leading to abundance for all is now the determined champion of the conservative fear of change and the longing for the green pastures and idyllic times based back in the Middle Ages or in a mythical golden age of the past. I believe that Jean-Francois Revel said it best in his thought provoking book *Without Marx or Jesus*:

> What is happening today is that the left is succumbing to a sort of pseudo-leftist rigidity, which consists of being mesmerized and immobilized by the past to such an extent that one is unable to derive any profit from it. It is really a political neurosis–in the strictest clinical meaning of the term–by virtue of which one is imprisoned by stereotypes treated in one's childhood and unable to benefit from later experience. To create a revolution means to create new patterns of behavior–or at least interpretations of behavioral patterns ... Thus every economic system which is incapable of ensuring growth is doomed by the verdict of history. And that, as hard as it may be to admit, is a situation of the socialist countries ... Growth is that which is absolutely necessary in order for us to be able to accomplish anything; but what we can accomplish on the basis of growth can be either for the better or the worst ... Revolution, therefore, must bring about, in the present state of affairs, the separation of political power and economic power–the separation which, exists hardly anywhere in the world today.[163]

Servan-Schreiber–a contemporary of Revel in the Radical Party–wrote this startling conclusion:

---

163 Jean-François Revel, *Without Marx or Jesus: The New American Revolution Has Begun* (New York: Doubleday & Co, 1970), 54.

Economic development is transforming all aspects of human societies. In all fields, man's traditional situation in the face of the nature of things is becoming reversed. [A] [s]tatic economy generates the eternal "Josephine" Cycle-the succession of years of the fat kine and years of the lien kine,[164] leaving man a stranger to the notion of progress. One can thus understand why, from Virgil to Milton, all golden ages, all paradises lost [were] situated in the past: *in illo tempore*.[165] This conception is at the heart of Judeo-Christian thought. [In] the Old Testament, the idea of salvation is associated with that idea of returning to the poverty of the patriarchal era ... The social relationships which pervade our life are inherited from the static economy, the one in which, Colbert puts it: "What we give to some, we take from others." Who, in any case, does not continue to behave as though this were true? ... In a developed economy wealth proceeds from collective creation, but in a more-or-less static economy, it cannot spring from anything other than a predatory action exerted by the strong over the weak ... In moving from scarcity to creation [i.e. abundance], men have not only transformed their attitude towards nature, but have acquired the capacity, if they so desire, to modify their respective positions as regards each other. They are called upon to assert their solidarity: developed economies have, as distinctive characteristics, a complexity, a complementary nature, and an interdependence. Interdependence and economic progress go hand-in-hand.[166]

Later on in the book he dedicates an entire chapter to the necessity of the *Separation of Political Power and Economic Power* a shocking proposal for a socialist to make as it is typically a classical liberal and libertarian position. The recognition of the failures of past socialist endeavors

---

164 An allusion to the Old Testament biblical story of Joseph's prediction that Egypt would suffer a period of abundance followed by a period of famine and scarcity.

165 Latin for, *in that time*, or *in the beginning*, the Author is making an allusion to the opening phrase of Genesis in the Bible.

166 Jean Jacques Servan-Schreiber, *The Radical Alternative* (New York: W.W. Norton & Co. Inc., 1971), 37.

along with the burgeoning acknowledgement of the necessity for the productive material forces, the Technium, to evolve, led for a brief period of time in the 1970's within The Radical Party of French socialists to this quite shocking libertarian conclusion. Tom G. Palmer discusses the classical liberal view:

> Classical liberals have persistently worked to debunk the false image of the past–common to socialists and conservatives alike, in which happy peasants gamboled on the village green, life was tranquil and unstressed, and each peasant family enjoyed a snug little college. The common yearning for a past "golden age," a yearning that is still with us ("Ah, for the 1950s, when everyone…").

And he goes on to uncover the cart before the horse mentality that grips us where poverty is concerned:

> Classical liberals have insisted that the question of the "wealth of nations" comes logically before "the poverty of nations." Poverty is meaningful only in comparison to wealth, and wealth must be produced. Poverty is a natural baseline against which wealth is measured; poverty is what you have if wealth is not produced. The classical liberal economist Peter Bauer of the London School of Economics famously retorted to John Kenneth Galbraith's discussion of the "causes of poverty": "Poverty has no causes. Wealth has causes." As the historians Nathan Rosenberg and L. D. Birdzell Jr. put the matter, "if we take the long view of human history and judge the economic lives of our ancestors by modern standards, it is a story of almost unrelieved wretchedness." Widespread poverty is the historical norm; the wealth explosion of the past two centuries is the aberration that requires explanation.

Prosperity, as is understood today, is a uniquely modern phenomenon. The experience of the great bulk of the human race for most of its existence, up until quite recently, has been the experience of early death, sickness, ignorance, almost unrelieved physical toil, and uncertain access to sufficient food to sustain life. The picture of the past, carried by so many intellectuals is deeply misleading... Such [idyllic] accounts are hardly representative of the lives of the great bulk of the human race.... It is a sudden shift from a nearly horizontal line to nearly vertical line (fig. 7) that demands explanation. The conditions of most previous generations of humans-as judged by the standards of the present-are no less than horrifying.... Poverty is what results if wealth production does not take place, whereas wealth is not what results if poverty production does not take place.[167]

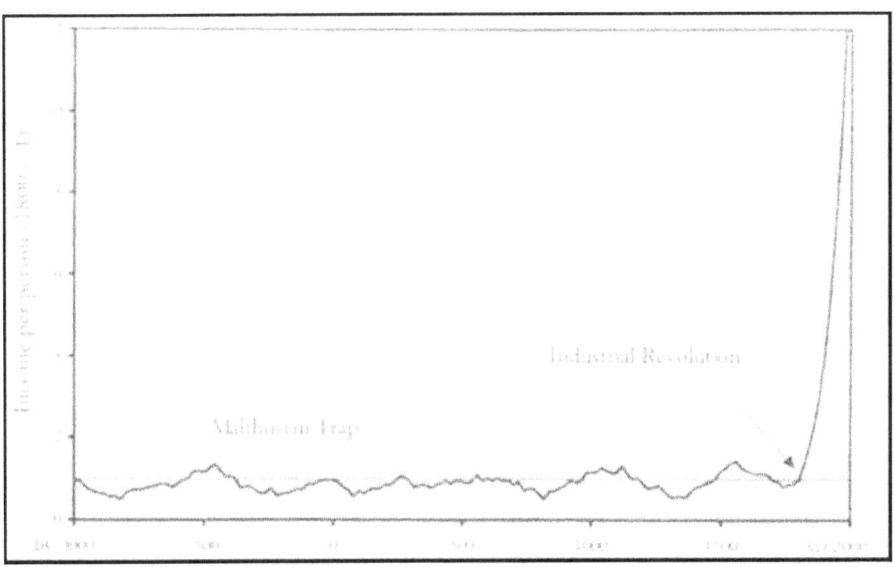

7 World Wealth[168]

167   Tom G. Palmer, "Poverty, Morality, and Liberty," in *After the Welfare State*, ed. Tom G. Palmer (Ottawa, IL: Jameson Books, Inc.), 111-113.

168   D.B. Halling, "Source of Economic Growth" (Blog), *State of Innovation*, Tuesday May 11, 2010, (8:50 AM), http://hallingblog.com/source-of-economic-growth/

Ideological convergence was already beginning to manifest itself some fifty years ago among French socialists and continues to do so though still mostly unrecognized. That socialists and classical liberals could agree on issues sounds astounding and incredible to us today. The Techno-optimists have proven Marx's intuition for the need for capitalism to evolve to the point of its bursting correct. All of their data have proven it irrefutably. The utopia we all dream of living in does not lie behind us in the past; it awaits us in a greatly advanced future that we are racing toward at an ever increasing velocity fueled by ever accelerating technological developments.

9

The Real Contradiction in Capitalist Production

What shape is the socialist world economy to assume? We have seen that Marx and his followers were primarily concerned with depicting capitalist society in its historical development; very rare and short are the passages in Capital that refer to the guiding principles of the system which is to replace the existing one. But one need not be too surprised at this fact: if it is History which ultimately governs human affairs, there is as yet no necessity (it is in fact quite out of place) to speculate on the details of the future order. When the time becomes ripe, all questions will be resolved and the parts will merge into a marvelous whole.[169]

-ELISABETH L. TAMEDLY

David Ricardo, writing in the early nineteenth century, was one of the most influential political and economic philosophers of his day. He and his followers and friends began an analysis of the new Industrial Revolution and came up with a perplexing discovery. As the

---

169   Elisabeth L. Tamedly, *Socialism and International Economic Order* (Auburn, AL: Ludwig von Mises Institute Press, 2007), 65.

industrial age advanced and production became more and more efficient as machine use was readily adopted throughout the production
process, the price of any x unit of product produced was continually
dropping. Meghnad Desai details the history of this theory:

> Every classical economist, from Adam Smith onwards, had a theory
> of the falling rate of profit. The idea that the rate of profit would fall
> as the economy progressed was central to classical political economy,
> though the reasons why this happened varied with different authors.
> Economy could run out of profitable opportunities (Smith), or run
> into the barrier of inflexible supply of land, so that rent which ate
> up profits (Ricardo), and so on. It was also a matter of taste whether
> the eventual state reached in such a case–the stationary state–was a
> happy one or a dire one.

> Marx's method of imminent criticism meant that he had to fight the
> classical economists on their own ground. They had a theory of the
> falling rate of profit, so would he. Of course, given his prognosis of
> the eventual breakdown of capitalism, his theory of the falling rate
> was bound to lead not to a stationary state but to another mode of
> production.[170] Marx, of course, avoided any speculation about the
> nature of socialism in his life's greatest work [Capital]. The falling
> rate of profit was a standard piece of political economy.[171]

This led the classical economists to the erroneous conclusion that since
all wages and profits to the entrepreneur were paid out of sales and since
the profit on every x unit of production sold was dropping, therefore
eventually at some future stage of capitalist production the worker and
the capitalist would both become immiserated. This idea was adopted

---

170 N.B. It is one of those funny twists in the history of political thought that modern greens and
the neo: left, socialists and communists of all stripes have abandoned Marx for the old classical
economic position that capitalism will break down and a static steady state system at equilibrium
will arise, which Karl Marx absolutely refuted.
171 Desai, *Marx's Revenge*, 75.

by Karl Marx as the breakdown of capitalism and was foundational in his later works and his economic magnum opus, *Das Kapital.*

The economic philosophers of the time were at their wits' end trying to come up with a scientific understanding of the basis for this deflationary process inherent in industrialization. One of the early explanations was based upon Smith's disastrous labor theory of value adhered to by Ricardo and was used to explain the natural deflationary trend in industrial production. This theory held that since all value was imputed to a product produced by the labor it contained from a human worker, and since machines do not impute human labor into the products that they produce as they are not human, then the phenomenon of the lowering of prices must be due to the absence of human labor value in the products produced by machinery.[172] Early on this explanation seemed plausible until around 1820 when the labor theory of value began to be heavily disputed and eventually fell out of favor by mainstream economic philosophers and was all but dead outside of socialist circles by 1830. Thus a new solution to the problem of value was searched for and a *cost of production theory of value* came into vogue, later itself to be found erroneous, but it did help lead to a beginning awareness of the phenomenon that became known in the late nineteenth century as the *Increasing Economy and Scope of Scale.*

Whether David Ricardo was heavily influenced by the pessimism brought on by the economic depression after the end of the Napoleonic wars (caused by England's inflating the money supply) or, if it was his own short sightedness that caused him to go so wide of the mark remains uncertain. His disastrous influence on continuing to promote Adam Smith's value error to later economists is to his lasting shame. By the late 1850's, a new phenomenon was showing up in capitalist production that again had the classical economists puzzled. Economic statistics showed that as more and more capital was being invested per

---

172 N.B. It is a funny twist of ideology that "scientific" movements such as The Venus Project and The Zeitgeist Movement that claim to base themselves upon empirical science use the machine theory of missing labor value from the early 19th century to try to describe the process of the law of increasing returns. See their Orientation Guide.

worker, and the more productive and specialized the worker became, the more their wage rates were actually raising. Coupled with the constant phenomenon of the continually declining price of goods sold, a new *phantom menace*[173] was all the rage in economic circles, especially among the American economists. It was one thing if the workers and the capitalists would both share immiseration by the evolution of the capitalist industrial system, but it would be quite a different matter if the workers, instead of sharing the capitalist's fate of being destined to eventual pauperdom, were instead guaranteed a future status of increasing wealth! Now it appeared that the worker would gain all of the profits and the owner of the industry doing the production would obtain a falling share of the proceeds until such time in the future when labor would absorb all of the profits entirely. Thus was born many fallacious ideas on "how to save capitalism from itself" and the poisoning of the economy by "excess savings" or capital accumulation. One of the most readily accepted ideas of saving capitalism was the idea promulgated by a new form of economic thought–Imperialist Economics. This form of neo-colonialism stated that the industrializing countries of Europe and America would have to shed their excess capital by exporting it to other underdeveloped countries in order to save the profit margins of the capitalists in the developed countries. Colonization was now reinvigorated and raised its ugly head again under this ideal of Imperialism, as Vladimir Lenin wrote:

> As long as capitalism remains what it is, surplus capital will never be utilized for the purpose of raising the standard of living of the masses in a given country, for this would mean a decline in profits for the capitalists; it will be used for the purpose of increasing those profits by exporting capital abroad to the backward countries. In these backward countries, profit usually are high, for capital scarce,

---

173 To borrow a term made famous by George Lukas' movie title.

the price of land is relatively low, wages are low, raw materials are cheap.[174]

Thus was born the mythos of the Leninist idea "that capitalist economies are inherently imperialistic." As stated above however this idea did not originate with any communist or socialist theorist, as the libertarian Lew Rockwell explains:

The view that sustaining capitalism requires aggressive war is usually said to originate with V. I. Lenin as a way of rescuing Marxism from a serious problem. The problem was that capitalism was not collapsing in the 19th century. It was getting more and more productive, and the workers were getting richer, not poorer–all facts that weighed heavily against the Marxist historical trajectory [of immiseration]. The Leninist answer to the puzzle was that capitalism was surviving only thanks to its military aggression ... But was Lenin really the originator of the theory? Not at all. The capitalists beat him to it ... The idea began with a group of Republican Party theoreticians during the late Gilded Age, who were concerned that the falling rate of profits would end up crippling capitalism and that the only salvation was a forced opening of foreign markets to US exports. These were the brain-trustors of Theodore Roosevelt, who ended up heralding US aggression against Spain in 1898. The fear of falling profits stemmed from David Ricardo's mistaken theory that the rate of profit is determined by the stock of capital investment. In fact, the rate of profit, over the long run, is determined by the rate of time preference in society. All else being equal, as savings rise, profits fall, which doesn't at all spell disaster for Capitalism ... But the theorists of Imperialism didn't believe it. Economist Charles Conant developed the theory in a series of essays beginning in 1896, including *"The Economic Basis of Imperialism,"*... In this piece, Conant argued

---

174 V.I. Lenin, *Imperialism, Highest Stage of Capitalism*, in *The Essential Works of Lenin: "What Is To Be Done?" And Other Writings*, ed. Henry M. Chrisman (New York: Dover publications, Inc., 1987), 216.

that advanced countries have too much savings, too much production, and not enough consumption, and that this was crowding out profitable investment opportunities for the largest corporations.[175]

What Rockwell did not mention was that this idea of divesting of 'surplus capital' is much older and goes all the way back to Jeremy Bentham and John Stuart Mill, as Murray Rothbard discloses:

Bentham had succumbed to worries about 'surplus' capital at home, to be relieved by imperial expansion, but James Mill had succeeded in persuading Bentham otherwise. As an adherent and virtual co-founder of Say's Law, the elder Mill had realized that Say's Law meant that there would be no 'gluts' from overproduction or excess capital; therefore, no colonial or imperial safety valve was necessary. John Stuart Mill, (John Mill's son) however, was converted to the idea of surplus capital by his old friend Edward Gibbon Wakefield (1796-1862)... A philosophical radical friend of Bentham and James Mill... Young Wakefield began the radical pro-imperialist movement with his *Letter from Sydney* (1829)... With this track, Wakefield launched the 'colonial reformer' movement, and John [Stuart] Mill proudly proclaimed himself Wakefield's first convert... Thus, by being converted to Wakefield's fallacy of the inevitable accumulation of surplus capital in advanced capitalist countries, John Stuart Mill lent his great prestige to the notion that capitalism economically requires empire in order to divest, to get rid of, allegedly surplus savings or capital. In short, [J.S.] Mill was one of the ultimate founders of the Leninist theory of imperialism.[176]

And that Lenin himself was influenced by an earlier book written by two Fabian socialists, "J.A. Hobson, together with G. D. H. Cole ... au-

---

175 Llewellyn H. Rockwell, *The Left, The Right, & The State* (Auburn, AL: Ludwig von Mises Institute Press, 2008), 272.

176 Murray N. Rothbard, *Classical Economics: An Austrian Perspective on the History of Economic Thought* (Auburn, AL: Mises Institute, 2006), 287.

thored *Imperialism*, published in 1902. This book inspired Lenin to write his pamphlet *Imperialism as the last Stage of Capitalism* which came out in 1915." [177] As the old adage goes, 'old fallacies never die, they just get continuously rediscovered and recycled by a new era of shallow ideological thinkers.'

As discussed above, the classical economists in their reified economic beliefs saw too much savings as detrimental as it caused prices and profits to fall. Thus was born the disastrous central idea of our age, first promulgated by classical economists in the 19th century and then later by Republican theorists influenced by this economic fallacy and after that to be picked up by the Fabian socialist John Maynard Keynes in his *General Theory*. These economic theorists thus surmised that capitalism with its incredible ever rising surplus of capital would eventually drown in its own savings causing its own immiserated demise by driving the prices of the goods produced and thus the profit rate to zero, as Marx himself thought it would and actually looked forward to.[178] For Marx this didn't mean immiseration forever, it meant revolution and a new form of production. This idea greatly influenced Keynes who became the champion of almost every economic fallacy of the eighteenth and nineteenth centuries which included this imperialistic idea in his economic system. His entire inflationary system was sold as a way to lower the real wage rate of the workers by the hidden mechanism of inflating the money supply, as Mises discusses:

> Lord Keynes's plan for the attainment of full employment, so enthusiastically endorsed by all "progressives," is essentially based on a reduction of the height of real wage rates. Keynes recommends the policy of credit expansion because he believes that "the gradual and automatic lowering of real wages as a result of rising prices" would

---

177   Erik von Kuehnelt-Leddihn, *Leftism Revisited*, 126.
178   N.B. For the Sci-fi nerds out there, imagine the Sandworm from Dune being drowned in water to get the spice Mélange from it.

not be so strongly resisted by labor as any attempt to lower [real] money wage rates.[179]

F.A. Hayek further elucidates Keynes' errors:

> The development of Lord Keynes's theories started from the correct insight that the regular cause of extensive unemployment is real wages that are too high. The next step consisted in the proposition that a direct lowering of money wages could be brought about only by a struggle so painful and prolonged that it could not be contemplated. Hence he concluded that real wages must be lowered by the process of lowering the value of money. This is really the reasoning underlying the whole "full-employment" policy, now so widely accepted. If labor insists on a level of money wages too high to allow full employment, the supply of money must be so increased as to raise prices to a level where the real value of the prevailing money wages is no longer greater than the productivity of the workers seeking employment. In practice, this necessarily means that each separate union, in its attempt to overtake the value of money, will never cease to insist on further increases in money wages and that the aggregate effort of the unions will thus bring about progressive inflation.[180]

A hidden pillorying of the worker was thus theorized by Keynes as a way to placate the capitalists to sign on to his flawed economic system of thought. However, hidden within the inflationary program is a much more devious ploy, as Keynes himself in a moment of glaring honesty stated:

> Lenin is said to have declared that the best way to destroy the capitalist system was to debauch the currency. By a continuing process

---

179 Ludwig von Mises, *The Clash of Group Interests* [1945] (Auburn, AL: Ludwig von Mises Institute Press, 2011), 22.
180 F.A. Hayek, *The Constitution of Liberty* (Chicago: The University of Chicago Press, 1960), 280.

of inflation, governments can confiscate, secretly and unobserved, an important part of the wealth of their citizens. By this method they not only confiscate, but they confiscate arbitrarily; and, while the process impoverishes many, it actually enriches some. The sight of this arbitrary rearrangement of riches strikes not only at security, but at confidence in the equity of the existing distribution of wealth. Those to whom the system brings windfalls, beyond their desserts and even beyond their expectations or desires, become 'profiteers,' who are the object of the hatred of the bourgeoisie, whom the inflationism has impoverished, not less than of the proletariat. As the inflation proceeds and the real value of the currency fluctuates wildly from month to month, all permanent relations between debtors and creditors, which form the ultimate foundation of capitalism, become so utterly disordered as to be almost meaningless; and the process of wealth-getting degenerates into a gamble and a lottery.

Lenin was certainly right. There is no subtler, no surer means of overturning the existing basis of society than to debauch the currency. The process engages all the hidden forces of economic law on the side of destruction, and does it in a manner which not one man in a million is able to diagnose.[181]

So, it seems that the idea hidden within the Keynesian system was a devious plan to bring down capitalism through the mechanism of inflation, while pretending to save capitalism from immiseration. However as revisionists, both Lenin and Keynes failed to realize that the exact same inflationary process could and would bring down communism and socialism as well and derail the evolution of the productive material forces as intuited by Marx. Robbing the economic system of capital (savings) is like pulling the electrical plug on a machine, it brings its smooth running operation as well as its evolution to a total halt.

---

181 John M. Keynes, *The General Theory of Employment, Interest and Money* (London: Macmillan, 1939), Chapter VI, 235. Note: there is some disagreement over whether Lenin ever said what Keynes quoted him as saying.

As Keynes reasoned, inflation lowered the purchasing power of the currency and by doing so it would cause the real wage rate to also similarly be reduced.[182] As prices in the economy rose and the real wage rate dropped below the market rate of labor, theoretically full employment would ensue. Since inflation would work to the benefit of the debtor–as the debt would be paid back in increasingly devalued currency–inflation would benefit the largest debt holders: government, bankers, corporations and capitalists, while debauching the workers' wages and their savings. The entire inflationary central banking system of the Federal Reserve was early on conceived as a way to inculcate this economic fallacy of the nineteenth century economists and Keynes gave the theoretical basis and support for it in his *General Theory* in the 1930's. Inflation would save capitalism as the more money that was printed the lower the actual real wage rate became and the more those holding debt were alleviated of it. It also had the other effect of "stabilizing prices," one of the main jobs tasked to the Federal Reserve as the ever shrinking purchasing power of the currency made it appear that prices were stable or at least increasing over time, and not deflating, as you had to use more fiat dollars with less purchasing power to buy goods. As Jörg Hülsmann stated so perspicaciously:

> Inflation is an unjustifiable redistribution of income in favor of those who receive the new money and money titles first, and to the detriment of those who receive them last. In practice the redistribution always works out in favor of the fiat-money producers themselves (whom we misleadingly call "central banks") and of their partners in the banking sector and at the stock exchange. And of course inflation works out to the advantage of governments and their closest allies in the business world. Inflation is the vehicle through which

---

182 Rough example: an inflation rate of 10% would theoretically eventually lower the purchasing power of wages by that amount, while raising consumer prices. While the worker would think their wage rate was rising, in real dollar terms it would actually be falling. Since wage rates do not rise as fast as inflationary prices the worker would be running a perpetual losing race between wage hikes and the government printing presses pumping out new currency.

these individuals and groups enrich themselves, unjustifiably, at the expense of the citizenry at large. If there is any truth to the socialist caricature of capitalism–an economic system that exploits the poor to the benefit of the rich–then this caricature holds true for a capitalist system strangulated by inflation. The relentless influx of paper money makes the wealthy and powerful richer and more powerful than they would be if they depended exclusively on the voluntary support of their fellow citizens. And because it shields the political and economic establishment of the country from the competition emanating from the rest of society, inflation puts a brake on social mobility. The rich stay rich (longer) and the poor stay poor (longer) than they would in a free society.[183]

All of which are the very problems which social justice reformers decry about the crony capitalist system of today. D'Amato disjointedly comprehends this process when he states:

> [T]he decline in profits can also be offset by siphoning off some of the funds that could be used to invest in new machinery ... High levels of U.S. government spending on the arms race siphoned off money that otherwise would have led to accelerated growth.[184]

Inflationary spending in all of its many forms: higher taxation, inflating the money supply, military spending, artificially restricting resources, union demands for higher wages etc. robs the Technium of the means to evolve at an ever accelerating rate, thus keeping prices and profits artificially higher for longer periods of time, thus bucking the natural

---

183 Jorg Guido Hulsmann, *Deflation & Liberty* (Auburn, AL: Ludwig Von Mises Institute, 2008), 34.
184 D'Amato, *The Meaning of Marxism*, 67.
N.B. The arms race/cold war was a quixotic event. On the one hand it drained away capital savings that would have gone to greater production, on the other hand the incredible amount of technological invention created to win the arms race increased production. But it is estimated that if all that spending had been allowed to stay in the economy the U.S. would be far wealthier and more technologically advanced then it is today.

deflationary trend in prices and profits of the capitalist market production system. This entire inflation–debt machine was actually created to stop the process of the natural deflation in prices and profits.

What most of the economists currying for political favor never seemed to fully realize, as they were blinded by the fear and greed of their own self-interest, was the real mechanism behind the historical process that was actually causing the natural deflation in prices. Karl Marx came closest to intuiting it in the nineteenth century and called it the productive material forces, but being a faithful follower of David Ricardo and his adherence to his own and earlier socialist writers, he failed to grasp it correctly and continued to adhere to the felonious idea of exploitation through the confiscation of *surplus value*. Even Lenin in his work discussed earlier failed to notice that when the developing Western industrialized countries exported their "excess capital" they exported it not to their colonies exclusively, but rather to each other. America exported capital to England, France and Germany. England invested in America and the Continent and so did France and Germany far more than they did to any of their undeveloped colonies. They imported the cheap raw goods from their colonies and then exported to the world finished goods, which the richer industrialized countries could afford in greater numbers than the poorer colonies. The exportation of capital theory, like the labor theory of value, failed as it was an economic fallacy from the very beginning and did not describe economic reality.

That did not stop it from becoming the hidden economic policy of today as America is drastically trying to export dollars through so called free-trade agreements so as to create a sea of dollars offshore which are needed to be imported back into the U.S. to buy burgeoning government debt so that our centralized banking Ponzi system can continue to operate. What began in the Nixon administration in the 1970's as a deal with the O.P.E.C. nations to denominate oil in U.S. dollars, and as part of the agreement that, "we would buy all of their oil if they would buy our debt," continues on with China and the rest of the world as America's number one export today is U.S. dollars. The American government is in the business of producing and selling its debt to whomever is stupid enough to buy it, and it needs as many dollars shipped to other countries as it can in order for them to come back and buy what the U.S. government is producing–massive debt. So if you ever wondered why the US government actually does anything and everything it can to keep us energy dependent, or pays and pushes manufacturers to leave the US, you have to understand this one point. In order for the Federal Reserve to create one dollar, it must create one dollar of debt and then commoditize it by having someone buy that debt and since we cannot buy our own debt using inflated money, we have to export dollars to other countries so that they can buy it.[185] As our federal government spends more, it thus has to outsource more U.S. production; if that fails it will have to dramatically increase taxes and confiscate savings and retirement accounts in order to shore up the system. One can readily realize that this feeding of the law of decreasing returns cannot continue on forever as Europe and all other countries using a centralized banking system is doing the exact same thing as the US.

This outsourcing of our debt caused another unforeseen problem which led up to the boom of the early 2000's as the excess exported US dollars from the loose monetary policies of the Federal Reserve came flowing back into the US economy from abroad seeking investment opportunities. This caused a fiscal supply shock, as this overabundance of savings began to help inflate the economy and drive the creation of riskier financial instruments in order to sop up all of this excess foreign liquidity. A. David Beckworth and Christopher Crowe mention in their book *Boom and Bust Banking*:

---

185 Mike Maloney, The Biggest Scam in the History of Mankind: Hidden Secrets of Money 4, https://www.youtube.com/watch?v=iFDe5kUUyT0. This is a good primer on how the monetary system works.

The monetary superpower hypothesis claims not only that the Federal Reserve is a monetary superpower, but also that because of its unusually accommodative monetary policy in the early-to-mid 2000's, it created a global liquidity boom and the related economic imbalances. Key part of the story is that the dollar-pegging countries had to acquire vast sums of foreign exchange reserves to counteract the loosening of US monetary policy. This buildup of foreign exchange reserves, in turn, got recycled back to the United States as these countries bought up US securities. This increased the demand for safe US assets and put downward pressure on long-term interest rates. For this story to hold, then, it must be established that the loose US monetary policy was closely tied to buildup of foreign exchange reserves during this time.[186]

The desire to save capitalism by exporting excess savings, monetary liquidity, or capital accumulation is thus a complete failure. All the economic ideologues have been able to do is to slow down the evolution of the Technium; they have not been able to arrest it.[187]

A Kevin Kelly states, "in 1957 Robert Shaw, an economist working at MIT, calculated that technology is responsible for about 80% of [US] growth. We see now, particularly with the advent of the network economy that technology is not the residual, but the dynamo. In the new order, technology is the Prime Mover." [188] As technology took off at ever increasing speeds it has caused a capital savings "boom" as the prices of the means of production continue to fall in both producers goods as well as consumer goods. This phenomenon outstripped the erroneous inflationary monetary policies of the Western Nation's central banks, actually saving capitalism from collapsing by supporting the value of the currency. So while in trying to save capitalism the inflationary monetary

---

186 David Beckworth and Christopher Crowe, ed. *Boom and Bust Banking: The Causes and Cures of the Great Recession* (Oakland, CA: The Independent Institute, 2012), 118.
187 Only an ideologically driven draconian *precautionary principle* can do that.
188 Kevin Kelly, *New Rules*, 156.

policies have been driving the West toward bankruptcy and collapse, the aggregate supply shocks caused by the law of increasing returns, which continues to drop the real prices and costs of production, has actually been saving them from collapse allowing the Western inflationists to continue on with their ill-advised credit expansion for decades longer than they would have been able to otherwise as Hans Sennholtz states:

> Yet, this purchasing power loss of the dollar would have been far greater if a remarkable rise in industrial productivity had not occurred. In spite of the heavy burden of government and the phenomenal increase in the supply of money..., both of which exerted their influences toward [a] lower dollar value, American commerce and industry managed to increase the supply of marketable goods and thereby retained or restored some purchasing power to the United States dollar. Under most difficult circumstances they managed to form more capital and improve production technology, and thus made available more and better economic goods which in turn helped to stabilize the dollar. Without this remarkable achievement by American entrepreneurs and capitalists, [the] United States dollar would have already followed the way of many other national currencies to radical depreciation and devaluation.[189]

The other theory of how to save capitalism was to stabilize prices to keep them from falling. This is the one of the main ideas underlying monetary theory and Keynesian and neo-Keynesian economics. One of the Federal Reserve's main missions is this one and after the Great Recession the new policy adopted by the Fed is now to increase prices by 2% a year. As Peter Schiff says about this new disastrous policy:

> Up until recently, promoting price stability was part of the Fed's dual mandate, the other part being maximum employment. However,

---

189 Hans R. Sennholtz, *Age of Inflation* (Belmont, MA: Western Islands, 1979), 16.

without any congressional action, the Fed changed its mandate. According to Ben Bernanke, the Fed's new mandate is to ensure that consumer prices, as measured by the CPI, rise by at least 2% per annum. Anything less risks the possibility that prices might fall, which according to Bernanke would be a disaster. However, for prices to remain stable over time, prices must fall during some years to offset rises in other years. Prior to the Fed we did not have stable prices, we had prices that gradually declined over time. The government told us that falling prices were bad, and that price stability would better promote economic growth. Now they are telling us that stable prices are bad, and that rising prices are more desirable. Think about this. When the Fed's goal was price stability we experienced steadily rising prices instead. Now that the Fed is pursuing rising prices as its official policy objective, imagine how much higher they will soar.

To make matters worse, the 2% annual consumer price increases the Fed considers a must are based on the CPI. However, thanks to the Boskin Commission, the CPI no longer accurately measures price increases. Instead a complex methodology using geometric weighing, substitution, and hedonics results in a CPI that rises more slowly than the general price level. So a 2% CPI might actually equate to annual price increases of 6% or more. The people running the Fed may be completely inept at most things, but the one thing they do well is create inflation.[190]

Here is the historical CPI index figures since 1800:

---

190 Peter D. Schiff, *The Real Crash: How to Save Yourself and Your Country* (New York, NY: St. Martin's Press, 2012), 124.

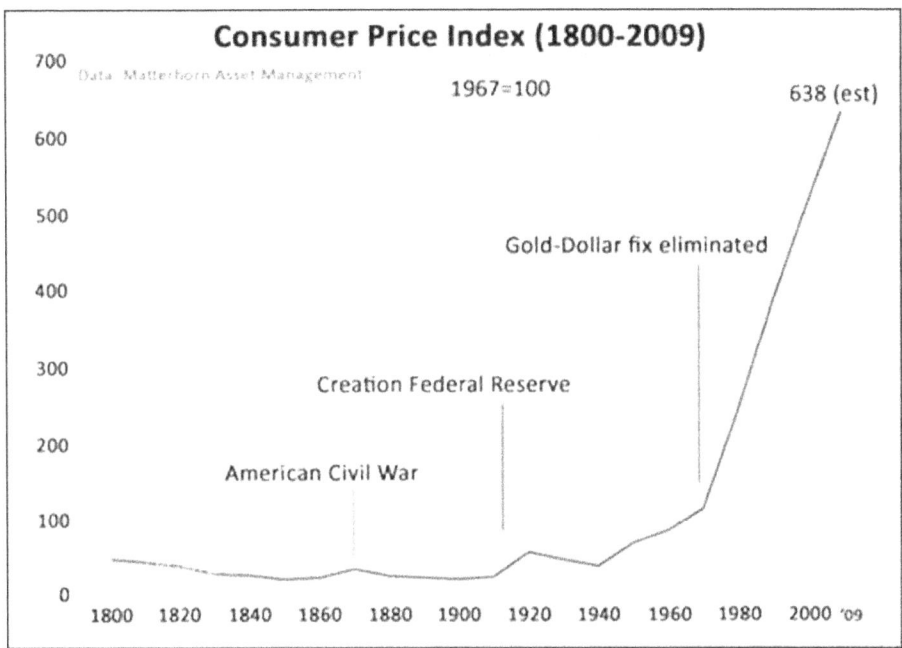

Consumer Price Index (1800-2009)

8 CPI Index 1800 – 2009 [191]

As we can see fear of deflation is fallacious and the great bugaboo of modern monetary economists and it has had disastrous results as Beckworth details about the Fed's bungling of the Great Recession:

> The Fed's actions are the consequence of its inability to handle the US productivity boom at the time. Between 2002 and 2004, total factor productivity grew at an average rate of about 2.5% year. This was a vast increase over the average growth of just under 0.9–percent growth over the previous 30 years. This productivity surge reduced upward pressures on the price level by expanding the capacity of the economy. These changes in turn meant that the federal funds rate needed to be higher to prevent monetary policy from becoming too expansionary. The Fed had a hard time seeing these developments

191   Joe Wiesenthal, "Chart of the Day: A Really Long View of Inflation Shows That it is All the Fed's Fault," *Business Insider* (blog), August 16, 2010 (11:51 AM), http://www.businessinsider.com/chart-of-the-day-inflation-1800-2009-2010-8.

this way. The Fed assumed that the disinflation was a result of harmful deflationary pressures and that the excess capacity was a symptom of slack demand. Raising the federal funds rate, therefore, would be contractionary. In short, the Fed approached these developments as though they were the result of a decline in aggregate demand rather than an increase in aggregate supply. Consequently, the Fed kept monetary policy excessively accommodative for extended period of time. Ironically, at the time, the Fed recognized that the productivity gains were contributing to the deflationary pressures in the growing economic capacity. Yet they could not get past its fear of these developments to see the implications of this understanding: further monetary easing was not necessary for most of the 2002-2004 period.[192]

This is not the first time that the Federal Reserve made the same mistake of confusing slack demand with an aggregate supply shock.[193] The Fed did the exact same thing throughout the 1920s as productivity greatly increased throughout that decade in the United States. Keynes comments on this fact, "In the United States factory output per head was 40 per cent greater in 1925 than in 1919."[194] The natural fall in prices during this time was seen by the Fed as a fall in aggregate demand so that the Federal Reserve pumped liquidity into the economy in order to fight this natural deflation rate created by the law of increasing returns. Beckworth elucidates further;

> Ben Bernanke, in his 2002 deflation speech, says that the "source of the deflation is not a mystery. Deflation is in almost all cases the side effect of a collapse in aggregate demand--a drop in spending so severe that producers must cut prices on an ongoing basis in order to find buyers."... The second type of deflationary pressure, on

---

192 Beckworth *Boom and Bust*, 27.
193 The term *aggregate supply shock* used by economists I feel is too vague and confusing to the average non-economist, the reader should think of the Law of Increasing Returns whenever they see this term used.
194 John M. Keynes, *Economic Possibilities for our Grandchildren.*

the other hand, is result of positive aggregate supply shocks. Such aggregate supply shocks are the result of surges in productivity or factor input growth that lower per-unit costs of production and, in conjunction with competitive market forces, create downward pressure on output prices. Unlike a collapse in aggregate demand, positive aggregate supply shocks generate benign deflationary pressures that are entirely consistent with robust economic activity. Consider, for example, the case of the sustained increase in the productivity growth rate. In this case, not only are deflationary pressures associated with strong economic growth, but also financial intermediation is not being harmed as asset prices are increasing and any unexpected increases in real debt burdens are being offset by unexpected increases in real income.[195]

He goes on to state a truly incomprehensible conundrum;

Bernanke acknowledges this type of deflationary pressure in his 2002 deflation speech: "deflation could also be caused by a sudden, large expansion in aggregate supply, rising, for example, from rapid gains in productivity and broadly declining costs.… Note that a supply-side deflation would be associated with an economic boom rather than recession." Although rare today, deflationary pressures like this did occur in the United States during the Postbellum period of 1866-97… During this time, real GNP growth averaged about 4% a year, while the price level declined on average about 2% a year… Deflationary pressures, therefore, are not necessarily associated with economic weakness and a breakdown of financial intermediation. It all depends on the source of the downward price pressures.[196]

The Federal chairman himself fully acknowledges that an aggregate supply shock caused by greater productivity would naturally deflate

---

195 Ibid. *Boom and Bust,* 32.
196 Ibid. *Boom and Bust,* 32. See his book for the graphs showing the economic figures for the late 19th century.

prices in the economy but quixotically he and the entire Federal Reserve system fights this effect by greatly inflating the money supply and/or expanding credit. Even Beckworth gets it wrong as he thinks that these aggregate supply shocks are rare today, what he himself fails to recognize is that they are about to become far more frequent and with much larger price drops as nanotechnology and meta-material production comes online in the next decade. As we accelerate toward the coming economic singularity's event horizon there will be no way to stop the precipitous fall in prices without inflating the money supply to such an extent that the nations adopting the Imperialist welfare state system will eventually collapse their own economies under an avalanche of public debt and a thoroughly devalued currency.

The real contradiction in capitalist production is thus not one of bringing on immiseration for everyone. The real contradiction is that as prices fall and profits average out to the marginal cost of production, the real value of the currency rises thus increasing the natural wage rate and savings. I go into more detail of what this actually means in the following chapters.

10

The Law of Increasing Returns

The most interesting thing to observe is the complete lack of imagination which [the] vision [of Malthus, Mill, and Ricardo] reveals. Those writers lived at the threshold of the most spectacular economic developments ever witnessed. Vast possibilities matured into realities under their very eyes. Nevertheless, they saw nothing but cramped economies, struggling with ever-decreasing success for their daily bread. They were convinced that technological improvement and increase in capital would in the end fail to counteract the fateful law of decreasing returns. James Mill, in his Elements, even offered a "proof" for this. In other words, they were all stagnationists. Or, to use their own term, they all expected, for the future, the advent of a stationary state....

-JOSEPH A. SHUMPETER, HISTORY OF ECONOMIC ANALYSIS, **1954**[197]

The nineteenth century saw the greatest revolutionary change in human production in the entire history of the world. Every economic historian shows the incredible expansion of production coupled with the amazing fact that all of the commodities and goods produced fell in price over 200 years. At the same time, life expectancy went up as the death rate

---

197   As quoted by Julian Simon in *The Ultimate Resource II*, 471.

fell. Maternal and child mortality was especially curtailed. Every economic indicator shows this amazing fact, that humanity advanced in every area over the last two hundred years by every indicator one can use or imagine is firmly proven.[198] And to the utter horror and shock of most neo-socialists, capitalism has brought down the world poverty rate and dramatically increased life expectancy. Hans Rosling in his video "The Best Stats You've Ever Seen"[199] demonstrates superbly these amazing facts.

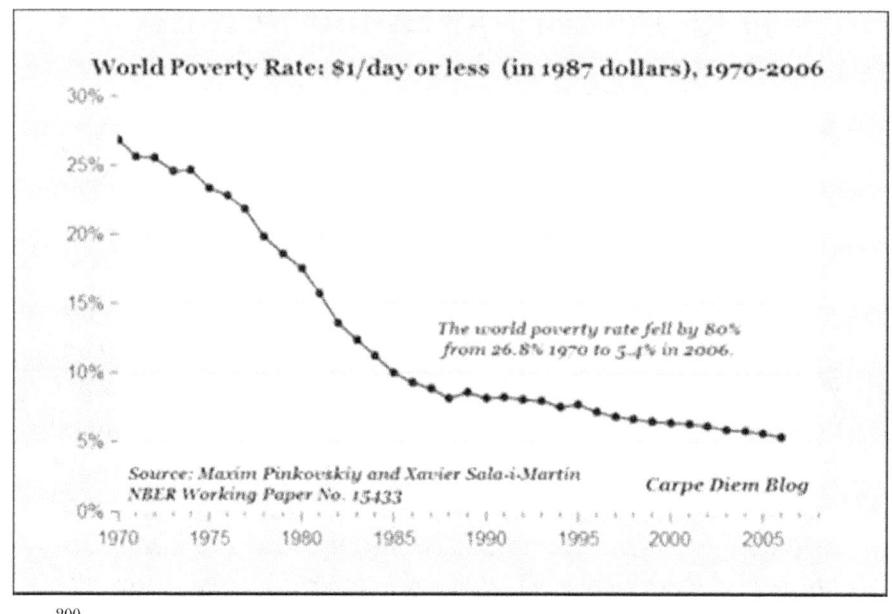

200

9 World Poverty Rate 1970-2006

What unbiased economic historians have uncovered is a shocking fact, which Marx himself intuited and foresaw. The evolution of the productive material forces–the Technium–improves the state of humanity

198   See Simon, Lomborg, Goklany, Diamandis et al.

199   Hans Rosling, "The Best Stats You've Ever Seen," TED, video, 2006 (19:53), http://www.ted.com/talks/hans_rosling_shows_the_best_stats_you_ve_ever_seen?language=en.

200   Mike J. Perry, "World Poverty Rate $1/day or less (in 1987 dollars), 1970-2006," *Carpe Diem* (Blog), www.aei-ideas.org/channel/carpe-diem.

as it continually evolves at an ever increasing rate of speed. What the early economic philosophers got incorrect was influenced by the undercurrent of pessimism, which greatly influenced the outlook of the nineteenth century. In the midst of growing abundance, scientific achievement and advancement doubt and uncertainty prevailed coupled to a disastrous eschatological outlook that said that "everything that could be invented had already been invented." As Lord Kelvin, one of the greatest physicists of his age, said, "There is nothing new to be discovered in physics now, all that remains is more and more precise measurement." The great mathematician Pierre Simon Laplace even fell for this archaic absurdity as Mitchell relates:

> Newtonian mechanics produce[s] a picture of a "clockwork universe," one that is wound up with the three laws [of dynamics] and then runs its mechanical course. The mathematician Pierre Simon Laplace saw the implication of this clockwork for prediction: in 1814 he asserted that, given Newton's laws and the current position and velocity of every particle in the universe, it was possible, in principle, to predict everything for all time.[201]

And as James Gleick rightfully states,

> The most passionate advocates of the new science [chaos theory] go so far as to say that twentieth-century science will be remembered for just three things: relativity, quantum mechanics, and chaos. Chaos, they contend, has become the century's third great revolution in the physical sciences. Like the first two revolutions, chaos cuts away at the tenets of Newton's physics. As one physicist put it: "relativity eliminated the Newtonian illusion of absolute space and time; quantum theory eliminated the Newtonian dream of a controllable

---

201 Mitchell, *Complexity a Guided Tour*, 13.

measurement process; and chaos eliminates the Laplacian fantasy of deterministic predictability."[202]

In the face of the old deterministic paradigm of science beginning to break down all around them the fading anthropomorphic and anthropocentric hubris of the 19th century created a bookend for itself. There was nowhere to go from the dead end this chiliastic thinking had engendered. For these last remaining intellectuals of the ancien regime humanity had obtained in the nineteenth century the height of technological and scientific achievement. All humanity could look forward to now was either a utopian system sustained in a dead static equilibrium brought about by more efficient management, or an eventual slow Malthusian decline into extinction as population exponentially buried us in human debris and detritus. This millennial historicist thinking kept the Marxian theorists in a box, which they could not escape with the advent of World War I. The crisis in Marxism was that the Victorian consciousness of the Marxian theorists was sadly still stuck in the previous century's millennial mindset. They looked around and thought that industrialization, science and technology had almost reached its zenith and thus the communist eschaton was about to commence, as Marx himself believed would happen during his own lifetime, as Mises states his mindset explicitly:

> Marx believed that socialism was just around the corner. After that, all history would come to an end. After that there could be no further development because once the class conflict was eliminated we would be living in a state in which no longer anything important could happen. Here is a quotation illustrating that point from Friedrich Engels ... In the first place the weapons used [for war] have reached such a stage of perfection that further progress which would

---

202 James Gleick, *Chaos: Making a New Science* (New York, NY: Penguin Books, 1987), 6.

have any revolutionizing influence is no longer possible. ... The era of evolution is therefore, in essentials, closed in this direction.[203]

It was this mistaken millennial ideal that was the real crisis in Marxist thought as it left no escape for the theory when the eschaton didn't readily materialize. They were left like the early Christians of the first century C.E. to scramble about and come up with a theological reason that explained why Jesus hadn't come as expected, just as Henry Marcuse and the Marxists of the *Frankfurt School* had to do for Marxism after 1914.

Looking back at all of the historical data that we now have, we can extrapolate that the real contradiction of capitalist production gleaned from the last two centuries of economic data and analysis that:

1. As the amount of capital invested per worker increases, the more labor becomes productive, distributed and specialized; the higher the wage rate naturally becomes.

2. At the same time the amount of products produced greatly increases it causes a natural fall in prices as economies of scale and scope expand. This natural fall in prices increases the purchasing power of money and all savings. We begin to climb the exponential curve upward as capitalism continuously evolves.

3. As the amount of product produced vastly increases, the profit to the entrepreneur actually increases. The profit per x unit of product produced does actually fall, but by producing a vastly greater amount of product to sell, the overall gross profit actually increases.

4. Capitalist profits allow the producers to continually invest in new machinery and methods of production under the pressure of

---

203 Ludwig von Mises, *The Free Market and Its Enemies: Pseudo-Science, Socialism, and Inflation* (New York: Foundation for Economic Education, 2004), 22.

market competition, thus causing the cycle to continue at ever increasing efficiencies, speeding up the evolutionary processes.

5. Synergy takes effect and the rate of *accelerating acceleration* continues to speed up and the *law of increasing returns* is now turning into the *law of exponential returns*.

This natural trend in capitalist production has a synergistic effect. The more that is produced at lower and lower prices the greater the wage rate of the worker rises in two dramatic ways. First, she is paid more as she becomes more productive, efficient and specialized. Second, she has a hidden wage increase as the cost of living constantly falls[204] in constant uninflated dollars. Her savings also increases in value. The phenomenon of the decline of prices 37% for the last three decades of the nineteenth century is readily explained by this process. That this process has continued under the cover of a greatly expanded inflation rate throughout the twentieth century is astounding.

Capitalist production—as an evolutionary ecosystem as expressed by complexity theory and the techno-optimists—is creating its own negation as Marx theorized, but not in the actual way he surmised, as it is not through continually increasing crises that capitalism will fail and bring about the immiseration of the workers and capitalists leading to the revolution. Rather it is through the evolution of exponential deflationary effects that exponential capitalism will actually transcend itself bringing about not immiseration but universal wealth. It awaited the discoveries of the cornucopians, techno-optimists, and Complexity economists to uncover this process and define it even further. With the recognition of the law of exponential returns, a paradigm shift is happening that will transform our understanding of interrelated economics and market

---

204 In a noninflationary monetary system these effects would be readily apparent to everyone. Inflation masks the actual fall in prices in terms of constant uninflated dollars, an effect seen throughout the twentieth century even with the interference in prices by several bouts of ever greater inflation by the FED.

forces. Without inflation we have to realize that prices would have continually fallen throughout the twentieth century to such an extent that poverty as we know it today would have vanished decades ago. Worldwide absolute poverty rates declined from 50% of the world's population in the 1960s to 5.4% today.[205] Absent the Malthusian lunacy of the Club of Rome and its fellow travelling Chicken Little Luddites, this effect would have happened decades earlier.

A negative exponential function can then be theorized in the absence of inflation, where the synergistic effects of deflation coupled with technological development would have so reinforced each other that a fall toward zero costs following an asymptote, as Kevin Kelly surmises in his books and blog,[206] is more than possible. It is in fact highly probable, as he said:

> The very best gets cheaper each year. This principle is so ingrained in our lifestyle that we bank on it without marveling at it. But marvel we should because this paradox is a major engine of the new economy. ... with the arrival of automation and cheap energy in the industrial age, manufacturers could invert the [cost] equation: they offered lower costs and increased quality. Between 1906, when autos were first being made, [and] in 1910, only four years later, the cost of the average car had dropped 24%, while its quality rose by 31%. By 1918, the average car was 53% cheaper than its 1906 counterpart, and 100% better in performance quality. The better–gets–cheaper magic had begun.

> The arrival of the microprocessor accelerated this wizardry. ... So certain is the plummet of prices that economists have mapped the curve of their fall. The cost of making something–whether it is steel, light bulbs, airplanes, flower pots, insurance policies, or bread-will

---

205 As defined by the U.N. as a person living on one US dollar a day or less.
206 Kevin Kelly, *New Rules for the New Economy:10 Radical Strategies for a Connected World* (New York: Penguin Books, 1999), The Technium blog at www.kk/thetechnium.com.

drop over time as a function of the cumulative number of units produced. The more an industry makes, the better it learns how to make
them, the more the cost drops. The downward price curve, propelled
by organizational learning, is sometimes called the learning curve.
Although it varies slightly in each industry, generally doubling the
total output of something will reduce unit costs on average by 20%.
… Computer chips further compound the learning curve. Better
chips lower the cost of all manufactured goods, including new chips.
Engineers use the virtues of computers to directly and indirectly create the next improved version of computers, quickening the rate at
which chips are made, and their prices drop, which speed the rate at
which all goods become cheaper. Around the circle the virtues go.[207]

This process is readily seen throughout the nineteenth and twentieth
centuries, and here in the early twenty-first century it is only accelerating.

Marx briefly broke out of the immiseration fallacy gained from reading David Ricardo and intuited the incredible synergistic force driving
capitalism to a culmination point where it transcends itself, but because
of the many errors of the classical economists of the nineteenth century,
he mixed error with insight, fact with fiction, reason with emotion and
missed the full implication of his own insight. He needed to keep the
Hegelian alienation mythos alive as it promulgated the propaganda that
the evil capitalists stole the worker's *surplus labor* and this fallacy could
only be kept alive by continuing to cling to the labor theory of value.
One real casualty of this ideological need was that when one reads the
first chapter in *Das Kapital* on commodities, one realizes that Marx is so
close to discovering the *subjective theory of value* that it is heartbreaking.
It was staring up from the page at him as he wrote and yet he never realized it. Carl Menger, the founder of the Austrian School of Economics,
almost two decades later intuited the *subjective theory of value* and went on
to define the law of *marginal utility theory of value*. If not for ideological

---

207 Kelly, *New Rules*, 51.

fixation, Marx would have beaten him to it as in many of his writings he himself mentions the subjective value of money and so many other economic and social elements in human praxis.

Marx's dedicated followers, confused and bewildered by the inner contradictions and omissions in his works, as he never gave an exact blueprint of how to get to the promised land of communism from here, were left to piece together a revolutionary catechism from which they could have a more secure foundation for their faith which would guide them in the revolutionary task at hand. A task which unfortunately became one of slowing down, derailing and bringing to a stop as much as possible the evolution of the productive material forces, an interventionism which Marx himself decried. Whether or not socialism today can free itself of its revisionism and recapture the Promethean evolutionary vision of the founder of *scientific socialism* is uncertain. That it must adhere more to science today and less to emotive, reactionary and truly conservative Romantic idealism is apparent. If and until neo-socialism cures itself of its reactionary ideological sympathies picked up from Ricardo, Malthus, Lenin, Stalin and Mao, the evolutionary forces have left it up to the techno-libertarian-optimist contingent to move humanity forward by using science and technology to discover the incredible exponential forces of the universe unleashed today by advancing exponential techno-capitalism, the real terminus stage before the transcendence and transformation of all human society.

Incredibly Simon, Lomborg, Goklany, Ridley, Kelly, Diamandis, Naam and Kurzweil solved the early twentieth century Marxian Crisis problem. It appears Marx was right all along and that the historical evolutionary process was primary and the discovery of the science of this nonlinear process was absolutely necessary in order to comprehend the evolution of the system as it approaches the point of real societal revolution, the economic singularity's event horizon. Complexity theory, complexity economics, and nonlinear mathematics are now doing so. The crisis in Marxism came to an end over three decades ago and Julian Simon and the other cornucopians ended it through the statistical analysis of the world's economic data. If in the rush to maintain the combative zeitgeist ideologues have unknowingly fought this shocking realization and reality, then they have done it to their own and the real progressive movement's detriment.

Henry Marcuse and the Frankfurt School of Marxism's revisionism, in trying to solve the early crises in Marxism, brought it to an antiscientific ideological dead end with the neo-left running after an ever shrinking minority population of new proletariats to free by contrived social revolutions brought about by legislative means while using bourgeois rights as their excuse. Postmodernism which is their ultimate creation and its ultra-subjectivism and antilogism, denies all science, reason and logic, leaves us nowhere to turn and paints the ideology into a corner from which there is no way out. In denying reason, logic and science in order to save neo-socialist ideology from its opponents who were readily showing all of the inherent contradictions and errors within it The neo-left ended up denying Marx and scientific socialism and fell headlong into "vulgar socialism" and emotive reactionary *bourgeois* sentimentality, the neo-left raises a fist above the quicksand they are immersed in not realizing that they themselves cut off all of the intellectual vines above them which could have been used to pull themselves out of the quagmire to save themselves. The problem society is in today cannot be solved by returning to a *golden age* before either industrialization or rationality. Myth and magic are not appropriate substitutions for physics and science. No matter how much the 1960's neo-left Hippie movement tried to revive magic, primitivism, Zen or the Gnosticism of the past, reified in a New Age movement, as a viable alternative to science and technology. It all failed, leading to a resurgence of nihilism. A dark pathos that infected the Romantics of the early 19th century when their movement failed as poetry and the poetic imagination couldn't change reality, which the neo-left sadly rediscovered as well for neither drums, nor guitars, nor free love, nor drugs could alter reality either. Our problems can only be solved by taking up once again the weapons of the Enlightenment: reason, logic, and science as they and they alone have been shown to be effective and can change reality. All of the Grimoires and Alchemical texts written throughout the Middle Ages lie moldering on library shelves irrelevant and worthless and the Tarot, Ouija boards and the I Ching that so mesmerized us in our naïve youth couldn't help us divine a path to escape our own irrationalist subjectivist Waterloos.

Whatever our ideological beliefs, the road to an exponential future is self-assembling before us and ideologues can either join the road crew helping to build it, or stand around griping and running around in circles impotently while being left behind to become increasingly irrelevant. Or worse yet, they can take up the anti-evolutionary stasist ideological stance and try to stop and dismantle evolution by "monkey wrenching" through regulation and legislation. The dynamist and technologically evolutionary stance creates the situation in the quote by Elisabeth Tamedly at the beginning of the last chapter in which "all questions will be resolved and the parts will merge into a marvelous whole," while the devolutionary verge leads us back to primitivism and privation. Karl Marx himself stood solidly within the evolutionary dynamist camp and with the advent of complexity theory and complexity economics a merging into a "marvelous whole" at last finally appears to be possible.

11

The True Mechanisms of Capitalist Re-evolution

[I]f capitalism repeated its past performance for another half century starting with 1928, this would do away with anything that according to present standards could be called poverty, even in the lowest strata of society.

-JOSEPH A. SCHUMPETER

The historical forces responsible for the evolution of capitalist production and its resulting natural deflationary rate have been recognized, discovered and rediscovered over the past 200 years. Sometimes it was intuited by economists, other times individuals outside of the economics field happened to discover this phenomenon. Either way, it is always an individual with an open mind, willing to look at the historical evidence that intuits the incredible synergistic processes of a spontaneously emerging and evolving complex system.[208] The following are the most compelling discoveries that synergistically comprise the Law

208 N.B. It is exceedingly sad that the "intellectuals" in The Venus Project and The Zeitgeist Movement ignore the evolutionary forces inherent in the Market System which is leading to its own transcendence and instead stay stuck in the old petrified catechism of a shopworn neo-Marxism that needs to blame the market system for every and all failures to live up to their perfect utopian fantasies and to see it as inherently flawed and evil. This keeps them stuck in the same old corner that all forms of neo-Marxism have been stuck in since 1914. This entire chapter explodes this totem fetish consciousness with the evidence of economic history.

of Increasing and Exponential Returns that are emerging in and from today's market system.

I.   The Increasing Economy and Scope of Scale

The Increasing Economy and Scope of Scale are defined as follows:

> The basic notion behind economies of scale is well known: As a plant gets larger and volume increases, the average cost per unit of output is expected to drop. This is partially because relative operating and capital costs decline, since a piece of equipment with twice the capacity of another piece does not cost twice as much to purchase or operate. If average unit production cost = variable costs + fixed costs/output, one can see that as output increases the fixed costs/output figure decreases, resulting in decreased overall costs. Plants also gain efficiencies when they become large enough to fully utilize dedicated resources for tasks such as materials handling. The remaining cost reductions come from the ability to distribute non-manufacturing costs, such as marketing and research and development, over a greater number of products.[209]

As firms get bigger they are able to buy more production inputs at greater volume and at lower prices. They are able to upgrade machinery to newer more efficient models, retiring less efficient models faster than smaller firms. They are able to boost production output to greater and greater levels, lowering the overall cost to produce any x unit of production. Thus as the scale and scope of the industry grows the more efficient it becomes until it reaches a size where internal information constraints (Hayek's knowledge problem) stop its growth. Economy of scope and scale is one of the earliest recognitions of the process of increasing productive efficiency recognized by economics, but it is not the only process driving capitalism's evolution.

---

209   Definition from enotes.com. http://www.enotes.com/economies-scale-economies-scope-reference/economies-scale-economies-scope.

II. BUCKMINSTER FULLER AND THE PROCESS OF EPHEMERALIZATION.

Buckminster Fuller was a physicist and a self-described comprehensivist. He strove to understand everything broadly, rather than becoming too narrow and specialized in any one field of study. This visionary could be considered the first techno-optimist and cornucopian and was a forerunner of Simon, Lomborg, Goklany, Ridley, Kelly, Diamandis and Kurzweil by decades. His discovery of the process of ephemeralization he himself describes:

In 1917, in the U.S. Navy, I studied these questions Chronofile disclosed a technological–environment–regenerated acceleration of technical evolution. This concept of *accelerating acceleration*, which had been discovered by Galileo was later identified with gravity by Newton, had not been conceived as accelerating social evolution. During 1922-1927 the Chronofile also disclosed a trend of comprehensive ephemeralization-i.e., the doing of evermore with ever less, per given resource units of pounds, time, and energy. Ephemeralization was vastly augmenting the standards of living of ever-increasing numbers ... Ephemeralization, which constantly does more with visibly less–as does, for instance, the one-quarter-ton communications satellite outperform 150,000 tons of transoceanic cables–has not as yet been formally isolated, recognized, and discussed in print as such by any economists. Until economists recognize it, ephemeralization cannot be properly comprehended and be adopted in public policy formulations.

However, as the years have gone by the combined effects of accelerating acceleration and ephemeralization account primarily for the technical and economic augmentations which are now overwhelming man–trying to make him a success in universe despite his age-old Malthus-supported conviction that humanity, regardless of its composite significance and fate, is, with but a few exceptions, destined to demonstrate personal economic failure and premature death. Public policy the world around as yet assumes that Malthus was right–ergo, the vital necessity of defense in view of the inexorability of the next great war... My Chronofile gradually disclosed the invalidity of that great superstition.[210]

By studying various information sources, which included the newspaper besides technical journals, Fuller was able to recognize that something amazing was happening with ever increasing scientific discoveries and the resultant technological advances put forward in the process of market production. He went on to formally define ephemeralization as, "Doing more and more with less and less until you are able to do everything with practically nothing." He also perceived the evolutionary aspects of the industrial revolution:

World society is as yet unappreciative of industrialization's significance. Its super evolutionary stature and the nature of its comprehensive functioning are as yet obscured by thick overlays of the essentially irrelevant theories of its political and economic profit involvements. World students, will, in due course, discover that world industrialization is an evolutionary transformation, as fundamental as that of caterpillars and butterflies. Man's originally internal and corporeally integral functions and organic processes are inventively externalized by man, all together to provide a world-around metabolic regeneration system of mutually sustaining significance.[211]

As a futurist, Fuller saw an incredible pattern accelerating in the world and he searched out any and all information related to it. He then reported it to anyone who would listen, but because he was averse to politics and political solutions and critical of the growing neo-Malthusian beliefs then arising, he was eventually relegated to obscurity by the new left. As a scientist who was conversant with systems theory, game the-

---

210 Fuller, *Utopia*, 24.
211 Ibid., 149.

ory, cybernetics etc., he can also bear the appellation "grandfather of complexity theory." Everything contained in the techno-optimists works upholds his insights and discovery of the process of ephemeralization. He recognized clearly that there was a positive feedback mechanism operating in human society and that a law of increasing returns was the real evolutionary force transforming human productivity. His graph on the Industrial Revolution's innovation below shows clearly the exponential discovery rate of elements on the periodic table.

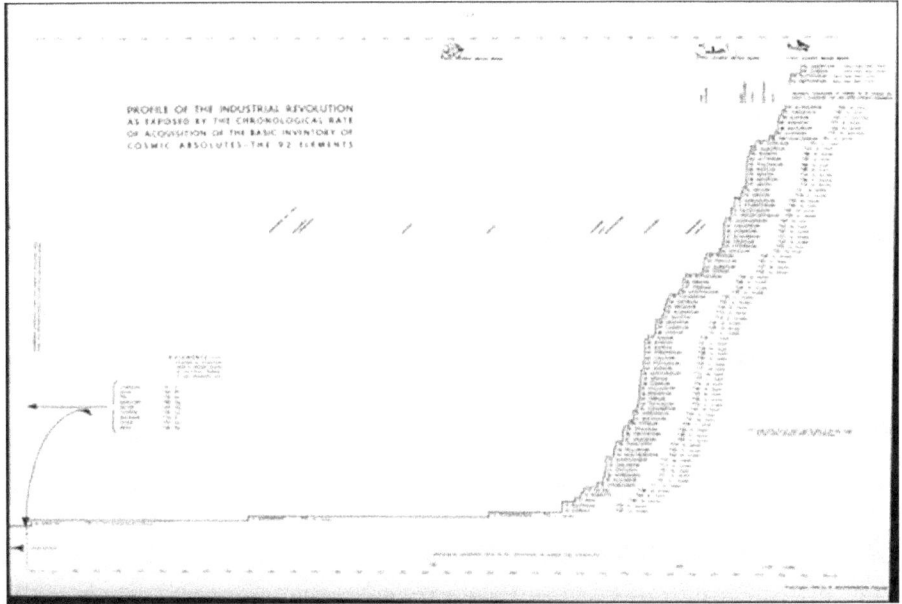

10 Rate of Acquisition of the Basic Inventory of Cosmic Absolutes-The 92 Elements. [212]

This exponential function continually pops up throughout ones research regardless of what historical statistics and area of research one engages in. It appears in economic statistics and history, scientific discovery rates, the rate of innovation, the production of resources, the

212   Ibid., 78-79, "Rate of Acquisition of the Basic Inventory of Cosmic Absolutes-The 92 Elements." Here Fuller expresses the great acceleration of knowledge throughout the eighteenth, nineteenth and into the early twentieth century for the discovery of the elements on the periodic table.

computing power of computers, Moore's Law, Mead's Law, data storage, etc. It is beginning to look like it is a natural function of universal evolutionary forces that humanity unleashes as we, the market and the Technium co-evolve.

III. The Know-More Factor.

Buckminster Fuller also described the phenomenon of the *Know-More Factor* in productive evolutionary transformation. This idea is simple and yet profound. As humanity knows more, it opens up the possibility of knowing more and so on to infinity as the process is synergistic. The horizon of our potential knowledge expands ever outward with no boundaries in sight. As the universe is infinite, the potential knowledge human beings may be able to discover is also infinite. Matt Ridley describes this process as, "the dissemination of useful knowledge causes that useful knowledge to breed more useful knowledge"[213] This process is only accelerating as Kevin Kelly states, "We are adding 400 exabyte's of new information to the technium each year, so the rate of our technological evolution is a billion billion times as fast as the evolution of [our] DNA.[214] As the rate at which humanity increases scientific knowledge and builds technology the faster the rate of the know-more factor becomes. Kevin Kelly calls this process the evolution of "The Technium," and Ray Kurzweil "The Law of Exponential Returns" and it appears that it is an inherent evolutionary process that humanity is intimately involved in. Kevin Kelly talks about this synergistic process further:

> George Gilder once noted there was a self-reinforcing positive feedback loop in miniaturization of technology. Smaller chips ran cooler, which allowed them to run faster, which allowed them to run cooler, which allowed them to be made smaller. And so on. There is

---

213 Ridley, *The Rational Optimist*, 249.
214 Kelly, *What Technology*, 334.

a similar self-reinforcing positive feedback loop in the free-ization of technology. Nearly-free goods permit waste and experimentation, which breed new options for that good, which increase its abundance and lower its price, which generate more new options, which permit further novelty. And so on. These loops work on each other, compounding the effects between techniques and goods, and supercharging the entire ecology of technologies with an unstoppable momentum towards the free and towards unleashing new capabilities and possibilities. [215]

The more we know: the more we learn, the more we invent, transform, substitute and rearrange matter, and commodities. Now with meta-materials and nanotechnology scientists and technologists are learning to manipulate and create new substances at the atomic level that have never existed before. All of this creates an abundance effect since, "The more we have to work with, the more we have to work with." Science and technology continuously expands our horizons in infinite directions as it discovers and invents more building blocks with which to work. Humanity lives in an expanding universe of knowledge and human beings are a major extropic element in the universe as many believers in the Anthropic Principle[216] expound.

IV. THE LEARNING/EXPERIENCE CURVE

The *learning curve* is the material component of the know-more factor and it is a well-known economic phenomenon. Chris Anderson describes this process:

Most industrial processes get better over time and skill through an effect known as the learning curve ... The learning curve was introduced by the 19th-century German psychologist Hermann

---

215 Kevin Kelly, "Technology Wants to Be Free," *The Technium* (blog), November 14, 2007, http://www.kk.org/thetechnium/archives/2007/11/technology_want.php.
216 The Anthropic Principle, http://en.wikipedia.org/wiki/Anthropic_principle.

Ebbinghouse to describe improvements he observed when people memorize tasks over many repetitions. But it soon took on a broader meaning … "The principle states that the more times a task is performed, the less time will be required for each subsequent iteration." An early example of this was observed in 1936 at Wright Patterson Air Force Base, where managers calculated that every time total aircraft production doubled, the required labor time decreased by 10 to 15 percent.

In the late 1960s, the Boston Consulting Group (BCG) started looking at technology industries and saw improvements that were often faster than simple learning curves could explain. Where the learning curve was mostly about human learning, these larger effects seemed to have more to do with scale: as products were manufactured in larger numbers, the costs fell by a constant and predictable percentage (10 to 25 percent) with every doubling of volume. BCG called this the "experience curve" to encompass institutional learning, ranging from administrative efficiencies to supply chain optimization, as well as individual learning of the workers.[217]

This accumulation of knowledge and experience synergistically brings down the prices of all goods produced. As one industry learns to make products faster, all industry learns to make all products faster; the synergy spreads out to effect all production and the costs to produce those goods continually falls. This leads to the *Compound Learning Curve* phenomenon, as Anderson describes about Mead's Law:

> Like Moore [of Moore's Law] before him, [Mead] could see that the eighteen-month doublings in [computer] performance would continue to stretch out as far as anyone could see. This was driven not just by the standard learning and experience curves, but also by what

---

217 Anderson, *Free*, 82.

he called the "compound learning curve," which is a combination of learning curves and frequent new inventions.

For more than a half-century, semiconductor researchers have come up with a major innovation every decade or so that kicks the industry into the sharp-decline part of the curve again. As one production process nears the tail of its efficiency improvement cycle, the incentive to come up with something radically new and better increases… Each time, whether it's a new material, a new etching process, the new chip architecture, or an entirely new dimension such as parallel processing, the learning curve starts again at its most vertiginous slope. When you combine all these innovations and learning curves across the entire computer industry, you end up with a pace of cost decline never before seen.[218]

The increasing rate of accelerating acceleration is compounding productivities learning curve and many closely working within the field of technology readily see it. Everything is now becoming exponential and knowledge and productivity are about to explode upward into a world of such abundance and wonder as only our ancestors in their wildest dreams could have imagined.

V.   THE LAW OF COMPARATIVE ADVANTAGE

There is an old economic fallacy, still very much alive today that states that all trade is a *zero sum* game. This fallacious idea goes like this: if I make a spear and you make fishnets and we trade them, we have not increased the overall wealth of either of us. All we did was trade one thing for another which each of us thought was of equal value (per Aristotle's idea of value). When cities, nations and states do the same thing, we, all of us, do not add one iota to our wealth; we only trade equal values for equal values which leaves us all the same, if not poorer,

---

218   Ibid., 84.

before we traded. This economic fallacy was refuted long ago by David Ricardo, and yet like most economic fallacies it endures into the twenty-first century. Matt Ridley in his book *The Rational Optimist*,[219] and in his TED talk, *When Ideas Have Sex*, refutes this fallacious zero sum idea brilliantly as do so many other economists like Peter Schiff in his elementary economics book *Why an Economy Grows and Why it Crashes*.[220]

What the law of comparative advantage describes is that when a producer of a product (who is more knowledgeable and skilled at producing that product) trades their product for another made by an individual or firm that specializes in producing that other product (which those others are skilled at producing) gains a comparative advantage over doing the production themselves. One of the main things they gain is time. A *Jack of All Trades*, or a *Robinson Crusoe*, has to produce everything himself. Survival thus becomes very time consuming as they have to make and produce solely everything they need in order to live. Comparative advantage divides the knowledge and labor among various producers all making a different product to the best of their ability. When individuals then trade, they are trading what they do not want as much for something they want and value more (the Marginal Utility Theory of Value), and by doing so they all gain a product they don't have and more free time in their lives. Trade is thus actually a *positive sum* game.

The term labor saving device is no misnomer. Here I myself sit typing a book on a computer, plugged into the Internet that gives me the ability to have several libraries at my disposal without my ever having to leave my chair or even my house. I can type and retype sections, move them about, spell check them, use my Dragon[221] speech recognition software to speak in long quotes, and do everything a student of 50 years ago could do with a ten person research team; and I do it faster and without the need for spending hundreds of hours searching through a score of

---

219 Matt Ridley, *The Rational Optimist* (New York: Harper Perennial, 2010).

220 Peter Schiff, *Why an Economy Grows and Why it Crashes* (New Jersey: Wiley & Sons, Inc. 2010). A more "intellectual" presentation of these ideas can be found in *"Not a Zero Sum Game"* by Manuel F. Ayau (Guatemala: Universidad Francisco Marroquin, 2007).

221 Dragon is a registered trademark of Nuance Inc., http://www.nuance.com/dragon/index. htm.

libraries, and employing a typist or two to do all of the manual typing and retyping that was once required. Hundreds of people, maybe even thousands, have helped me to be able to create written works at a cost and time savings to myself in the thousands of dollars by working in the computer manufacturing business. I traded my $400 dollars for this computer which in turn has given me hundreds of hours of time back to me while greatly expanding my creative ability. I do not need to know how to mine copper, drill for oil to make plastic, generate electricity, manufacture electronic components etc. to use this wondrous device. As Ridley relates in his video, "No one knows how to make a computer mouse [themselves], but we all know how to use one, and as the author of *I Pencil* so aptly describes about creating the "simple" pencil:

No One Knows- Does anyone wish to challenge my earlier assertion that no single person on the face of this earth knows how to make me? Actually, millions of human beings have had a hand in my creation, no one of whom even knows more than a very few of the others. Now, you may say that I go too far in relating the picker of a coffee berry in far-off Brazil and food growers elsewhere to my creation; that this is an extreme position. I shall stand by my claim. There isn't a single person in all these millions, including the president of the pencil company, who contributes more than a tiny, infinitesimal bit of know-how…

No Master Mind-There is a fact still more astounding: The absence of a master mind, of anyone dictating or forcibly directing these countless actions which bring me into being. No trace of such a person can be found. Instead, we find the Invisible Hand at work. This is the mystery to which I earlier referred.[222]

---

222 Leonard E. Read, *I Pencil: My Family Tree as Told to Leonard E. Read* (New York: Foundation for Economic Education, 1958), 8.

There is a great video on TED from Thomas Thwaites entitled, *How I built a Toaster–from scratch.*[223] Thwaites decided to go out and try to make his own toaster from scratch that is an incredible representation of this law of comparative advantage. In the end, his toaster looked terrible, was not very safe to use, and cost him thousands of dollars and hundreds of hours to produce himself. *I Toaster* would have been a much better title for the video, but it remarkably demonstrated the law of comparative advantage. We don't need to make our own toasters, we can go out and buy one for under $30 and we all save a tremendous amount of time, energy, money and resources doing it.

VI. SPECIALIZATION AND DIVISION OF KNOWLEDGE AND LABOR

The *Division of Labor* was known and understood as far back as the eighteenth century and Adam Smith commented upon it in his *Wealth of Nations* with his example of the manufacturing of pins. Though readily understandable, it didn't stop it from being vilified, first by Tory conservatives and Romantics as attacking the old guild system and the privileges of Mercantilism and then by the socialists who disastrously took up most of the conservative propaganda ready made against classical liberalism's revolution against the *ancien regime*.[224] Dividing labor into specialized fields was seen as dividing human beings themselves into alienated parts. A person's full powers could then not be "harmoniously developed," as Marx put it. The ideal of making everyone into a jack-of-all-trades so that they can develop their human and social powers fully seemed a good idea back at the beginning of the nineteenth century when so many people were engaged in agricultural production and technology and science were still in their early stages. The idyll of the Romantics was then in full swing, even Buckminster Fuller fell under

---

223   Thomas Thwaites, *How I built a Toaster-from scratch*, Ted.com Video, 10.52 min, 2010, http://www.ted.com/talks/thomas_thwaites_how_i_built_a_toaster_from_scratch.html.
224   For more in-depth information on the subject see *Capitalism and the Historians*, ed. F.A. Hayek (Chicago: University of Chicago Press, 1954).

the aegis of this fallacy and denounced the increasing specialization of knowledge in science, yet it is, and has ever been, a social and economic fallacy. Thoreau on Walden's pond and Ted Kaczynski–the Unabomber– were not entirely self-sufficient even though their ideology touted that ideal. Each went to the local store to get the staples they needed to survive, each gained from the division of labor and knowledge that their era had to offer all the while they idealized pristine nature and advocated a return to Mother Earth. Kevin Kelly goes into this in more detail in his work, *What Technology Wants*,[225] as he describes both Thoreau and Kaczynski's inherent contradiction of thought by their actions.

Like the law of comparative advantage in trade, the specialization of labor and knowledge is a form of interdependence and it gives everyone an advantage over doing and knowing everything oneself. As Ridley so cogently states, "prosperity, or growth, has been synonymous with moving from self-sufficiency to interdependence, transforming the family from a unit of laborious, slow and diverse production to a unit of easy, fast and diverse consumption paid for by a burst of specialized production."[226] The specialization of labor and knowledge leads to a more interrelated world, a socialization of labor and knowledge to a true socialization of production. Every person lives upon the shoulders not only of their predecessors but also their co-citizens the world over who produce products for their consumption. There is little need for a physicist or engineer on a desert island besides the inability to produce one. Today's modern highly technological society creates physicists, engineers, biotechnicians, computer science majors and all manner of specialized individuals. As our knowledge expands the need increases for more highly skilled people to work in the new areas of knowledge increases. The market is actually socializing the world.

The person who bought the machine, built by the technician, who received the knowledge from the scientist, needs the trained laborer to produce it and the repairman to fix it when it breaks down. There

---

225 Kevin Kelly, *What Technology Wants* (New York: Viking, 2010).
226 Ridley, *The Rational Optimist*, 41.

is a circle of interrelation that synergistically coordinates and develops science, technology and productivity. Instead of taking time away from being able to fully develop oneself, it has instead given all of us more time off work to pursue our own interests and our own development as Goklany relates from the historical economic evidence:

> Acceleration of economic growth began around 1800 and has been dramatic in recent years. Basic necessities such as food are much more easily obtained than they were even a few decades ago. For instance, between the years 1897 to 1902 and 1992 to 1994, U.S. retail prices of flour, bacon, and potatoes relative to per capita income dropped by 92 percent, 87 percent, and 80 percent, respectively. ...

> Not only is food cheaper and the average person's annual income higher, but workers spen[t] fewer hours on the job. Between 1870 and 1992, average hours worked per person employed declined 46, 48, and 36 percent for the U.S., France, and Japan, respectively. Ausubel and Grübler (1995) estimate that for the average British worker, total life hours worked declined from 124,000 in 1856 to 69,000 in 1981. Because the average Briton lives longer and works fewer hours each year, the life hours worked by the average British worker has declined from 50 percent to 20 percent of his or her disposable life hours. In other words, the average person has more disposable time for leisure, hobbies, and personal development.[227]

Julian Simon relates that this process is not new:

> Since the early nineteenth century, productivity–defined as output per unit of input–in the economy as a whole has doubled about every 75 years, while labor productivity growth has been somewhat more rapid.... Dramatic productivity gains are not just an artifact

---

227 Indur M. Goklany, "Economic Growth and the State of Humanity," *PERC Policy Series*, PS-21, Bozeman, MT: PERC, (April 2001): 9. http://www.perc.org/articles/article185.php.

of recent technological change. Prior to the Industrial Revolution, it took 50,000 hours or more to convert 100 pounds of raw cotton to thread by hand. The earliest spinning machines at the end of the eighteenth century accomplished the same task in 2,000 hours. Within 15 years, though, this had been cut to 300 hours, while today machines take less than 40. A late nineteenth-century study of 672 industrial processes recently converted from hand to machine production found similar dramatic gains in productivity from mechanization. For example, that the switch from hand to machine weaving of 36" wide gingham cloth reduced man-hours to produce 500 yards from 5,039 to 64, a 79-fold increase in labor productivity. Nor was this gain extraordinary. Machine printing and binding was 212 times more efficient than hand production, while machine production of screws was 4,032 times more efficient. During the initial phases of invention and innovation, productivity seems to grow exponentially as successive generations refine and improve the original idea.[228]

This outcome of capitalist (i.e. market) production– ever greater productivity–should be no surprise to old line Marxists, as Engels himself relates:

> Just as sharply as Marx stresses the evils of capitalist production, so also does he clearly prove that this social system has been necessary so as to develop the productive forces of society to a level which will make it possible for all members of society to develop equally in a manner worthy of human beings. All earlier forms of society have been too poor to do this.[229]

The evolution of the market economy has given every one more time off work to do the very thing that Marx's humanist ideal desired. The full and complete development of the individual is now in sight as capitalism

---

228 Julian Simon L. ed, *The State of Humanity* (Malden, MA: Blackwell Publishers Ltd.), 164.
229 Jose Miranda, *Marx Against the Marxists*, (New York: Orbis Books, 1986), 107.

evolves toward its exponential stage. Matt Ridley sums up this phenomenon brilliantly:

> The cumulative accretion of knowledge by specialists that allows us each to consume more and more different things by each producing fewer and fewer is, I submit, the central story of humanity. Innovation changes the world but only because it aids the elaboration of the division of labor and encourages the division of time. Forget wars, religions, famines and poems for the moment. This is history's greatest theme: the metastasis[230] of exchange, [the] specialization and the invention they have called forth, the 'creation' of time.[231]

Instead of fragmenting and alienating humanity the division of knowledge and labor, and its extension globally, has given humanity more of our life back to pursue those individual goals and dreams that each one of us individually desires in the free time we have away from work, while more closely integrating all of us. The modern reactionary position is that all production should be local and that the worldwide division of labor should be politically dismantled over fears of increasing carbon emissions and pollution. Ridley and so many economists explode these neo-Malthusian mercantilist myths:

> Two economists recently concluded, after studying the issue, that the entire concept of food miles 'is a profoundly flawed sustainability indicator'. Getting food from the farmer to the shop causes just four percent of all its lifetime emissions. Ten times as much carbon is emitted in refrigerating British food as in air-freighting it from abroad and fifty times as much is emitted by the customer traveling to the shops. A New Zealand lamb, shipped to England,

---

230 In an email with Matt Ridley he expressed to this author that he meant "metastases" in this case as "the increased spread of" and did not want to convey in any way a cancerous or malign impact or effect from trade. This is one of those cases where the English and American use of words and their various definitions can cause misunderstandings to arise. Permission to convey said correspondence given by Matt Ridley.
231 Ridley, *The Rational*, 46.

requires one-quarter as much carbon to get onto a London plate as a Welsh lamb; a Dutch rose, grown in a heated greenhouse and sold in London, has six times the carbon footprint of a Kenyan rose… In truth, far from being unsustainable, the interdependence of the world through [global] trade is the very thing that makes modern life as sustainable as it is.[232]

Jeffrey Tucker gives voice to a cry that so many well educated Marxists can echo today;

AH, FOR THE DAYS when the socialists believed in material progress! That is no longer the case. Now they propose poverty and advocate government regulations to bring it about…whereas socialism could not actually work to bring about greater productivity, it can do what the "postmaterialist" socialists desire. Socialistic means can work to bring about lower standards of living. In a strange way, this is a betrayal of Karl Marx. [233]

And he reminds us of the history of this dramatic change on the left;

Somewhere along the way, during the last 50 years, the critique of capitalism changed from condemning its failure to spread the wealth to condemning the very opposite. Suddenly the great sin of capitalism was that it was producing too much, making us all too materialistic,[234] fueling economic growth at the expense of other values, spreading middle-class decadence, and generally causing society to be too caught up in productivity and too focused on the standard of living.

---

232 Ibid., 41.
233 Jeffery Tucker, *It's a Jetsons World: Private Miracles and Public Crimes* (Auburn, Al: Mises Institute, 2011), 235.
234 I always find this charge: "that capitalism is making us too materialistic" quixotic, for it was socialism itself that preached materialism, under the auspices of dialectical materialism, for decades.

Noting this dramatic change, Murray N. Rothbard writes that the turning point might have been John Kenneth Galbraith's 1958 work titled *The Affluent Society*, which is one long harangue against consumerism, middle-class decadence, and the ever-increasing wealth of the average person under capitalism. Galbraith claimed that all this was coming at the expense of public institutions and public infrastructure.

This book became a bestseller. It changed the way the Left went about promoting government intervention and critiquing free markets. This book was the first of a half-century of similar books that recaptured that Rousseauian spirit, that penchant to romanticize the world before industrialization, to toy with the idea that the hunter-gatherer society has a lot going for it, to imagine that we can all live better by trading only at the level of the small tribe and raising our own food, and all the rest that comes with primitivism.[235]... this tendency to romanticize poverty and simplicity in a world without modern technology is an ideology that is animating the antics of many of today's intellectuals, politicians, and bureaucrats which set themselves up as the enemies of all that makes life grand, which is say that they set themselves up as enemies of freedom.[236]... To be sure, there are plenty of Americans who are firmly convinced that we would all be better off if we grew our own food, buy only locally, kept firms small, eschewed modern conveniences like home appliances, went back to using only natural products, expropriated wealthy savers, harassed the capitalistic class until it felt itself unwelcome and vanished. This paradise has a name, and it is Haiti.[237]

And as Matt Ridley reminds us:

---

235 Ibid. 235.
236 Ibid. 236.
237 Ibid. 162.

This notion dates from Herbert Marcuse, who turned Marx's notion of the 'immiseration of the proletariat' by steadily declining living standards on its head and argued that capitalism forced excessive consumption on the working class instead. It resonates well in the academic seminar, causing heads to nod in agreement, but it is sheer garbage in the real world."[238]

Karl Marx long ago was the champion of free trade among nations and world economic interdependency and superabundance making socialism at last possible. It is a sad commentary indeed that many of his heirs are working tirelessly to bring the worldwide division and extension of knowledge and labor to an end and institute in its place a production plan highly restricted to local producers. This is far more in line with the old Tory conservatives' protectionist mercantilist ideal of the nineteenth century and Fichte's disastrous Nationalist economic ideas, or Italian and German fascism in the 20th. Now, instead of protecting a nation's domestic industry from riotous competition, it is instead claimed to protect Mother Nature. The propaganda behind this economic fallacy is better, but the ideology behind it and its disastrous effects is exactly the same.

Ludwig von Mises waxes almost Teilhardian in his magnum opus *Human Action* when talking about the division of labor:

The principle of the division of labor <u>is one of the great basic principles of cosmic becoming and evolutionary change</u>. The biologists were right in borrowing the concept of the division of labor from social philosophy and adapting it to their field of investigation ... one must never forget that the characteristic feature of human society is purposeful cooperation; society is an outcome of human action, i.e., of a conscious aiming at the attainment of ends ... Human society is an intellectual and spiritual phenomenon. It is the outcome of a purposeful utilization of a universal law determining cosmic becoming,

---

238 Matt Ridley, *The Rational*, 291.

viz., the higher productivity of the division of labor. As with every instance of action, the recognition of the laws of nature is put into the service of man's efforts to improve his conditions.[239]

There are moments sprinkled throughout the writings of Mises and Hayek when one can readily see a convergence between all of the various philosophies and sciences, i.e. complexity theory, Marxism and millennial thinkers. The very idea of "cosmic becoming" and the Austrian School of Economics seem incongruent, contradictory, even farcical, and yet it is there. A deep evolutionary dynamist verge runs throughout their works. What one can learn from examining the various schools of thought and comparing their similarities is vastly more important than the inconsequential areas of conflict that seem to divide them.

VII. The Adjacent Possible

Peter Diamandis describes the adjacent possible in his book *Abundance: The Future is Better Than You Think*:

The true promise of abundance was one of creating a world of possibility: a world where everyone's days are spent dreaming and doing, not scrapping and scraping. Never before has such promise really been in the offing. Most of human history, life was a constrained affair. Just finding ways to survive took most of our energy. The gap between one's day-to-day reality and one's true potential was vast indeed. But in these extraordinary days, that chasm is beginning to close.

On a certain level, change is being driven by a fundamental property of technology: the fact that expands into what theoretical biologist Stuart Kauffman calls "the adjacent possible." Before the invention

---

239 Ludwig von Mises, *Human Action: A Treatise on Economics* [1949] (San Francisco: Fox & Wilkes, 1996), 145. Underline mine.

of the wheel, the cart, the carriage, the automobile, the wheelbarrow, the roller skate, and a million other offshoots of circularity were not imaginable. They existed in a realm that was off-limits until the wheel was discovered, but once discovered, these pathways became clear. This is the adjacent possible. It's the long list of first-order possibilities that open up whenever a new discovery is made.

"The strange and beautiful truth about the adjacent possible is that its boundaries grow as you explore them," wrote author Steven Johnson in the Wall Street Journal. "Each new combination opens up the possibility of other new combinations"... Our path of adjacent possibles has led us to a unique moment in time. We have wandered into a world where the expansive nature of technology has begun to connect with our inner desires. In *What Technology Wants*, Kevin Kelly explains it this way ... "As technology expands the possibility space, it expands the chance that someone can find an outlet for their personal traits. ... When we enlarge the variety and reach of technology, we increase options, not just for ourselves and not for others living, but for all generations to come."[240]

Steven Johnson describes the adjacent possible in these terms:

The adjacent possible is a kind of shadow future, hovering on the edges of the present state of things, a map of all the ways in which the present can reinvent itself. Yet is it not an infinite space, or a totally open playing field. The number of potential first-order relations is vast, but it is a finite number ... What the adjacent possible tells us is that at any moment the world is capable of extraordinary change, but only certain changes can happen ...The strange and beautiful truth about the adjacent possible is that its boundaries

---

240 Diamandis, *Abundance*, 236.

grow as you explore those boundaries. Each new combination ushers in new combinations into the adjacent possible.[241]

The adjacent possible is like exploring a mansion. As one enters one room, there are several doors leading out from that room to more rooms. As one goes through the rooms at an increasingly accelerating rate, the number of doors that each room contains begins to at first multiply linearly and then exponentially. As the number of people exploring the mansion increases the rate of discovery also advances outwards exponentially. Each new discovery makes possible the chance for more discoveries and the adjacent possible then expands exponentially. Each scientific discovery has surrounding it an almost infinite variety of other discoveries adjacent to it. It is the mother of two devices that becomes the mother of four devices that goes on to be the mother of sixteen devices and so on and so on and so on ad infinitum. The adjacent possible thus leads to a world of eventual abundance if no artificial precautionary ring of restriction is placed around it.

VIII.   THE CONTINUOUSLY FALLING RATE OF PROFIT AND PRICES

As mentioned before, this phenomenon was recognized by many economists in the nineteenth century that all production was constantly tending toward a unified rate of profit. It was also seen that a continually falling rate of prices was also occurring; even Marx comments on this fact. After the mid-twentieth century, this phenomenon was so well known as to be ubiquitous. George Reisman in his work, *The Government Against the Economy*, details why profit rates fall as capitalism evolves:

The influx of additional capital in an initially more profitable industry, however tends to reduce the rate of profit in that industry. Its

---

241 Steve Johnson, *Where Good Ideas Come From: The Natural History of Innovation* (New York: Riverhead Books, 2010), 11.

effect is to increase the industry's production and thus to drive down the selling prices of its products. As the selling prices of its products are driven down, closer to its costs of production, the rate of profit earned by the industry necessarily falls. Conversely, the withdrawal of capital from an initially less profitable industry tends to raise the rate of profit in that industry, because less capital means less production, higher selling prices on the reduced supply, and thus a higher rate of profit on the capital that remains.[242]

This is one of the driving forces of a freer economic system. The more capital that is available to be put back into the lines of production, the lower the profit rate will be driven downward. All interventions that siphon away capital through higher taxation, legislation, regulation, wage and price controls, and increasing inflation, all tend to raise the profit rate or to keep it artificially higher then it naturally would be. This phenomenon of the falling rate of profit Riesman goes on to explain:

> In order to earn a rate of profit that is above average, it is necessary for businessmen to anticipate changes in consumer demand ahead of their rivals, to introduce new and/or improved products ahead of their rivals, or to cut the costs of production ahead of their rivals. I say, "ahead of their rivals," because as soon as any innovation becomes general, then, in accordance with the uniformity-of-profit principle, no special profit can be made from it ... Sooner or later, virtually every innovation does become general. This implies that for any firm to continue to earn an above-average rate of profit, it must repeatedly outdistance its rivals: it must work as an agent of continuous progress ... what was good enough once to make a high profit, ceases to be good enough as soon as enough others are able to do the same thing. In order to go on earning an above-average profit, one must continue to stay ahead of the competition. By the same token, any business that

---

242 George Reisman, *The Government Against the Economy* (Ottawa, Canada: Jameson Books, 1979), 5.

stands pat is necessarily finished in a free economy, no matter how great its past successes. For the technological advances of any given time are further and further surpassed as time goes on.[243]

As the libertarian Kel Kelly[244]states in his first book:

> The greater our level of capitalism–in this case, paying for machines and labor–the greater our productivity (and real incomes). More capitalism means more would-be profits are instead used to pay labor and machines. Thus, if socialists want companies to earn lower profits, they should support [free-market] capitalism.[245]

Earlier on in his work he fully realizes the result of the natural rate of deflation in a free democratic market system that is left freer to continuously evolve:

> The phenomenon of people saving and investing part of their income for the future would mostly not exist if not for inflation. We are all forced to try and save because we know that the value of our wealth today will be worth less in the future when everything costs more. Imagine that we had a free market in money and prices actually did fall each year. How much money would you need to save if the lifestyle you have today (mortgage, food, vacations, medicine, entertainment, etc.) costs you, say $50,000 per year, but that same lifestyle in 30 years would cost you $15,000, because everything became cheaper? This would be a very realistic scenario since, without government printing money, the production of goods would increase about 4% per year, and prices would therefore fall by almost 4% per year.[246]

Rothbard comments on this effect many times throughout his works. Here is one such example:

---

243 Ibid., 9.
244 Not to be confused with Kevin Kelly of technium fame.
245 Kel Kelly, *The Case for Legalizing Capitalism* (Auburn, AL: Mises Institute Press, 2010), 227.
246 Ibid., 137.

During most of the 19th century (apart from the years of the war of 1812 and the Civil War), prices were falling, and yet the economy was growing and industrializing. Falling prices put no damper whatsoever on business or economic prosperity. Thus falling prices are apparently the normal functioning of a growing market economy so how is it that the very idea of steadily falling prices is so counter to our experience that seems a totally unrealistic dream world[247]... This quixotic goal of a stable price level contrasts with the 19th century economic view-and with the subsequent Austrian school. They hailed the results of the unhampered market, of laissez faire capitalism, invariably bringing about a steadily falling price level. For without the intervention of government, productivity in the supply of goods tends always to increase, causing a decline in prices. Thus, in the first half of the 19th century-the "Industrial Revolution"-prices tended to fall steadily, thus raising the real wage rates even without an increase of wages in money terms. We can see this steady price decline bringing the benefits of higher living standards to all consumers, and such examples as TV sets falling from $2000 when first put on the market to about $100 for far better set and this in a period of galloping inflation.[248]

Hunter Lewis weighs in on this phenomenon as well:

A steep price decline is a symptom of depression. Deflation in general, however, is a perfectly natural and normal phenomenon, not just a symptom of depression. As Keynes himself noted, profit-making firms are always striving to become more productive, which means being able to make products better and more cheaply. They may hope to make products more cheaply without reducing prices, thereby boosting profits. Over time, however, the need to keep the best workforce means that some of the savings from making products more cheaply goes to workers. And, if there is normal competition, lower costs also

---

247 Murray Rothbard, *Economic Controversies* (Auburn, AL: Ludwig Von Mises Institute Press, 2011), 778.
248 Ibid., 905. See economic figure 14 for only 5 years from 2005 to 10.

lead to lower consumer prices as well. Indeed, over time, all the cost savings typically go to workers and customers. Consequently a successful market economy is one where prices fall 2-3% a year, year in and year out, even when there is no sign of economic trouble.[249]

Peter Schiff states:

[The] steady devaluation of the dollar is a new practice, relatively speaking. For most of our country's history, the dollar gained value. The dollar was worth 75 percent more in 1912 than it was worth in 1800. You know the stories your parents or grandparents tell about how they used to buy a sandwich and a fountain soda for a dime? How everything was so much cheaper back in the day? If you were around in 1900, for instance, the old folk didn't tell those sorts of stories. What cost a dime in 1900 probably had cost fifteen cents in 1875, and twenty cents in 1800....

Deflation is Natural

Slow, steady deflation, though, is the natural state of things in an economy with sound, stable money. Think about it this way: does creating a particular product or performing a particular service generally become easier or harder over time? In most cases, it becomes easier: your computer becomes faster and the software gets better. Manufacturing equipment improves. Through practice, people figure out more efficient ways of doing the same thing. ...

So as widgets get easier to make, the cost of production goes down. In a competitive market, this will bring the price of the widget down. In other words, what we see with electronics would be the case with everything.[250]

---

249 Hunter Lewis, *Where Keynes Went Wrong: And Why World Governments Keep Creating Inflation, Bubbles, And Busts* (Mt. Jackson, TN: Axios Press, 2009), 315.
250 Peter Schiff, *The Real Crash*, 118.

The other boogeyman of the deflation fear mongers is that if deflation is allowed to happen then no one will buy, they will just sit on the sidelines and wait until prices fall to the lowest they can before they buy anything. Economist Mark Skousen explodes this fallacy:

> If a new technology reduces the costs of inputs or the price of outputs, more time and resources are freed up to expand in other areas. The reduction in prices and the increase in the volume of business would occur at stages closer to consumption. Ultimately, then, a technological advancement should mean an expansion in consumer goods through lower prices, increased volume, higher incomes, and better quality. The amount by which consumption increases depends on many factors. Because consumer prices are lower, consumer demand increases. Consumers pay less but buy more, so that total spending on final consumer goods may actually remain the same, even though people are clearly better off. In real terms the volume of consumer goods has definitely increased, and probably in nominal terms as well. Thus, the standard of living improves. If the new products are universally useful in both industrial and consumer sectors, such as computers and word processors, then the standard of living increases almost universally.… An increase in the production of technologically advanced equipment and products will also encourage a dramatic increase in savings and capital formation. As Böhm-Bawerk argues, savings and innovation are "interrelated."[251]

Peter Schiff also addresses this bit of cognitive incoherence about falling consumer demand:

> Falling prices do not discourage people from buying; they entice people to buy. The lower prices fall, the more people can afford to buy! When confronted with real-world examples of consumer electronics, economists often dismiss them as the exceptions that prove

---

251 Mark Skousen, *The Structure of Production* (New York, NY: New York University Press, 1990), 228.

the rule. However, apply the same logic to other prices. What if someone made an invention that could create a mansion for ten dollars. Think about that: a 99.999 percent deflation in housing prices. Would that be disastrous? No. It would be the greatest advance in human prosperity ever. But it would be vastly deflationary. Would it really be so bad if gas prices fell? How about healthcare-would it really be so bad if insurance premiums fell each year instead of rising? What about food? Would it be such a disaster if food became less expensive? How about education? Would parents really consider it a tragedy if college tuitions went down instead of up? You get the point. For all the talk about the horrors of deflation, I do not know anyone who would not benefit were it actually allowed to happen.[252]

Both Kevin Kelley and Chris Anderson state the same phenomenon as Schiff. As Anderson states about the French mathematician Joseph Bertrand's own analysis after reviewing Antoine Cournot's economic theories:

> Bertrand concluded that rather than limit output to raise prices and increase profits [which Cournot theorized], companies would more likely lower prices to gain market share. Indeed, they would attempt to undercut each other until the price was just above the cost of production, which is called "marginal cost pricing." And if the lower prices encouraged greater demand, so much the better. Bertrand competition can be shorthanded like this: in a competitive market, price falls to the marginal cost.... In abundant markets, where it's easy to make more stuff ... Price often does fall to the marginal cost.... Today we are building the most competitive market the world has ever seen, one where the marginal cost of products and services is close to zero. Online, where information is a commodity and products and services can be easily copied, we are seeing Bertrand competition playing out in a way that would have amazed even Bertrand.

---

252 Ibid., 123.

If "price falls to the marginal cost" is the law, then free is not just an option it's the inevitable endpoint. It's the force of economic gravity, and you can only fight it for so long.[253]

As prices have fallen and the long tail of more products for sale has expanded, sales have actually increased.[254] The continuing falling rate of profit and prices is generally agreed upon by many economists whether classical liberal, Austrian, neoclassical, Keynesian or socialist, and it is in the two initial enclaves that the realization that the evolution of capitalism won't lead to the immiseration as foretold by Ricardo, Mill and Marx. It will instead lead to what Schumpeter refers to as an *embarrass de richesse*,[255] which the deflationary continuously falling rate of profit and prices foreshadows.

As Marx ingenuously glimpsed so long ago, capitalism is evolving toward a system that will transcend what has been known before. What that new system will be, what it will be called, is unknown at this time, but the economic data show that it will be one where all prices for goods and services have dropped dramatically toward Kevin Kelly's and Chris Anderson's "Free." Money for all extent and purposes would become so valuable as to be worthless as Kel Kelly's and the libertarian's line of reasoning intuits.[256] If the natural rate of deflation during the last three decades of the nineteenth century had been allowed to continue without intervention, all prices would have continued to drop at least 1.2% or more a year, which means that over the twentieth century prices would have naturally declined over 120%! If we take Kel Kelly's 4% figure as factually possible due to greater productivity brought about through technological advancement, and many economists acknowledge that figure as reasonable, the price drop would have been well over 400%. If

---

253   Chris Anderson, *FREE*, 172.

254   Note: Production created its own demand just as Say theorized; in fact the entire new economy has proven Say's Law.

255   French, "embarrassing surplus of riches."

256   By turning the figures around and hypothesizing a deflation rate of 2,500% since 1913 instead. What cost you $18,616.00.48 in 1913 would cost you roughly $800 today. See the CPI Inflation Calculator at the United States Department of Labor, http://www.bls.gov/data/inflation_calculator.htm, and invert the results.

the law of increasing returns was allowed to continue (uninterrupted by the theft of inflation) the real cost reduction may well have been over 4,000%. Why didn't society see this natural decline in prices over the last 100 years? Quite simply, the Federal Reserve's inflating the money supply and its credit expansion caused all prices to increase 2,500% since 1913, or to put it more accurately, inflation caused the value of the dollar to decrease in purchasing power almost 2,500%! Today's dollar is worth less than 2 cents of the 1913 value of the dollar.[257]

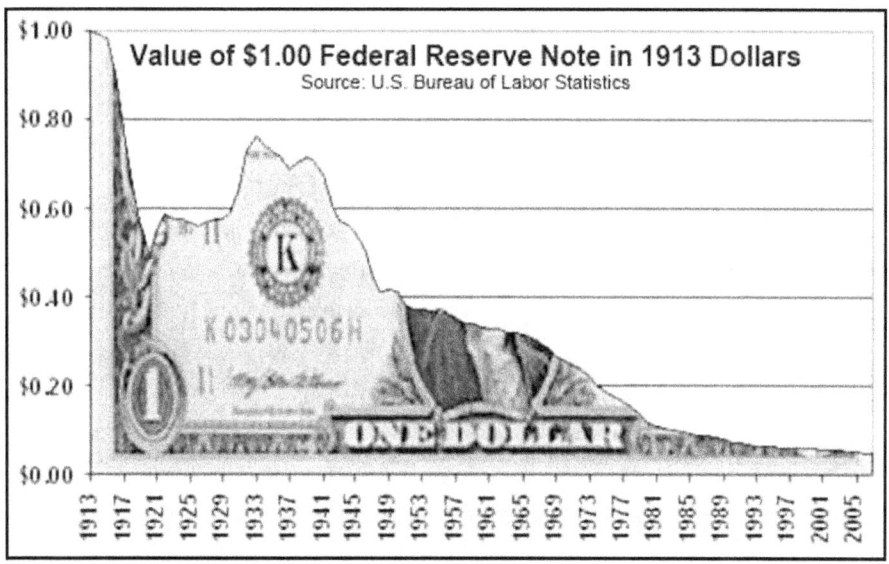

11 The Continuing Devaluation of the Dollar.[258]

Inflation, over-regulation, legislation, overzealous environmental restrictions, union bargaining for wages exceeding the market rate of labor,[259] higher tax rates, and increasing government spending at all

257 CPI figures are from the U.S. Dept. of Consumer Affairs.
258 Editor, "Minimum Wage Supporters Minds Blown after Learning Secrets of the Federal Reserve," AgainstCronyCapitalism.org (blog), May 8, 2014, http://www.againstcronycapitalism.org/2014/05/minimum-wage-supporters-minds-blown-after-learning-secrets-of-the-federal-reserve-video/.
259 Union bargaining is an epiphenomenon of inflation as in a non-inflationary and or deflationary economic system there would be no need for unions to raise wages. Wages would naturally increase as the value of the currency and productivity of labor continued to increase and as prices continued to naturally decline.

levels have caused the vast price increases and the draining away of capital accumulation, which would have fed a naturally rising wage rate and the falling rate of profit and prices. Inflation thus artificially supported and kept the rate of profit higher than it would have been naturally. "Inflationary Imperialism"[260] theoretically saved crony capitalism from the "phantom menace" of falling prices and higher wage rates that the previous century's theorists feared would erode away the capital needed to keep ephemeralization from greatly accelerating. Utopia was derailed and kept from appearing decades ago by the very inflationary economic system that far too many progressives and neo-socialists defend and uphold today out of sheer economic ignorance and their uninformed emotional need to blame the market economy for not being perfect.

Property as a Derivative of Scarcity and Abundance

One of the results of this natural deflationary rate is that it dovetails in with the main ideal that most socialist and communist ideology had as a platform and which Marx put center stage in the *Communist Manifesto*, which is the elimination of private property. Marx conceived it as an integral part of the evolution of capitalism that private property would come to an end. If we understand substantiated economic theory and the evolution of the Technium, we readily see that this epiphenomenon of exponential capitalism is a natural part of the deflationary process. If the market had been allowed to continue its evolution untroubled by huge amounts of inflation by central banks, the need or desire to own property would eventually have been eliminated. Taking out a long term mortgage in a market system where the money is worth 10% to 20% more each decade is disastrous for those who take on long term debt, as they are paying back that debt with dollars that are increasingly gaining value as one's debt would also appreciate in value at the same rate. Therefore all debt would have to be very short term if one didn't want

---

260 Or the "imperialism of inflation."

to be immiserated completely. The other side of technological advancement also goes against long-term property ownership as things became more abundant and cheaper, and scarcity begins to vanish, all products would overtime lose their value and become basically free. Reynolds clearly sees this eventual possibility:

> The widespread availability of such devices [nanoassemblers] would make things very, very different. Material goods wouldn't be quite free, but they would be nearly so. In such a world, personal property would become almost meaningless. Some actual physical items would retain sentimental value, but everything else could be produced as needed, then recycled as soon as the need passed. ... Value usually describes an objects ability to be exchanged for another item. But with personal property creatable on-demand from sunlight and dirt, it is not clear what a medium of exchange would be. Value comes from scarcity, and most goods wouldn't be scarce. ... Even without nanotechnology, the prices of many goods are falling. Televisions, once expensive, are near-commodity goods, as are computers, stereos, and just about all other electronics. It's cheaper to build new ones than to fix old ones, and prices continue to fall as capabilities increase. Nanotechnology would simply accelerate this trend and extend it to everything else. Ironically, it may be the combination of capitalism and technology that brings about a utopia unblemished by the need for ownership, the sort that socialists (usually no fans of capitalism) and romantics (no fans of technology) have long dreamed of.[261]

An idea which is seconded by Hans-Hermann Hoppe:

> For a concept of property to arise, there must be a scarcity of goods. Should there be no scarcity, and should all goods be so-called "free goods" whose use by any one person for any one purpose would not

---

261 Reynolds, *An Army*, 158.

in any way exclude (or interfere with or restrict) its use by any other person or for any other purpose, then there would be no need for property.... To develop the concept of property, it is necessary for goods to be scarce, so that conflicts over the use of these goods can possibly arise. It is a function of property rights to avoid such possible clashes over the use of scarce resources by assigning rights of exclusive ownership. Property is thus a normative concept: a concept designed to make a conflict-free interaction possible by stipulating mutually binding rules of conduct (norms) regarding scarce resources.[262]

Property can thus be seen as a derivative of the level of the scientific, technological and economic means of production. As these means become ever more exponential and the prices for all goods produced drop down an asymptote toward zero, property rights and their value decrease in importance. The evolution of nanotechnology through the Technium actually promises to bring about so much of what is in the socialist platform without any need to forcefully put it into place by political interventionism as Marx later in his life began to theorize. The full evolution of capitalism by the productive material forces of the Technium bode the utopia that both Marxists and techno-optimist libertarians desire. Thus neo-Marxist Michael Rechtenwald's statement in his article of the same name as my book states that, "The [Singularitan] movement is a carrier of an ideology [which] would leave the social order in place as it ignores the antagonisms of class society to focus on technological management" [263] is a statement based on his own ideological biases and not on facts. Kurzweil and other Singularitarians are very much aware and state many times in their works that the technological

262 Hans-Hermann Hoppe, *A Theory of Socialism and Capitalism* (Auburn, Alabama: Ludwig von Mises Institute, 2010), 18.
263 Michael Rechtenwald, "The Singularity and Socialism, Journal of Communist Theory and Practice," *Insurgent Notes*, October 5, 2013, http://insurgentnotes.com/2013/10/the-singularity-and-socialism/.
NB: I became aware of Mr. Rechtenwald's article and its title many months after having chosen the title of my own book. It is one of those weird cases of serendipity that my book and his article are titled the same.

forces now being unleashed will greatly change all of human society, nothing will be left intact. As Marx himself stated, and Rechtenwald seems to have missed in his reading of Marx, a change in the economic and productive processes would axiomatically change the social order's political and legal superstructure. Most of the Singularitarians are also well versed in complexity theory so "technological management" of the top down command and control type desired by Technocrats is not in most of their complex thinking.

The quixotic conundrum of it all has been that neo-socialist and neo-Marxist interventionism, in trying to make capitalism fairer and to redistribute the wealth and bring about the socialist utopia now, while sticking it to big business, has actually worked with the imperialistic capitalists to derail the evolutionary deflationary processes that boded their being eventually cast into the tar pit of history. Inadvertently social activists have caused the crony capitalist [neo-mercantilist] system we have today, which impoverishes the poor and lower classes worldwide while greatly increasing the profits of the big corporations and the wealth of the 1%. The more social activists intervene in the system's natural evolution, the more they stop it from evolving and the more they actually help big corporations in bed with big government keep their profits artificially higher than they would have been otherwise.[264] By remaining economically and historically ignorant and in refusing to accept the techno-optimist's data, progressive apparatchiks have inadvertently derailed the coming of the "messianic age" they all ardently hoped for. Murray Rothbard goes on to wax poetically in a manner reminiscent of the old utopian socialists:

> I envision the free-market world of the future ... the scourge of inflation will finally be lifted from the world; prices will fall, and the more productive the economy, and the more the increase in the supply of

---

264 I fully realize that inflation makes it appear that corporations and businesses are making profits or even higher profits, when in actuality their profits are being eroded away by inflation as well. In an inflationary regime everyone is actually being despoiled. That is why it is necessary for big business to gain governmental favor to keep their profits above the rate of inflation.

goods, the more prices will fall, the cost of living will decline, and the greater will be the increase in the standard of living for everyone. And without fractional reserve banking, there will be no more booms and busts, no more terrible malinvestments, distortions, and shocks of euphoria and distress brought about by business cycles. Investment will be limited to voluntary savings, and therefore there will be no periodic outbreaks of unsound investments that will have to be liquidated by recession. The world *oecumene*[265] will at last be secured by the money required for freedom: a metallic money, produced by the market and the value of which is decided totally by the market and not at all by government. Consumers and the economy will be immeasurably freer and sounder, and the only ones who will lose from the development of this market *oecumene* are the special interest groups who benefit from government and bank-controlled inflation and who constitute the ruling power elites in our increasingly state-dominated economy.[266]

A vision whose elements so many progressives today also readily share. The antagonistic ideologies have so much in common, right and left, and they share the same dream, a utopian world where each human being lives in a society that has the abundant resources that allows each individual to develop and reach their full potential and by the individual doing so, society also. As Marx, Engels, Simon, Diamandis et al. realize, this utopian future lies ahead for humanity through the evolution of the Technium, not behind us in a past non-technological golden age which actually never existed.

IX. Dematerialization

Dematerialization of objects has been going on all around us for decades, but it mostly flies under many people's radar and many do not recognize that it is actually happening. When Buckminster Fuller

---

265 Greek for economy.
266 Murray N. Rothbard, *Economic Controversies* (Auburn, AL: Ludwig von Mises Institute Press, 2011), 217.

used to ask people strange questions like, "How much does your building weigh," they thought he was crazy. His ideas and discovery of the process of ephemeralization were really remarkable for their time as dematerialization was only just then at its earliest stages. Today it is all around us and more and more people are readily apprehending it. Peter Diamandis explains this phenomenon:

> With *One Planet Living*, Jay Witherspoon explained that if everyone on earth wants to live like a North American, then we are going to need five planets worth of resources to do so-but is this really the case anymore? Bill Joy, cofounder of Sun Microsystems turned venture capitalist, feels that one of the advantages of contemporary technology is "dematerialization," which he described as one of the benefits of miniaturization: a radical decrease in footprint size for a great many of the items we use in our lives ... Just think of all the consumer goods and services that are now available on the average smartphone: cameras, radios, televisions, web browsers, recording studios, editing suites, movie theaters, GPS navigators, word processors, spreadsheets, stereos, flashlights, board games, card games, videogames, whole range of medical devices, maps, atlases, encyclopedias, dictionaries, translators, textbooks, world-class educations ... And the ever-growing smorgasbord known as the app store.
>
> Moreover, all of these now dematerialized goods and services used to require significant natural resources to produce, a physical distribution system to disperse, and a cadre of highly trained professionals to make sure that everything ran smoothly. None of these elements remain in the picture. And the list of those items no longer necessary keeps growing. When you also consider that robotics and AI will soon be replacing material possessions such as the automobile... The potential for sustainably increasing standards of living becomes much more apparent.[267]

---

267 Diamandis, *Abundance*, 150.

Everywhere one looks with an open mind, one sees this process working dramatically. The amount of steel and aluminum in cars has been decreasing steadily over the decades. With the advent of Boeing's new 787 *Dreamliner*[268] aircraft whose fuselage and interior is mostly constructed out of composite materials, the amount of aluminum being used in aircraft manufacturing is about to plummet throughout the industry. This is also apparent in computer production. The big computer towers in older models began shrinking over the last decade and now they have dematerialized completely and the CPU is being included with in the monitor. Now, the keyboard is about to vanish as the Celluon Company has invented a laser projection keyboard and touchpad.[269] With the widespread adoption of flash memory, standard motorized hard drives are about to vanish as well. Rooms that used to be full of internet servers in companies have now been replaced by one server, saving a great deal of material resources and energy and this one server is getting smaller and smaller every year as well. High technology is shrinking as the price drops while their features dramatically and exponentially increase.

With the advent of email, digital cameras and scanners, fax machines are no longer used. One can photograph a document using ones cell phone and then email it to a recipient. Digital cameras did away with film cameras and film processing. Tons of silver were then freed up to be used elsewhere in the economy. Today digital cameras are vanishing into our phones. Digital x-rays made x-ray photography instantly available in the ER and can be sent to a specialist hundreds of miles away to read instantaneously. Books are dematerializing with the invention of Kindle[270] and other such media devices. Now, many bestselling books are not even being printed anymore, they are available without having to drive to the bookstore or having it delivered, saving millions of dollars on paper production, ink, fuel costs etc. The Phone book doesn't need to be printed anymore and it is a big waste of resources and money

268 See this innovation at: http://boeing.com/stories/videos/vid_02_787. html?cm_mmc=Link-_-INNOVATION-_-Outbrain-_-787.
269 See this impressive invention at: http://www.techthisone.com/celluon-magic-cube-laser-projection-keyboard-and-touchpad/.
270 Trademark of Amazon.com.

as most people dump them into the recycling bin the moment they receive them![271]

The invention of fiber optic cable permitted millions of tons of copper wire to be recycled as it was replaced by the new technology. Soon carbon nanotube wire will replace millions of tons more copper used in electrical transmission lines. This process also includes CFL and LED light bulbs. As Charles Fishman states:

> One thing hasn't changed: the energy savings. Compact fluorescents emit the same light as classic incandescents but use 75% or 80% less electricity.

> What that means is that if every one of 110 million American households bought just one ice-cream-cone bulb, took it home, and screwed it in the place of an ordinary 60-watt bulb, the energy saved would be enough to power a city of 1.5 million people. One bulb swapped out, enough electricity saved to power all the homes in Delaware and Rhode Island. In terms of oil not burned, or greenhouse gases not exhausted into the atmosphere, one bulb is equivalent to taking 1.3 million cars off the roads.[272]

Or as Lester Brown states:

> Shifting to CFLs in homes, to the most advanced linear fluorescents in office buildings, commercial outlets, and factories, and to LEDs in traffic lights would cut the world share of electricity used for

---

271 "The environmental impact and economic costs are mind-boggling: White Pages estimates that 5M trees need to be harvested each year to print~147M white pages phone books. And the costs to recycle these books each year costs taxpayers an estimated $17M... State laws exist that require telephone companies to print and distribute WPPB: It's not that the phone companies want to print these wasteful books (it's a pretty big cost for them). They're required by law to deliver a phone book to every landline customer!" Jon Lusk, "Ban the White Pages Phone Book" *Whitepages* (Blog), August 13, 2009, http://blog.whitepages.com/2009/08/13/ban-the-white-pages-phone-book.

272 Charles Fishman, "How Many Light Bulbs Does it Take to Change the World? One. And You're Looking At It," *Fast Company* (Blog), September 2006, http://www.fastcompany.com/57676/how-many-lightbulbs-does-it-take-change-world-one-and-youre-looking-it.

lighting from 19 percent to 7 percent. This would save enough electricity to close 705 of the world's 2,670 coal-fired plants. If the high cost of LEDs drops faster than we have assumed, making widespread use feasible, lighting efficiency gains will come even faster than we have projected.[273]

So ephemeralization through new lighting technology would shrink the equivalent of 1.3 million cars and 705 coal power plants into nonexistence causing all of their materials to be recycled and reused elsewhere. The switch to LED lights is only accelerating this phenomenon. Soon smart transportation PODs callable at a few minutes' notice from your smart phone, will take you where you want to go (ride share companies are already providing this service and it is estimated to do nothing but grow) and millions of cars will vanish as the need to own a car of your own will disappear.

Everywhere one looks everything is dematerializing. With the creation of the 3D and now the 4D printer,[274] all production will soon be revolutionized as well. As these very expensive units fall down the asymptote in price, soon every home will have one. Children will use software to make their own toys. A person can either design their own clothing or buy someone else's designs and print it out for themselves to wear. Need a new tool, or have a great idea for a new tool? A person will be able to design one and print it out, or sell their design online for everyone else to print out and use. Imagine the burst of creativity that will explode in the world once this device is in every home. Factories and the old way of producing and distributing many or most products will soon vanish from the face of the earth. Artists and sculptors can create a work of art on their computers and then have it for sale throughout the internet ready for customers to print out. An even more amazing idea brought up by the biochemist Lee Cronin is to create a 3D printer

---

273 Lester Brown, "How Many Light Bulbs Does it Take to Close Down 705 Coal Plants?", *Book Bytes* (blog) June 16, 2010, http://www.earth-policy.org/book_bytes/2010/pb4ch04_ss2.
274 To see this amazing device see the TED.com video by Lisa Harouni: *A Primer on 3D Printing*, http://www.ted.com/talks/lisa_harouni_a_primer_on_3d_printing.html.

that can print molecules.[275] This would dramatically change our world. We are now beginning to print even human organs for transplant, so medicine is about to be transformed as well. Even food is now being 3D printed. The neo-Malthusians have been wrong all along; humanity won't need five, or even three Earths, to give everyone in the world the lifestyle of the developed world as the future will give everyone in the world a lifestyle well above what humanity has today at far far lower prices and with greater abundance of resources and materials most of which haven't even been invented yet. The promise of nanotechnology already predicts that nano-production will use 80% less energy and resources to produce its products, and cost 80% less than present products to produce, a truly dramatic exponential cost decline of all products thus awaits humanity in the very near future.

X. The Law of Accelerating Returns

Ray Kurzweil gives a list of the Law of Accelerating Returns on his blog:

The Law of Accelerating Returns

We can organize these observations into what I call the law of accelerating (LOAR) returns as follows:

- Evolution applies positive feedback in that the more capable methods resulting from one stage of evolutionary progress are used to create the next stage. As a result, the:

- Rate of progress of an evolutionary process increases exponentially over time. Over time, the "order" of the information embedded in the evolutionary process (i.e., the measure of how well

---

275 Lee Cronin, "A 3D Printer of Molecules", *Technology Education Development* (blog), June 2012, http://blog.ted.com/2012/06/26/lee-cronin-at-tedglobal2012/.

the information fits a purpose, which in evolution is survival) increases.

- A correlate of the above observation is that the "returns" of an evolutionary process (e.g., the speed, cost-effectiveness, or over-all "power" of a process) increase exponentially over time.

- In another positive feedback loop, as a particular evolutionary process (e.g., computation) becomes more effective (e.g., cost effective), greater resources are deployed toward the further progress of that process. This results in a second level of exponential growth (i.e., the rate of exponential growth itself grows exponentially).

- Biological evolution is one such evolutionary process.

- Technological evolution is another such evolutionary process. Indeed, the emergence of the first technology creating species resulted in the new evolutionary process of technology. Therefore, technological evolution is an outgrowth of–and a continuation of–biological evolution.

- A specific paradigm (a method or approach to solving a problem, e.g., shrinking transistors on an integrated circuit as an approach to making more powerful computers) provides exponential growth until the method exhausts its potential. When this happens, a paradigm shift (i.e., a fundamental change in the approach) occurs, which enables exponential growth to continue.[276]

---

276 Ray Kurzweil, "The Law of Increasing Returns," *Accelerating Intelligence* (blog), March 2001, http://www.kurzweilai.net/the-law-of-accelerating-returns.

The implications of this law are world changing and are almost unbelievable. Kurzweil himself discusses the resistance this new paradigm receives:

> I can understand why many observers do not readily embrace the obvious implications what I have called the law of accelerating returns (the inherent acceleration of the rate of evolution, with technological evolution as a continuation of biological evolution). After all, it took me forty years to be able to see what was right in front of me, and I still cannot say that I am entirely comfortable with all those consequences.

> The key idea underlying the impending Singularity is that the pace of change of our human-created technology is accelerating and its powers are expanding at an exponential pace.[277]

As an amazing result of this exponential acceleration in technology, all prices are now sliding down an asymptote toward becoming so cheap that they may become free, as Kevin Kelly in his blog post *Technology Wants to be Free*, describes this exponential negative sloping decline in prices:

> If technology wants to be free, where does this compulsion reside? I believe it emanates from the networks of communication within the technium which surrounds each good. Orthodox economics teaches that every producer is trying to maximize price but will "minimize the maximum" in response to competition. The more "perfect" the competition, the stronger the drive to lower prices. The major inventions in the last 20 years have been vast improvements in communication and market mechanisms, which have accelerated the 'perfection' of the market. Innovations such as easy reverse auctions,

---

277 Kurzweil, *Singularity*, 7.

ubiquitous small-price auctions, searchable discounts, price aggregators, outsourcing clearinghouses, real time quotes, instant always on connection– all conditions [that] squeeze fluff out of the system all along the creation chain and push prices downward relentlessly. In this flat world there's no harbor from the natural pressure toward free.

Additionally, this same network of communications spreads learning fast and furious. The news of how to make something more efficient travels almost instantly from the inventor to the entire technium. Tools such as online patents and reverse engineering techniques as well as great mobility among workers all contribute to promiscuous exchange of learning. Further, advanced technologies that encourage cooperation and collaboration permit faster invention and distribution of those inventions, which in turn permit the competitive pressure for lower prices to take effect quicker and deeper. Finally, the market for the finished goods is boosted by easily assembled networks which can gain members quickly. The more units produced or consumed, the faster the learning cycle for efficiency and price reduction. These five traits of networked technology–perfect market competition, price transparency, innovation sharing, collaboration, and expanding markets–ceaselessly push technology toward the free.[278]

The law of increasing returns was the acknowledgement that humanity is on the rising portion of an exponential curve transitioning from linearity to accelerating nonlinearity, but even that curve is accelerating leading to Kurzweil's incredible insight of the Law of Exponential Returns.

---

278 Kevin Kelly, "Technology Wants to Be Free," *The Technium* (blog), November 14, 2007, http://www.kk.org/thetechnium/archives/2007/11/technology_want.php.

XI. Kurzweil's Law: The Law of Exponential Returns.

As technological production increases it takes on the slope of an exponential function, the rate of *accelerating acceleration* increases and it approaches the upward curve toward infinity, or the singularity, using a physics term borrowed for describing the event horizon of black holes. This Singularity is what Kurzweil sees technology and humanity co-evolving toward in a synergistic interrelated fashion. It is his great insight into exponential systems and in the data which proves his insight that gives his vision such power, as he himself states:

The evolutionary process of technology seeks to improve capabilities in an exponential fashion. Innovators seek to improve things by multiples. Innovation is multiplicative, not additive. Technology, like any evolutionary process, builds on itself. This aspect will continue to accelerate when the technology itself takes full control of its own progression.

We can thus conclude the following with regard to the evolution of life-forms, and of technology: the law of accelerating returns as applied to an evolutionary process: An evolutionary process is not a closed system; therefore, evolution draws upon the chaos in the larger system in which it takes place for its options for diversity; and evolution builds on its own increasing order. Therefore, in an evolutionary process, order increases exponentially.

A correlate of the above observation is that the "returns" of an evolutionary process (e.g., the speed, cost-effectiveness, or overall "power" of a process) increase exponentially over time. We see this in Moore's law, in which each new generation of computer chip (now spaced about two years apart) provides twice as many components, each of which operates substantially faster (because of the smaller distances required for the electrons to travel, and other innovations). This exponential growth in the power and price-performance of information-based technologies – now roughly doubling every year – is not limited to computers, but is true for a wide range of technologies, measured many different ways.

In another positive feedback loop, as a particular evolutionary process (e.g., computation) becomes more effective (e.g., cost effective), greater resources are deployed towards the further progress of that process. This results in a second level of exponential growth (i.e., the rate of exponential growth itself grows exponentially). For example, it took three years to double the price-performance of computation at the beginning of the twentieth century, two years around 1950, and is now doubling about once a year. Not only is each chip doubling in power each year for the same unit cost, but the number of chips being manufactured is growing exponentially.[279]

He sees no limit to this constantly accelerating evolutionary process. He theorizes the approach of the Singularity, "we'll get to a point where technological progress will be so fast that unenhanced human intelligence will be unable to follow it. That will mark the Singularity."[280] It is "a future period during which the pace of technological change will be so rapid, its impact so deep, that human life will be irreversibly transformed."[281]

XII. There Are No Limits to Human Knowledge

The main and fundamental feature underlying the techno-optimist vision is the idea that there are no actual limits to human knowledge.

---

279 Ray Kurzweil, "Kurzweil's Law," *Kurzweil Accelerating Intelligence*, (blog), January 12, 2004, http://www.kurzweilai.net/kurzweils-law-aka-the-law-of-accelerating-returns.
280 Reynolds, *An Army of Davids*, 246.
281 Ibid., 244.

That as long as human minds, hearts, imaginations and souls are left free to inquire, investigate, invent, and discover, the horizons of human understanding and knowledge will continue to expand outward almost infinitely. This is at the heart of entrepreneurial activity as well as scientific discovery; it is an integral part of what it truly means to be human. In a footnote of his book Hans de Soto states this revolutionary fact:

> The entrepreneurial process gives rise to sort of continuous social "Big Bang" which permits the boundless growth of knowledge. According to Frank J. Tipler, professor of mathematics and physics at Tulane University, the limit to the expansion of knowledge on earth is 10^{64} bits (and thus it would be possible to multiply by 100 billion the physical limits to growth which have been considered up to now), and it can be mathematically demonstrated that a human civilization based in space could expand its knowledge, wealth, and population without limit. Tipler concludes: "much nonsense has been written on the physical limits to economic growth by physicists who are ignorant of economics. A correct analysis of the physical limits to growth is possible only *if one appreciates Hayek's insight that what the economic system produces is not material things, but immaterial knowledge.*"[282]

Intellectual freedom is an indispensable requirement for spontaneous emergent evolutionary forces which led to the development of technological density as the economist Brad DeLong describes in his article "Slouching Toward Utopia:"

Causes of Growth: Technological Density

Even the conjunction of market economic organizations and political democracy is insufficient to account for the economic miracle

---

[282] Jesus Huerta De Soto, *Socialism, Economic Calculation and Entrepreneurship* (London: MPG Books Group, 2010). 46.

of the twentieth century. Both of these factors are only tangentially related to the extraordinary explosion of technology–of scientific knowledge and its application to production in everyday life–in this century. In order to achieve this 'centuries' revolutions in science and technology, we need "technological density" as well: research and development has to become an industry in itself, rather than an avocation of a few learned gentlemen reading papers before a Royal Society, to maintain the pace of invention and innovation that we now take for granted. Only the confluence of all three, market institutions, political democracy, and high technological density, could generate the economic revolutions of the twentieth century.[283]

And besides density there must be a networked system:

When economic systems shift from feudal structures to the nascent forms of modern capitalism, they became less hierarchical and more networked. Society organized around marketplaces, instead of castles or cloisters, distributes decision-making authority across a much larger network of individual minds. The innovation power of the marketplace derives, in part, from this most elemental math: no matter how smart the "authorities" may be, if they are outnumbered 1000 to one by the marketplace, there'll be more good ideas lurking in the market than in the feudal castle. Cities and markets recruit more minds into the collective project of exploring the adjacent possible. As long as there is spillover between those minds, useful innovations will be more likely to appear and spread to the population at large. In thinking about network innovation this way, I am specifically not talking about a "global brain," or a "hive mind.".… Large collectives are rarely capable of true creativity or innovation…when the first market towns emerged in Italy, they didn't magically create some higher-level group consciousness. They simply widened the

283 J Bradford DeLong, "Slouching Towards Utopia?: The Economic Meaning of the Twentieth Century-III The Meaning of Economic Growth," http://econ161.berkeley.edu/TCEH/Slouch_causes3.html.

pool of minds that could come up with and share good ideas. This is not the wisdom of the crowd, but the wisdom of *someone* in the crowd. It's not that the network itself is smart; it's that the individuals get smarter because they are connected to the network.[284]

Kevin Kelly talks about the "Great Asymmetry" the interrelated density that creates the force that overwhelms entropy:

"Humans on average build a bit more than they destroy, and create a bit more than they use up," writes economist Julian Simon. That's about right, what enables humans, on average, to ratchet up such significant accumulations? The ratchet is the Great Asymmetry, says evolutionist Stephen Jay Gould. This is the remarkable ability of evolution to create a bit more, on average, than it destroys. Against the great drain of entropy, life ratchets up irreversible gains. The Greatest Asymmetry is rooted in webs, in tightly interlinked entities, in self-reinforcing feedback, in co-evolution, and in the many loops of increasing returns that fill an ecosystem. Because every new species in life co-creates a niche for yet other new species to occupy, because every additional organism presents a chance for other organisms to live upon it, the cumulative total multiplies up faster than the inputs add up; thus the perennial one-way surplus of opportunities. We call the Great Asymmetry in human affairs "the economy."[285]

As the techno-optimists have discovered, interrelated knowledge in a networked distributed system is the evolving force of both evolution and the Technium and it is driving technology upward in an exponential arc as prices are also declining in an exponentially reverse direction. Utopia is thus envisioned as a matter of time, in evolutionary terms, and not a matter of imposed ideology. It is a bottom-up, democratic, spontaneous, emergent, chaotic and complex phenomenon and not a: top-down, command and control dictated program.

---

284 Steve Johnson, *Where Good Ideas*, 17.
285 Kelly, *New Rules*, 141.

12

The Coming Economic Singularity

*"You never change things by fighting the existing reality.
To change something, build a better model that makes
the existing model obsolete."*

-BUCKMINSTER FULLER

At this point you must feel like you have taken Mr. Toad's Wild Ride through the history of political and economic philosophy and techno-optimism. By now though you have assembled enough basic facts and ideas so that I can finally come more fully to the main premise of my entire work, which is that we are evolving economically as well as scientifically and technologically toward an event horizon that will forever change our world. In fact it is the changes brought about in and by the market by science and technology that is the main driving force propelling us toward this economic singularity–the omega point. Where the present economic system is transcended and a new one begins, a concept that Desai calls *Socialism beyond Capitalism*. Desai spent his entire book *Marx's Revenge* promising the reader that he would reveal a great secret on how to obtain socialism found within Marx's later evolutionary thought, and in the last page of his book he seemed to have pulled his punch. A punch that I shall let loose later on in this chapter, but the last page of his important book is worth quoting in full here:

> Marx's challenge to Adam Smith therefore remains yet to be met. Knowing full well the potential capitalism had to eliminate scarcity, Marx did not see that inequality as well as poverty could be eliminated in a capitalist society. Yet between his juvenilia in the 1840s and his mature writing in *Capital*, he became less sure that the system would disappear imminently. Sadly, his youthful rhetoric rather than his mature analysis became his legacy. Untold crimes were committed in his name, provoking the prophecy that capitalism would die soon, defeated by the new order created in the Soviet Union. **The idea that capitalism, while it lasted, was a progressive mode of production whose unfettered development was preferable to reactionary alternatives was forgotten.** Now it has come back with a vengeance. Capitalism has become truly global, and it has not yet reached its limits. So what happens to Marx?

> Recall Marx's reluctance to prophesy what would follow capitalism in any detail. It was to be socialism, followed after some time by communism. Yet how it would come about and what it would look like, how it works, are all issues he left untouched. After twenty years devoted to the critique of political economy–an analysis of how capitalism worked–he never came back to the questions he posed in his youthful manuscripts. Is it possible to have a society that is not merely self-organizing, but consciously so? A society fully self-conscious of its own workings, and able to direct them, where individuals are not alienated from their work, or from themselves, but fully participate in their self-emancipation, and realize the full potential of the species-beings that they are-in other words, Socialism beyond Capitalism?

Marx diverted himself from the task of answering these questions to studying capitalism, and excoriating contemporary socialists for their illusions about the prospect of achieving socialism. Yet these delusions reappeared after his death, and had murderous consequences after 1917. That sad, violent and barbaric episode in the world's history is over. Marx has had his revenge. But will he ever get his reward? Will there [ever] be Socialism beyond Capitalism?[286]

Socialism has forgotten its evolutionary roots and by forgetting it and falling headlong into reactionary interventionist practices has done nothing but delay the ripening of capitalism and its eventual transcendence. This idea that capitalism would evolve to transcend itself is not a new discovery or intuition on my part, it is in fact very old and belongs both to the classical liberal philosophers and to the socialists, especially Marx and Engels' "scientific socialism." Murray Rothbard recounts the classical liberal economic philosopher John Baptiste Say's ideas on the subject:

> [Say] pointed out, the wants of man are unlimited, and will continue to be until we achieve genuine superabundance –a world marked by the prices of all goods and services falling to zero. But at that point there would be no problem in finding consumer demand, or, indeed any economic problem at all.... The essay postulates a situation where all costs of production are at last reduced to zero: 'in which case, it is evident there can no longer be rent for land, interest upon capital, or wages on labor, and consequently, no longer any revenue to the productive classes'. What will happen then?

---

286 Meghnad Desai, *Marx's Revenge*, 315. Bold mine.

What then, I say, these classes would no longer exist. Every object of human want would stand in the same predicament as the air or the water, which are consumed without the necessity of being either produced or purchased. In like manner as everyone is rich enough to provide himself with air, so would he be to provide himself with every other imaginable product. This would be the very acme of wealth. Political economy would no longer be a science; we should have no occasion to learn the mode of acquiring wealth; for we should find it ready made to our hands.[287]

Which correspond exactly with Marx's and Engels' own ideas:

In 'The Principles of Communism', an essay written in late 1847 that became the first draft for the *Communist Manifesto*, Engels laid bare one of the crucial, usually implicit, assumptions of the communist society–that superabundance will have eliminated the problem of scarcity:

Private property can be abolished only when the economy is capable of producing the volume of goods needed to satisfy everyone's requirements... The new rate of industrial growth will produce enough goods to satisfy all the demands of society... Society will achieve an output sufficient for the needs of all members.

This superabundant production somehow will have been achieved by a wondrous technological progress.[288]

287 Murray N. Rothbard, *Classical Economics: An Austrian Perspective on the History of Economic Thought*, Volume II (Auburn, Al: Mises Institute, 2006), 28.
288 Ibid., 327.

When you combine all of the insights and discoveries of Marx, the classical liberal and complexity economists, and the techno-optimist's, which I have mentioned throughout the previous chapters, you can readily surmise that given the natural deflationary rate of a complex, emergent, spontaneously evolving, dynamic system driven by ever accelerating scientific and technological progress, that all prices would eventually fall down a asymptote toward zero, as resources greatly expanded in the absence of central banking's monetary inflation and ideologically driven artificial resource constraints.

We have two exponential functions going on in the world today in our economies; 1. A positive production curve and 2. A negative price curve operating at the same time. (see figure below)When these two achieve a certain point, what I call the Omega Point, the present economic system is dramatically changed, transformed and transcended. Without inflation and interventionism by the reactionaries and revisionists, crony-capitalists and crony-socialists alike, the entire system would naturally evolve to this Omega Point, the economic event horizon, and Marx's vision of the necessity for "the full evolution of capitalism" will be fully vindicated and the fulfillment of both the classical liberal and scientific socialist dream of utopia would arrive. Socialism beyond Capitalism would arise spontaneously from the bottom up brought about by the fuller evolution of the scientific and technological historical forces (The Technium). This socialism is and would be unlike any other social system ever imagined or influenced by the old notions of the past. It will be something completely new and different, organized and brought about by the new rules and laws of exponential production, and organized by spontaneous emergent complex forces. This society and culture is 180 degrees from what we have all thought of as "socialist" or "libertarian" in the past, while containing their essential humanistic and praxeological elements, but realized in a new evolutionary complex way.

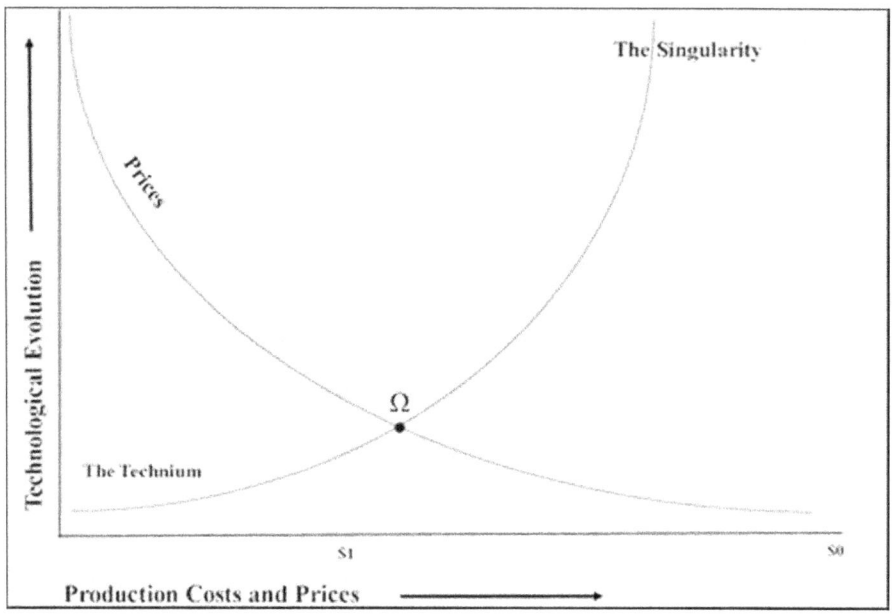

12 The Omega Point

This future would not be a moneyless society in the sense that all currency was abolished or banished by decree. In actuality the money would over time become so valuable as to be in all essentials worthless to carry.[289] Imagine a world where a gourmet dinner out might cost .0001 cents, a new vehicle less than $5.00 USD. One's savings would increase in value every year to the point that everyone would become virtually wealthy. The short term thinking that an inflationary economy drives people to adopt would be eliminated and very long term thought processes and expectations would become common in a natural deflationary market. As the cost to produce products continued to drop as production became ever more exponential, making everything out of "sunlight and dirt" using nanoassemblers, the products would begin to incorporate the best materials and technology efficiently feasible as these

---

289 Not worthless in the value sense, or in the absolute necessary function that monetary prices serve in distributing knowledge, information and making the efficiency of production possible, but only in the need to carry it and save it as we do now under an inflationary system that causes all savings to evaporate.

materials would consistently drop in price and increase in availability and quality each year as well as be transcended by new meta-materials created by the Technium. The old saw against "planned obsolescence" driven by producers desperately scrambling to try to lower production costs through substituting cheaper materials so as to keep retail prices lower in a constantly inflationary economic system driving up prices, would no longer be necessary.

A huge savings glut would naturally drive interest rates toward zero[290] down an asymptote vastly increasing even more production and innovation. As I mentioned in a previous chapter, "in the realm of incredible or super abundance property rights do not have the same meaning that they have in the realm of scarcity." Everyone could afford the luxuries society has to produce as their cost will have plummeted as the value of the currency naturally increased through the law of exponential returns. Everything that the monetary cranks and inflationist have desired over the last two centuries will actually be brought about, not through inflation, but by a huge savings and productivity aggregate supply shock (The Law of Exponential Returns) feeding technological growth that would create a supply tsunami. We could finally afford everything that is produced because the price of everything will have fallen as the value of the currency naturally increased along with the vast increase in more efficient production. As Albert Einstein once said, "Compound interest is the most powerful force in the universe." Technological evolution and its resulting deflation is the almost magical compound force that can bring us to the futuristic utopian world that we all desire and want to live in.

If you wished to build the most modern up-to-date building or device using the most advanced physics, engineering and material science available today, would you recommend first banishing all numbers, calculation

---

290 It must be remembered though that the interest rate could never reach or actually become zero. As Steele correctly mentions, "A zero rate of interest would have bizarre results: for instance numerous projects with slight but perpetual yields would all have to be accorded an infinite value." Steele, *From Marx to Mises*, 293. And Skousen states, "As long as life is finite and resources are limited, a zero interest rate will be impossible." Skousen, *The Structure*, 230.

and Newtonian and quantum mechanics in order to achieve this goal? Would you recommend banishing measurement, length, weight, width and height? Of course not, that would be ludicrous. What you would do is you would use the most advanced science, technology and building techniques efficiently known at the time to realize your dream. You wouldn't recommend and promulgate an entirely new scientific system, as of yet completely untried, in order to fulfill your project's realization. Yet today the Resource Based Economists, the Venus Project-ers and the Zeitgeist Movement all recommend the ludicrous actions I just mentioned in order to stay faithful to older utopian socialist ideas. The most important thing about my discovery of how to reach the economic event horizon and thus realize utopia, is that it doesn't go against or violate any of the economic theories and forces surmised by either older Marxists, the Classical liberals, or the Austrian School of Economics. It uses the present discoveries of the scientific, technological and economic system to reach its goals, just as one would use existing science to build a futuristic high rise building or any scientific device, or to invent the technology of tomorrow that will revolutionize and make outmoded the technology of today. It is a natural process of technological evolution and not an ideological intervention that will bring about utopia.

Both Marxists and Libertarians can agree and sign on to the means that are necessary to reach this utopian goal as it involves withering away the state upfront and the eventual transference of all political power to social forces now evolving through the Internet as it moves to becoming the Global Brain. You don't have to stop the world and put into place a new untried static "utopian" economic system. You don't have to count all of the available resources in order to begin more efficient production (an impossibility that violates complexity theory), you don't have to promulgate a pie in the sky system that has never worked, been tested, or breathed the air of reality as a possible way to reach utopia. What I have rediscovered is that you only have to allow scientific, technological and economic evolution to pursue its natural extropic course and the utopian world we all dream of arises spontaneously with the full evolution of the Technium. Marx, Mises, Complexity theory, the techno-optimists and the full evolution of capitalism merges dialectically into a syncretic whole which culminates at the event horizon of the omega point. "That which evolves eventually converges" and this is the unseen force that is driving the world today, a force that is impelling us to convergence and transcend the present political, economic and social system steeped in polarized delusional dialectical gridlock.

Imagine a world where the Tea Party and the Occupy Movement could actually come together and work to achieve the goal of the Economic Singularity, since agitating for union, minimum or living wage increases are only necessary in an inflationary environment. Inflation keeps feeding and growing the rich 1%, deflation redistributes income to the lower classes automatically as Hülsmann states in his insightful work *Deflation & Liberty*, which I quoted from above and which Murray Rothbard seconds below:

> Credit expansion has, of course, the same effect as any sort of inflation: prices tend to rise as the money supply increases. Like any inflation, it is a process of redistribution, whereby the inflators, and the part of the economy selling to them, gain at the expense of those who come last in line in the spending process. This is the charm of inflation—for the beneficiaries—and the reason why it has been so popular, particularly since modern banking processes have camouflaged its significance for those losers who are far removed from banking operations. The gains to the inflators are visible and dramatic; the losses to others hidden and unseen, but just as effective for all that. Just as half the economy are taxpayers and half tax-consumers, so half the economy are inflation-payers and the rest inflation-consumers.[291]

Once we set a course on allowing evolutionary technical deflation, everyone's wage rates and savings will naturally increase each year

---

291   Murray Rothbard, *Man, Economy and State, with Power and Market*, scholars edition [1962] (Auburn, Al: Ludwig von Mises Institute, 2004), 990.

without the need for any political involvement or agitation. Everyone will get a real wage increase every year automatically tied to the technological deflation rate, right now estimated at 4% a year. Everyone will receive over a 48% real wage increase every decade. If you had invested only $10,000 at 4% a year compounded annually incredible things happen. At 10 years without any new funds added it only grows to $14,802. At 50 years it has grown to $71,066 and after 100 years it has grown to a whopping $505,049. Savings would grow exponentially with just a small 4% deflation rate a year. We would live in a world not where the candy bars, cereal boxes, and the content of shopping carts get smaller every year as their size diminishes and their prices increase, but the opposite. We would get more and more for our money until such a time as having a price for most things would become almost impractical. Imagine a world where the graph of the falling value of the US dollar (fig. 11) I presented several chapters ago was flipped along its horizontal axis (fig 13 below) so that the value of the currency would actually rise every year.

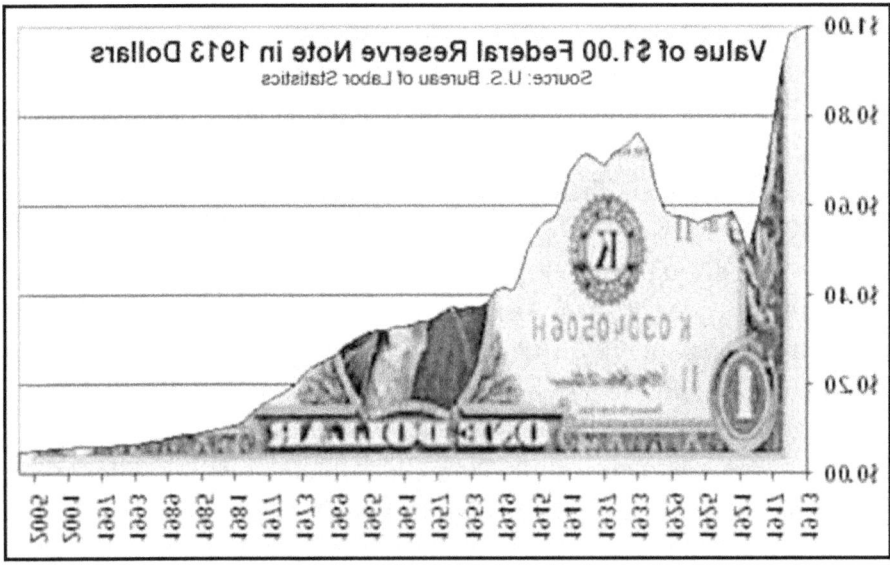

13. What if the dollar increased in value every year? (fig 11 reversed).

Take as our starting date 2014 and our ending date of 2114, the reverse of what has happened from 1913 to today would have happened. Prices will drop 2,500% instead of having gone up as the value of the dollar dramatically increased. You, your children and grandchildren's savings and investments will also increase by more than that amount as well. Rich Karlgaard imagines this process using only a 2% rate of production:

> Suppose the U.S. economy, since 1949, were giving up 2% extra growth per year because of bad economic policy. Or, as Ramsey might say, because Presidents, legislators and unelected regulators were born stupid or try their best to act that way.

> Now, 2% a year doesn't sound like much. Most of us could spend 98% of our budget next year without too much pain. The quip about compound interest is noteworthy only because it would take a genius like Einstein to observe something so profoundly simple yet subtly opaque. But run the numbers yourself–and prepare for a shock. If the U.S. economy had grown an extra 2% per year since 1949, 2014's GDP would be about $58 trillion, not $17 trillion. [292]

And if the U.S. had only had an extra 1% increase in productivity a year since 1949 we would have had the following:

- The 2014 GDP would be $32 trillion, not $17 trillion.

- Per capita income would be $101,000, not $54,000.

- Per capita wealth would be $480,000, not $260,000. It would probably be higher than that, since savings rates might be higher.

---

[292] Rich Karlgaard, "Americas Missing Wealth," *Forbes*, October 20, 2014. http://www.forbes.com/sites/richkarlgaard/2014/09/30/americas-missing-wealth.

- The U.S. would have no federal, state or municipal debts or deficits.

- Pensions would be solid. So would Social Security.[293]

Though Karlgaard's article focuses entirely on the dire effect of government over-regulation and doesn't mention the effects of inflation, it is a sobering experience to comprehend the synergistic effects that disastrous interventionism, both monetary and regulatory, has had on keeping us all poorer. Keith Weiner, also of Forbes, gives us the inflationary side of this issue:

> We need constant-value money to compare current profits to historically invested capital, and calculate the real rate of return. We have to sort good investments from bad, increasing the good and liquidating the bad.

> The dollar is not constant, so we struggle with how to compensate. Using consumer prices to adjust it is fatally flawed. Every farmer, miner, manufacturer, and distributor constantly works to improve its efficiency. Real costs are falling. Prices follow costs (though it's a complex relationship).

> The dollar is falling [in value] and real prices are falling too. By using prices to measure the dollar, we can only see the difference between the two rates of descent. In some areas, like electronics, prices fall faster than the dollar. For example, the iPhone today is more powerful than supercomputers that used to cost millions.

> By contrast, the price of milk is falling slower than the dollar. In 1965, a gallon sold for about $0.37 (wholesale). By 2012, it was about $2.42. The conventional view measures only the difference—$2.05

---

293 Ibid.

or 554 percent. However, it misses most of the real drop in the dollar. I calculated that the real cost of producing milk fell at least 87 percent since 1965. If the dollar had kept its value, then grocers should be paying about a nickel and milk would retail for ten cents.

Using the price of milk, the dollar appears to inflate 554 percent. That's bad enough, but it misses the massive reduction in costs. In reality, the loss is about ten times worse—over 5,000 percent.

We use the dollar to measure prices. Then we turn around, and attempt to use prices to measure the dollar. It's circular.

There is a better way to measure the dollar: gold. In 1965, a dollar was worth 889mg gold. Today it's 25mg. The dollar has lost 97 percent of its value between 1965 and today.

The price of milk was 0.01oz gold in 1965. Now it's 0.002oz. Milk actually fell by 80 percent (despite increased taxes and regulations).[294]

To bring this issue home even more Craig Smith elucidates just how much this currency debasement has cost us:

How much has the Great Debasement cost America, at least in money? Using data compiled by the Bureau of Economic Analysis (BEA), *Forbes* columnist Louis Woodhill estimated in June 2012 that, in lost growth and value, the fiat dollar that Progressives imposed on America between the years 1974 and 2010 cost America more than $80 trillion.

These 36 years, it goes without saying, are only a fraction of the 100 years of the Great Debasement.

---

294 Keith Weiner, "Prices Provide a Misleading Measure of Dollar Devaluation," *Forbes*, October 13, 2014, http://www.forbes.com/sites/keithweiner/2014/10/13/prices-provide-a-misleading-measure-of-dollar-devaluation.

If the annual loss over these entire 100 years averaged the same as during the 36 years of Woodhill's calculation, then the great debasement in dollars has cost the United States at least $222 trillion.

Speaking of coincidence, the "fiscal gap" between US projected long-term debt and projected revenues–the debt that could bring America's economy and dollar crashing down in ruins–has been calculated by Boston University economist Kotlikoff to be $222 Trillion.[295]

This makes sense as every dollar created by the Federal Reserve System creates a dollar of debt. We paid for today's (vote buying) social services and largesse out of tomorrow's income and productivity and loaded up a massive tsunami of debt that is coming toward us at an ever increasing speed.

Tasking up Bastiat's challenge and learning to "see the unseen," imagine what an aggregate supply shock (Law of Increasing Returns) of 3% to 4% a year without any inflation would bring us? We can now begin to imagine a world of such economic abundance that money doesn't have the necessity or need it once had. Where a penny buys what $100 does today and in time it will buy eventually what $10,000, or even millions do today. This is the natural course that the centralized banking bureaucracies and inflationary monetary policies purposely tried to stop and derail and which the evolution of the productive material forces through the Technium continues to fight as it brings down prices every year despite the inflation the central banks and governments disastrously create. We are in a race between two dueling exponential functions, the one of the Economic Singularity and the other of inflationary debt and money creation through government control of the economy in league with crony bankers and businesses.

---

295 Craig R. Smith and Lowell Ponte, *The Great Debasement: The 100 Year Dying of the Dollar and How to Get America's Money Back* (Phoenix, AZ: Idea Factory Press, 2012) 125.

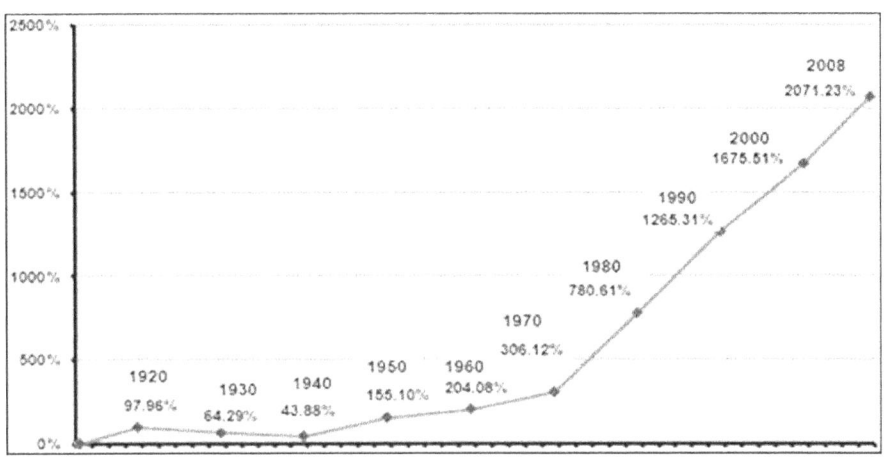

14. Cumulative Inflation Since 1913. [296]

If we take a average of the inflation rate that we obtain from the above graph we obtain an average inflation rate of 21.35% per year over the last 97 years the Federal Reserve has existed (from 2007). Using the inflation rate above and flipping the concept to one of deflation, an ever rising value for the dollar and if we use a compound interest calculation using only 2 cents as our staring point we would have obtained a value of $5,070,001 after 100 years. Our 2 cents has grown to over $5 million dollars! This is the power of exponential functions! This is the way we can reach an almost utopian economic system with real abundance for everyone.

---

296 Robert Jackson Smith, "Chart of the Cumulative Past Acts of the FED in its Inflation-Fighting Efforts," from *The Fate of the US Dollar: Talk is Cheap. It's Action That Counts*, Inflationomics.com (Blog), http://www.inflationomics.com/article.php?article=Talk%20is%20Cheap.

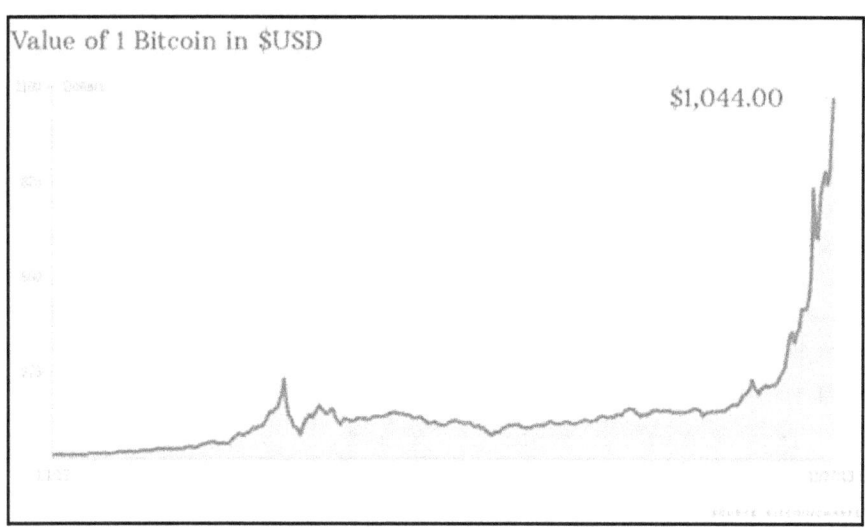

15 Value of Bitcoin. [297]

This is where national and then global competing currencies can greatly help as Bitcoin has shown its tendency to increase greatly in value as demand for it has markedly increased (fig. 15). [298] Though this may well be a bubble for Bitcoin, which may collapse as it is trying to accomplish too quickly a currency value increase, it does show us what an appreciating currency can accomplish over a longer period of time based upon real production increases and technological deflation, say in one hundred or even two hundred years, where a currency that started out being only worth 4 cents grows to being worth over $849 dollars today. [299] Presently our US Dollar is worth only about 2 cents of the pre-Federal Reserve 1913 US dollar, so we have a long way to go. If we wish to realize a utopian system of the future that does away with all of the corruption, insider trading, cronyism and interference on behalf of well-connected politicians and corporations, there is only one evolutionary way to do it.

297 Ben Rooney, "Bitcoin Prices Top $1,000," *CNN Money* (Blog), November 27, 2013 (11:11 AM ET), http://money.cnn.com/2013/11/27/investing/bitcoin-1000/.
298 Hibah Yousuf, "Bitcoins are a bubble," *CNN Money* (Blog), April 5, 2013 (6:52 AM ET), http://buzz.money.cnn.com/2013/04/05/bitcoin-bubble/.
299 Value estimated on January 9, 2014 at 1:44 pm using http://preev.com/.

We must allow and help the full evolution of freer market capitalism to commence. We must understand valid economics and how it can help us achieve the futuristic dreams of such organizations as the Venus Project and Zeitgeist Movement, but by using complex spontaneous and emergent evolutionary forces to do so, free of the ideological cant, fallacies and blather of previous eras and their crank economic theories. As the evolution of the system advances capitalism is actually becoming more social, as the sharing economy readily shows.

We cannot banish monetary prices, commodity creation, the division of knowledge and labor, global trade, or the interest rate without destroying evolutionary processes, abandoning all efficiency and any sense of an economic system and world unification. We can only banish political control over the economy on behalf of cronies and preferred partners which demand that the currency and bank credit be inflated every year so that the wealth, power and control of the "ruling" class can continue to increase over us all. Imperial crony capitalism and its cousin crony socialism must be ended so that the forces of the Technium can work with evolutionary powers to bring us to the point of a new revolutionary system-holoarchy. The Law of the Falling Rate of Profit and Prices—the law of exponential returns—must be fully and finally unleashed! The Technium itself is the productive evolutionary force whose free operation is necessary to banish the baneful features of the present political and economic system that we all suffer under today.

13

Conclusion

As the technium expands, it accelerates the rate of evolution first begun with life, so that it now evolves the idea of change itself. This is more than simply the most powerful force in the world; the evolution of evolution is the most powerful force in the universe.

-KEVIN KELLY

As presented in the previous chapters the ideas and discoveries of the various schools of neo-mysticism, economic thought and the new scientific discoveries of complexity show an astounding interrelated quality. A holistic pattern interweaves throughout the once oppositional ideologies revealing lines of mutual attraction between them that if followed would eventually lead us to a unified world. The Austrians, the cornucopians, the techno-optimists, the complexity economists, older Marxists et al. all describe and detail out the road to a utopian future for all of humanity coalescing in an future Teilhardian omega point. This future is being self-assembled and will continue to assemble itself from the bottom up through the evolution of the Technium if allowed to remain free of all artificial constraints. The interconnectedness and interrelatedness of all systems and the emergent, spontaneous complex order that arises naturally as those systems evolve is showing us that the old top-down command

and control paradigms of previous centuries are wearing thin. As Butler Shaffer says in the conclusion of his book *Boundaries of Order*:

> To presume that a complex world can be rendered orderly through the imposition of elaborately structured systems and rigidly enforced rules, is to fail to comprehend nature's inherent orderliness, as well as the dangers associated with the disruption of such undirected regularities. As we learn more about chaos, including how our inherently limited knowledge and understanding can never keep up with the interconnected complexities of our world, we may discover that the quality of our lives depends on learning how to live with greater flexibility, diversity, spontaneity, and uncertainty than our institutionally structured systems allow–qualities demanded by the unpredictable and uncontrollable nature of a complex universe. ... If we think of order as a quality *imposed* upon the world–whether by divine forces or so-called "laws of nature"–we will be inclined to embrace social systems that reflect such a model. As our understanding of orderliness is transformed, we should expect our social systems and practices to reflect such changed awareness. Thus, if the study of chaos, complexity, and quantum mechanics, informs us that order is a quality that *arises from*–rather than being *mandated upon*–human behavior, we may find ourselves attracted to a holographic metaphor for society.[300]

Evolution is a force that cannot be legislated away since stasis and equilibrium in an ever expanding universe with ever increasing complexity is an impossibility. Our Western religious sympathies once inferred that the world was static, created and directed by a divine Imperator from on high and was just recently created in the last five or six thousand years, all elements now burst asunder by modern scientific discoveries. When the *divine right* of the Catholic Church was worn away by

---

300 Shaffer, *Boundaries*, 318-319.

the first revolution of Protestantism, the sympathy to worship the next great totem, the divine right of kings, was put in its place, quite possibly an intellectual reaction arising from the loss of the infallible direction of Church authorities. After the divine right of kings was toppled by the Enlightenment and classical liberalism the divine right of the state was substituted for that of kings by many thinkers, most notably, Hegel, Fichte, List and Lassalle. Old wine was continually poured into new ideological skins, yet the content was the same, the worship of the old totem fetish pyramidal shaped system whose power alienated human beings from the fullness of their very humanity. Tomorrow, the evolutionary hope can only be that the divine right of the individual and society, interconnected through the global brain, will bring about the withering away of this last false totem idol–The State–leading to a new holistic governance structure that some are tentatively calling omniarchy.

So many of today's arising discoveries and paradigms from complexity theory and the techno-optimists point strongly in this direction, which validates Marx's evolutionary vision that the revolution will come in time as it is moved along by an evolutionary historical process, which freer market capitalism is creating. With the acceptance of this phenomenon, we can realize that the messianic era still lies in its mother's womb awaiting its full gestation period to be born. As the Technium takes off into exponential territory at warp speed, the labor pangs can readily be felt. "We are living in exponential times" and it will take some time for scientific paradigms and human consciousness, previously conditioned by linearity, to catch up to the facts of non-linearity. Whether people like it or not the future is approaching us at an accelerating rate of speed, which cannot be stopped without disaster for the entire human race. Like all evolutionary processes our species has only two choices offered to us by the universe, either adaptation or extinction. Failure to choose the first is to axiomatically choose the second; there are no other choices as a static system itself is dead. As a species we can set our sails and "boldly go where humanity has not gone before," or we can try to stop evolution and turn back the hands of time and escape into a glorified "safe" golden age of a past that never was. Our ideologies, like the previous systems of production, are about to burst their old clothes as the gravitational pull of the Singularity before us greatly increases and they will be pulled apart and destroyed at the event horizon.

History shows us what came before modern industrial and technological society; it was static, unchanging and stable to the point of death where inventiveness was lacking for thousands of years, causing untold misery, suffering, privation and slavery for the entire human race. If humanity chooses that road (out of the comfort of familiarity) we choose the law of diminishing returns and slow death, or we can choose a dynamic ever changing future, propelled by the law of exponential returns, which will unfold before us as we journey upon its path. How humanity perceives and conceives ourselves (as either shrinking violets withdrawing from all uncertainty, risk and change, or as heroic beings determined to walk bravely forward harnessing the powers of chaos and complexity) will determine our ultimate evolutionary destiny. As Heraclitus understood so many centuries ago, "No man ever steps in the same river twice, for it's not the same river and he's not the same man." There is no going back again to one's childhood, not for each person individually nor for the entire species of humanity as a whole. We are stuck in our preadolescent phase, with part of ourselves longing wistfully for the idyll of childhood and our other half desiring to walk forward into full adulthood resolute to take on adult responsibilities. The techno-optimists show us that our adulthood will be far more magnificent than we could ever have hoped for or imagined, in which our new play may be in bringing the universe to life and full consciousness.

It is time for a new courageous paradigm to help propel humanity into that great "utopian" future. We shall converge with each other at a new level and curve of the upward spiral which is human evolution; and technology shall deliver us there. What humanity gives up of our past (its false security, the comfort of old routines and mostly nostalgia) for a "childhood" that was never as good as our reified fantasies of it, will be replaced by something far greater: the end of aging, disease, famine, poverty, starvation and possibly even death itself. Everything humanity has longed for and desired as far back as the first known written work in human history, *The Epic of Gilgamesh*, will finally be realized. Our putative original ancestors partook of the tree of knowledge and were kicked out of a static unchanging perfect garden ruled by an omnipotent deity who demanded that we never partake of knowledge. Humanity inherently hates stasis, we rebel against it, and boredom is our one hated enemy. We want to know, to discover, to venture out into the unknown and as we evolve we are creating a dynamic ever-changing new garden, which will be governed by a synergistic interrelated new "deified" and awakened cosmos with Humanity as co-creator. The children of the old god now grown to adulthood will become the children of God in every sense of the word. With Prometheus' fire and the Protean lightning of Zeus tamed in humanity's hands we can at last over throw the old ideological gods and build a new Olympus. Wessell reminds us that:

> Philosophy proclaims the Apollonian imperative to become a creator. … The struggle of the subjective consciousness with the recalcitrant world can only be described as a titanic battle… Out of the struggle between titan and chaos a new cosmos will emerge, a new creation shall arise. Garaudy was absolutely correct that the key to Marx's philosophy, economic, and politics, is the Apollonian imperative to turn man into a creator, an "untroubled God," which implies that Marx imagines man to be a titan. Phantasy is, indeed, the creator of worlds. The young Marx's philosophical imagination has projected the outlines of a cosmic poem of redemption, one in which man struggles against the powers of chaos. Marx's theoretical reflections were simply his attempt to write this Promethean poem in secular or prosaic language. The true poetic genius of Marx lies in his ability to create a scientific mythology, to dramatize the human condition in the exoteric dress of science.… Philosophy for Romantics is but a conceptual longing for infinity.[301]

---

301 Leonard P. Wessell, Jr., *Karl Marx, Romantic Irony*, 150.

There is no going back to a revisionist past, pessimism and nihilism have brought us to a dead end. There is no life in the mausoleum and playing at vampires, wizards and zombies doesn't give us any enduring comfort. Nihilism, death and decay is an absolute end from which there is no return, we have only one choice, the rising spiral of human evolution and its entwining nature with the entire cosmos in which both humanity and the universe become fully conscious and alive. That is the only choice we have or can ever make. The stairway to the stars is a limitless open-ended boundless future; we may tremble at what evolution in this grand commission asks and requires of us, but we cannot forsake or shirk from it. Earth is the cradle of humanity but like all children we reach a point where we must leave our cradle and first crawl, then walk and finally run to a new future. Life is predicated upon continued upward growth; extropy is evolution; and entropy is nothing but slow decline and eventual death. To break our chains and rise and take our place in this new era we must win the battle over all ideologies that proclaim the static, steady state ideal of full equilibrium as they are predicated upon an old idea that has never truly existed (and never will) in a real universe whose very processes and laws are dynamic and evolutionary.

Epilogue

All great truths begin as blasphemies.
-GEORGE BERNARD SHAW

Though some may say I am an anti-progressive in writing this book, they would be grossly mistaken and mischaracterizing me based on their own shallow notions and neo-ideological miseducation of what true progressivism is. From my childhood growing up in the heady futurist 1960's watching the original Star Trek series on TV, and the moon landings, to be a "progressive" is to be completely progressive in every meaning of the word, which includes a constant updating of one's ideology and beliefs with up-to-the-minute scientific discoveries. Our age instead has sadly become the age of denial, and we have developed strong reactionary defenses to counter any challenge to our firmly held ideocratic beliefs. Why is it that (when a work of such incredible insight arises, such as Jean Francois Revel's *The Last Exit to Utopia*) instead of doing the self-searching and mea culpas that are necessary, the neo-left goes into paroxysms? Only someone on the left can do the searing analysis of the inner contradictions in the left today as superbly as Revel; and he states the absolute truth:

> Throughout history up to the present day, humanity's ruling obses-
> sion has been to eliminate property. This indeed was a goal that
> the Communists said they alone could achieve. As we know, their

program was mostly a factory of famines, but abundance neverthe-less remained the ideal toward which their system aimed. Why is it, then, that when abundance does arrive but happens to be the fruit of capitalism, suddenly "consumption" becomes a curse?[302]

This continuing condemnation of capitalism's increasingly creating af-fluence and abundance and a consumerist society full of goods is thus nothing but a childish petulant reaction based on the neo-Marxist's re-visionism and denial of Marx's evolutionary thought. The left's own er-ror in not comprehending Marx's later works thus caused the defensive revisionist stance of ardent denial that Revel succinctly describes, the reaction ad revisionism that so many leftist intellectuals fell into when facing communism's continuing failures:

> The communism that failed was not real communism. To the end of time, real communism will remain both irreplaceable and never to be found, anywhere. It is thus immunized from all criticism. The urgent task, so clearly necessitated by socialism's failure, became cri-tiquing [classical] liberalism, and numerous intellectuals of the Old and the New Left, moderate or extreme, applied themselves tire-lessly to this project.[303]

This defensive mechanism is one of protective psychological projection designed to keep oneself and others blinded to reality. Thus if social-ism could not bring abundance, it could bring equality in penury. If it could not fill store shelves, it could instead use the praise of poverty and self-denial that medieval monastics and Proudhon once proclaimed, but instead of achieving sanctity of one's soul the environmentalist greens now claim that austerity will bring about the sanctification of the Earth. As the French intellectual Chantal Desol so intuitively stated:

---

302 Jean Francois Revel, *The Last Exit to Utopia: The Survival of Sovietism in a Post-Soviet Era* (New York, NY: Encounter Books, 2009), 21.
303 Ibid., 40.

Marx's successors hoped to eliminate scarcity by creating a society of abundance. Western socialism hoped for a kind of happy austerity, in which desires would be limited in proportion to the available goods, imagining that people would be content with a bare minimum made palatable by the attainment of equality for all. Here again the aim was to reconcile man with himself, to seek the ever-elusive unity by restricting desire.[304]

So if neo-socialism could not run a dynamic modern industrial society, it could use the old hackneyed Romantic and Tory conservative longings of going back to the Middle Ages and its static and slower tempo of existence, all done to entice people to march backwards, all the while being deluded into thinking that they were instead progressing. Is this not why there are so many calls and false studies telling us that too much consumer choice is confusing and bad for people? That "less is more" and that stopping consumption is in a sense virtuous? Every aspect of today's propaganda circles around the propaganda meme created by Malthus over a century ago with no acknowledgment that it has been exposed as the fraud it was over 40 years ago. The past is dead; a historical period which we can never return to, any belief that we can do so is inherently naïve, reactionary and conservative. To hate and fight the present system for having achieved what the left once said that only it could achieve is simply a ludicrous farce. Yet that is the modus operandi of today's neo-left and today the neo-left engages in a criticism of the market that is based on the fact that "Utopia is not under the slightest obligation to produce results: its sole function is to allow its devotees to condemn what exists in the name of what does not."[305] An anti-rational stance that the Occupy Movement, the Venus Project and The Zeitgeist Movement adhere to and espouse most rigorously.

---

304 Chantal Desol, *Icarus Fallen: The Search for Meaning in an Uncertain World* (Wilmington, DE: ISI Books, 2003), 19.
305 Ibid., 23.

The entire socialism calculation debate won by the Austrians[306] was not a defeat of progressivism's "liberal" world view absorbed from classical liberalism. It was a defeat of an old pseudo-scientific conservative paradigm common in the eighteenth and nineteenth centuries that socialism unfortunately inculcated into itself and that needed to be negated (as all contradictions, errors, emotional and quasi-religious thinking, need to be exploded and discarded) as it leads to what Jean-Francois Revel termed *leftist rigidity*. The fact that much of the left today rejects the techno-optimists, even though they have vindicated and proven Karl Marx's evolutionary insights correct, is *prima fascia* evidence of this reified ideological petrification the neo-left has undergone. Hans de Soto asked a rhetorical question in his book *Socialism, Economic Calculation and Entrepreneurship*, "Can the word socialism be redeemed?" His answer was in the negative as it has become too connected with collectivist and coercive ideals that lead to increasing despotism and the law of decreasing returns by an enforced QWERTY system that stems from the inherent "conservative" hatred of Progress itself.[307] From my own point of view, and from the research that I have conducted, for a New Socialism–a socialism of the twenty-first century–to arise it must do so like a phoenix from the flames of its past ideological biases, contradictions and errors. For a new scientific socialism to come into being, it must set as its main foundational goal the inalienable right of freedom of thought, expression and speech guaranteed to every person. Jean François Revel remarked four decades ago that:

> Scientific and technological progress itself was born of the right of free inquiry, of the right of free criticism-rights which were aspects of the liberal revolution. There will never be a socialist society unless it allows pursuit of scientific and technological progress; and therefore, there will never be a social society unless it allows cultural freedom. The connection between those two elements is not accidental,

---

306 See appendixes A and B in this book.
307 Note: The chapter in *The Last Exit to Utopia* entitled "Hating Progress" is well worth reading.

but essential. Socialism cannot exist without scientific progress because socialism cannot exist in penury. Poverty automatically causes the rebirth of inequality. The only possible form of socialism is that of "scientific socialism" –not in the sense in which Marx and Engels understood that expression, but in the sense that a society in which scientific activity exists can become a socialist society. Moreover, that scientific activity must enjoy complete freedom of research... The second world revolution will therefore consist in large part, and perhaps essentially, in the establishment of intellectual and informational autonomy with respect to political power. That is the key; and, under this aspect also, democracy is the matrix of socialism.[308]

Without free inquiry, there can be no authentic democracy and therefore no authentic socialism. The right to openly and authentically uncover contradictions, errors and omissions and disclose them is a fundamental aspect of all free scientific inquiry. The one constant feature that all conservative and totalitarian regimes have is the silencing of any and all views that contradict its rigidly held ideological beliefs. The consensus that today's neo-left claims to exist, in all its areas of ideological certainty, is one based on the old common front's ability to coerce and silence detractors while the so called settled "science" it adheres to lies untouchable in a utopian realm *Beyond the Looking Glass* in the land of Cockaigne. As long as everything is subjective and no objectivity is ever accepted, one's beliefs can stay inviolate and unrefutable, at least in theory. In reality it is a theological construct created in the childhood based beliefs of a Never Never Land. As long as political powers can be brought to bear and financial inducements can be used to guarantee the greedy compliance of corporate rent seekers, the Fairy Tale denial of objective reality can be kept alive a little while longer, but not forever. In the end you have to pay the piper: reality cannot be bamboozled as easily as naive human beings.

---

308 Revel, *Without Marx*, 98.

Inner contradictions are the first sign your ideas are false; the second is that they don't square with economic and historical facts; and the third is that they are based on wishes and beliefs. Nietzsche stated that humanity was poised halfway across a tight rope stretched over an abyss stuck between the primitive and the übermensch. Have we become so afraid of the responsibility and work that is required of becoming a Prometheus that we now run backward? Are the shadows, lies and pantomime of Dionysus, the perpetual adolescent religion of the untermensch enslaved by instinct, all that we can elicit and reach for today? Has the visionary reach of Postmodern Man (of late-modernity, late-Marxism and late-Capitalism) become too short for his intellectual grasp? Is Plato's cave the unthinking inclination and natural destination for a culture that has lost the desire, the will and the ability to risk and to dream? Is anarcho-primitivism the only anti-ideal that we can cling to in a world awash with complexity and change? Desol waxes eloquently on these subjects in her books:

> Nietzsche described the great questions about which humanity wondered as illusions. In fact it is the will to deny them that has turned out to be an illusion. In a wild maelstrom of irrationality, late modernity simultaneously derides spirituality and bemoans the triumph of materialism, proclaims moral relativism and becomes indignant over the spread of pedophilia, claims that all is in vain and deplores a society where boredom can lead to suicide. Every society expresses what it has been given. Even though they are always debatable, answers to the eternal questions of mankind are all that can raise barriers, however fragile, against the chaos of meaninglessness.[309]

Our crazy patchwork quilt of contradictory ideological memes only stays coherent if we are under the aegis of a very strong cognitive bias supported with large doses of Orwellian Double Think. The frosting of

---

309 Chantal Desol, *The Unlearned Lessons of the Twentieth Century: Essays on Late Modernity* (Wilmington, DE: ISI Books, 2006), 52.

cognitive bias keeps us from ever realizing the problems that we have with neo-leftist ideology today. Our program on the left is no longer about futuristic grand visions, with sweeping vistas and the type of expansive growth filled world that we will build benefiting all humanity. We are no longer builders, we are demolishers. What we can do, what we have the ability to do, about growth, vision, increasing technical improvements, a Promethean positive outlook, is all gone. We are inundated by ideologues that constantly bombard us with what we cannot do and sue in the courts to enforce their nihilism. It has become only about bringing it all down, ending, restricting, retracting, containing, "sustaining" and staying within "natural" limits, all the while denying that with human imagination and creativity there are no actual natural limits to the human enterprise.

If I have erred in my analysis, and I am sure there are many who will erroneously deem that I have, then I have "erred" while supporting the fundamental basis of a valid and thriving original progressive paradigm which was fundamentally based upon the full evolution of the productive material forces and the superabundance they would bring to all humanity through the evolution of the capitalist system, which Marx himself foresaw. Some would say that this is an antiquated view of socialism, and that it is no longer relevant for today due to environmental concerns. Yet having examined so much of the technological, economic and historical evidence, I know, whether anyone agrees with me or not, that the super-abundance of the Technium is fulfilling older socialism's prophesies while making the environment cleaner. The Technium seems to be that evolving independent synergistic force molding humanity and human society written about by so many intellectuals throughout history; we fight and resist it and try to derail it at our own peril. Humanity must embrace science and the new discoveries of *complexity theory* and the *law of exponential returns* as doing so will bring us to the transcendence of the present system and to a new order of society: Where each individual is owner and controller of the system of production and where the state withers away displaced by an emerging new social governance structure, Omniarchy, through the mechanism of the arising global brain–the distributed hyper-net. The political welfare-warfare state as we know it today is thus doomed; there is no saving the present order of things, nor should we even try as all older technological forms are always superseded by newer ones. Our social and political technologies are old, they are decaying, and it is time for their negation.

Leonard Wessell sums up the dynamic Promethean ideal at the heart of Marx's thought at the end of his work:

> Marx offered a program, a dramatic plan, for critical activity, the theoretical or practical. The telos of this program is nothing less than the creation of the mythic "Golden age."… The ideal of communism goes back deep into history, into the very depths of the lives of millions of the working people. Dreams of this ideal can already be found in folktales about the 'Golden Age' that were composed at the Dawn of time. Marxism is indeed the stuff folktales are made of! How then, does materialism further the pursuit of "dreams"? "Materialism is imbued with the utmost faith in the human intellect, in the power of knowledge, in man's ability to fathom all secrets of the world around him, and to create a social system based on reason and justice." And what is the content of the "Golden Age"? "The supreme goal of communism is to ensure *full freedom of development of the human personality,* to create conditions for the boundless development of the individual, for the physical and spiritual perfection of man." The "Golden Age" will be a time of boundless development, which is to say the limitations of empirical existence will be overcome. And who is to realize this "dream"? Man, for man possesses the cognitive power to fathom all the secrets of the universe and to transform dream into reality.[310]

---

310 Wessell, *Karl Marx, Romantic Irony,* 203.

Marx's "Golden Age" lies only in the future and for the first time we can now begin to see the coming economic event horizon and what the new dawn foretells is an amazing new world of abundance for all. These new discoveries give us the ability to end the wasteful and worthless fight between progressives and conservatives/libertarians and to join forces with them for true and faster change as they allow a convergence of all our foundational ideals. To fight this eventuality is not the revolutionary and historical mission of socialism and the proletariat; our fight and mission has always been to bring this new era for the flourishing of all humanity to reality. We were and are supposed to be midwives attending the birth of the new social order. Our Mother is reaching her term as exponentialism is beginning to burst her water. It is only a matter of time now, a few decades more, before we see the coming new messianic age springing from her loins. Ideologues can continue to stand around her with coat hangers seeking to abort her at every opportunity out of ideological fixation and rigidity because they are afraid of dynamic change, or we can become true midwives as Marx suggested and help bring this new child into the world. The decision is ours to make; dystopia or utopia is the result of our ultimate decision whether to abort capitalism now or to allow the gestation to come to its full term and deliver the coming messiah. Complexity theory has carved out the cave in which our new "Mary" lies in wait. Who will gather around the crèche to worship this new child will be a surprise to us all, yet the new star in the sky draws the old weary combatants together in wonder. I shall end this book with a long cogent quote from Virginia Postrel's *The Future and Its Enemies*:

> To create a dynamist alternative to the sterile stasist verge, then, means drawing together this wide array of passions and interests into a powerful fertile verge. It is better, Machiavelli famously said, to be feared than loved. And stasists claim fear as an ally: fear of change, fear of the unknown, fear of comfortable routines thrown into confusion. They promise to make the world safe and predictable, if only we will trust them to design the future, if only they can

impose their uniform plans. Those promises may be false, but they are also appealing. The open-ended future can be genuinely scary, the turmoil it creates genuinely painful.

Dynamists to have fear on their side: fear of stagnation, of poverty, of pain. Stasist prescriptions, we can say with conviction, stifle the very processes through which people improve their lives–from the invention of new medical treatments to the creation of art. In their quest for stability, stasists make society brittle, vulnerable to all sorts of disasters. They disregard and disrespect important knowledge, the specific knowledge through which we can shape our lives. They scorn pleasures not their own, and improvements they did not conceive. They lock individuals into narrow status boundaries, blocking opportunity and self-definition. They are frighteningly intolerant ... The dynamist verge must be bound by love: love of knowledge, love of exploration, love of adventure, and, just as much, love of small dreams, of the textures of life. These passions are broad enough to bring dynamists together across interests and disciplines, professional affiliations and cultural associations. Only then will the dynamist verge become truly fertile.

Some dynamists believe that the future must lie in bold ventures, private endeavors too grand to be contained in technocratic schemes: the terraforming and settlement of Mars, the doubling of human life span. Such big dreams, they argue, are important not only for their own sakes but help keep sclerosis at bay, to demonstrate that great things can still be done, that the sterile verge has not extinguished enterprise. The spirit of Tennyson's Ulysses– "to strive, to seek, to find, and not to yield"–is, they believe, the great tonic for youthful culture ... The dynamist verge ... Cares about intensive progress. And it perceives what stasists miss–the spectacular creativity and cumulative knowledge embedded in the things we take for granted ... We live in an enchanted world, a world suffused with intelligence, a world of our making. In such plenitude, too, lies an adventurous future.

"It is in the process of learning." Hayek reminds us, "in the effects of having learned something new, that man enjoys the gift of his intelligence." It is in curiosity, problem solving, and play we discover who we are. These are the very qualities and activities that make the future unknown, and unknowable. On the verge between centuries, the dynamist promise is not of a particular, carefully outlined future. The future will be as grand, and as particular, as we are. We cannot build a single bridge from here to there, for neither here nor there is a single point. And there is no abyss to cross.[311]

Here in Late Modernity an incredible convergence has already happened, when a "conservative" like Postrel can proclaim the dynamist dream that once lay at the heart of Marx's philosophy. In this crazy time it is the Transhumanists, the Singularitans, the Techno-Optimists and Techno-Libertarians that have become the true heirs of Marx for they are the only contingent that has taken up the visionary call of the extropic dynamist verge. Old age, sickness, poverty, lower intelligence, alienation and even death are finally within our grasp to conquer and eradicate. Prometheus is rising and Nature's restrictions on human potential may at last be in the process of being overthrown. Ray Kurzweil's six epochs is a proclamation that the Apollonian dream and program yet lives, that contingency can be overcome and that the physical and spiritual perfection of man is yet possible through the evolution of the Technium. Utopia lies just ahead for humanity, a point of convergence to a new harmonious social and economic arrangement, where total abundance and not scarcity for the first time in human history predominates. The cornucopian economists, techno-utopians and even Karl Marx each point out to us the emerging *omega point*, the economic singularity up

---

311 Reprinted from The Future and its Enemies by Virginia Postrel, published by the Free Press. © 1998 Virginia Postrel and used with permission. Found on pages 216-218.

ahead; it is up to us to choose the correct path. Up (extropy) or Down (entropy) are the only two choices we have, for Left and Right is a dialectical delusion that keeps us spinning in circles constantly fighting one another and keeping us from going anywhere. As Buckminster Fuller ominously warned us decades ago, "it is either utopia or bust," and it is time for humanity to finally choose irrevocably Up, to choose utopia. To paraphrase Marx at the end of the *communist manifesto*, "People of the World Unite! For in the coming economic and technological Singularity Humanity finally loses all Her chains!"

Appendix A.
The Socialist Calculation Debate Revisited

In 2010, Jesus Huerta De Soto, professor of Political Economy at the University of Juan Carlos in Spain published a seminal work, *Socialism, Economic Calculation and Entrepreneurship,* in which he did an extensive analysis and an update of the s*ocialist calculation* debate started by Ludwig Von Mises of the Austrian School of Economics back in the 1920's. This tour de force was a much welcome addition to the debate and framed it using historical sources in an in-depth way that made the entire issue much more comprehensible to scholars and novices, both pro and con, alike. For all of his great acumen expressed in the work, there was one glaring omission throughout the entire book which I found incomprehensible. That omission was that there was no mention of complexity theory or complexity economics. Neither in the bibliography nor in the index can the word complexity be found. Since the book was basically an in-depth review of the subject, tending more toward the historical argument than a strictly up to date reassessment, one could possibly overlook this glaring omission, but one has to wonder still, "why no mention of this emerging scientific field by name?" Especially when the basics of complexity theory and complexity ideas are to be found throughout the book? For example his entire first chapter on the entrepreneurial process is a primer on the complexity theory of interrelatedness, so the absence of stating the theory by name is perplexing to say the least, but I digress.

In order to comprehend the complexity issues foundational to the argument, the historical foundations of the *"socialist calculation"* and *"knowledge problem"* debate have to be covered. In 1920 Ludwig Von Mises, the leading economic theoretician of the Austrian School of Economics, wrote an essay entitled *Economic Calculation in the Socialist Commonwealth*,[312] which set off a firestorm in economic and socialist circles at the time. I shall let Mises speak for himself summing up his theory:

Where one cannot express hours of labor, iron, coal, all kinds of building material, machines and other things necessary for the construction and upkeep of the railroad in a common unit [money] it is not possible to make calculations at all. The drawing up of bills on an economic basis is only possible where all the goods concerned can be referred back to money. Admittedly, monetary calculation has its inconveniences and serious defects, but we have certainly nothing better to put in its place, and for the practical purposes of life monetary calculation as it exists **under a sound monetary system** always suffices. Were we to dispense with it, any economic system of calculation would become absolutely impossible.

The socialist society would know how to look after itself. It would issue an edict and decide for or against the projected building. Yet this decision would depend at best upon vague estimates; it would never be based upon the foundation of an exact calculation of value.

The static state can dispense with economic calculation. For here the same events in economic life are ever recurring; and if we assume that the first disposition of the static socialist economy follows on the basis of the final state of the competitive economy, we might at all events conceive of a socialist production system which is

---

312 Ludwig von Mises, *Economic Calculation in the Socialist Commonwealth* [1920] (Auburn, AL: Praxeology Press 1990).

rationally controlled from an economic point of view. But this is only conceptually possible. **For the moment, we leave aside the fact that a static state is impossible in real life, as our economic data are forever changing, so that the static nature of economic activity is only a theoretical assumption corresponding to no real state of affairs, however necessary it may be for our thinking and for the perfection of our knowledge of economics.** Even so, we must assume that the transition to socialism must, as a consequence of the leveling out of the differences in income and the resultant readjustments in consumption, and therefore production, change all economic data in such a way that a connecting link with the final state of affairs in the previously existing competitive economy becomes impossible. But then we have the spectacle of a socialist economic order floundering in the ocean of possible and conceivable economic combinations without the compass of economic calculation.

Thus in the socialist commonwealth every economic change becomes an undertaking whose success can be neither appraised in advance nor later retrospectively determined. There is only groping in the dark.[313] Socialism is the abolition of rational economy.[314]

Mises' theory is intricate and needs a much more in-depth study and analysis than can be presented here in this book. In dealing with complexity theory's discoveries the basis of the *social cooperation school of economics*[315] foundational ideas in this matter are actually proven. Complexity economics upheld the Austrian attack on socialism (any command and control system such as Fascism as well) and Walrasian econometrics i.e. the belief that a static, steady state, equilibrium condition of economics is possible and preferable to the present "chaotic" and "anarchic" methods of production. Of all the socialist apologists who rose up to attack von Mises and defend socialism only Oskar Lange, the socialist

---

313 N.B. As can be surmised Mises actually started the *knowledge problem* issue here.
314 Ibid., 25. Bold mine.
315 Another name for the Austrian School of Economics.

economist, stated that, "A statue of Professor Mises ought to occupy an honorable place in the great Hall of the Ministry of socialization or the central planning board of a socialist state ... both as an expression of recognition for the great service rendered by him and as a memento of the prime importance of sound economic accounting."[316] The firestorm that erupted at the time forced von Mises to go on to write his seminal tome *Socialism: An Economic and Sociological Analysis* in 1936 in which he fleshed out his argument in much more depth and detail adding onto his argument the historical, philosophical, ideological and sociological criteria against socialism to his economic calculation problem.

One can ignore Mises' great work, *Socialism*, out of ideological faithfulness, but in doing so one misses the essential elements that dovetail into today's complexity theory and complexity economics' challenge against the delusion of stationary states and mathematical models in neoclassical economics, which agree with the criticisms that the Austrian School first put forward against them as far back as the late nineteenth century. Popular socialist apologetics changed the argument that Mises made to one where he supposedly said that "socialism was itself impossible." That was never Mises' argument, as the following quote succinctly shows:

> A stationary society could, indeed, dispense with these [economic] calculations. For there, economic operations merely repeat themselves. So that, if we assume that the socialist system of production were based upon the last state of the system of economic freedom which it superseded, and that no changes were to take place in the future, we could indeed conceive a rational and economics socialism. But only in theory. **A stationary economic system can never exist**. Things are continually changing, and the stationary state, although necessary as an aid to [economic] speculation, is a theoretical assumption to which there is no counterpart in reality."[317]

---

316 De Soto, *S, EC&E*, footnote 20, page 127.
317 Mises, *Socialism*, 105. Bold mine.

Later on he states:

> To use a peculiar but not altogether satisfactory terminology we can
> say that the problem of economic calculation is of **economic dynam-
> ics**: it is no problem of economic statics. **The problem of economic
> calculation is a problem which arises in an economy which is per-
> petually subject to change**, an economy which every day is confront-
> ed with new problems which have to be solved.[318]

Mises entire argument can be boiled down to one that states that "socialism could manage a non-industrial, stationary, steady state, economic system that had come to full equilibrium; but managing an
industrial, highly technological, dynamic, constantly changing, emergent, spontaneous evolutionary social and economic system (i.e. a real
world economic system) would be an impossibility." The main constructivist, Cartesian and Newtonian mechanistic reductionist flaw of all
earlier forms of socialism, as well as conservatism, is that, "All socialist
theories and Utopias have always had only the stationary condition in
mind."[319] From Plato's *Republic* through Thomas Merton's *Utopia* all the
way to The Venus Project and The Zeitgeist Movement of today, the
static, steady state economic system ruled by a petrified precautionary
principle firmly entrenched in place to stop all technological change
is the stated, or unstated, ideal. However against these utopian static
socialists, Marx himself held instead the idea of the spontaneous or-
dering of the market:

> Mises repeatedly accused Marx and his followers of trying to inocu-
> late themselves against any critical analysis of the socialist system by
> simply arguing that such an analysis was irrelevant and utopian, since
> socialism would inexorably evolve from capitalism … and second,
> because Marx himself felt that within his theoretical framework,

---

318   Ibid., 121. Bold mine.
319   Ibid., 142.

meticulous or detailed speculation about the specific aspects of future socialism was not "scientific..." Marx was so influenced and obsessed by the Ricardian model of adjustment and equilibrium, that his entire theory is aimed at justifying a *normative* equilibrium, in the sense that, according to Marx, the proletariat should coercively impose from above a "coordination" which does away with the typical features of capitalism. As for the actual, detailed analysis of the economic realities of the capitalist system, we should stress that Marx focuses on the disequilibriums and maladjustments that emerge in the market and thus, Marxist theory is mainly a disequilibrium theory. Paradoxically, it occasionally coincides on some very curious points with the analysis of market processes carried out by Austrian economists, in general, and by Hayek and Mises himself, in particular. Therefore, curiously, Marx understood to a point how the market, as a spontaneous and impersonal order, acts as a process which creates and transmits the information that permits a certain coordination in society. In fact, in *Grundrisse* we read:

> "It has been said and may be said that this is precisely the beauty and the greatness of it, **this *spontaneous* interconnection, this material and *mental* metabolism which is independent of the knowing and willing of individuals, and which presupposes their reciprocal independence and indifference.** And certainly, this objective connection is preferable to the lack of any connection, or to a merely local connection resting on blood ties, or on primeval, natural or master-servant relations" (italics added).

Moreover, Marx explicitly recognizes both the role *institutions* play in enabling people to acquire and transmit practical information in the market, and their importance to the knowledge of economic agents: "Together with the development of this alienation, and on the same basis, efforts are made to overcome it: *institutions* emerge whereby each individual can acquire *information* about the activity of all others and attempt to adjust his own accordingly ... Although the total supply and demand are independent of the actions of each individual, everyone attempts to *inform* himself about them, and this *knowledge* then reacts back in practice on the total supply and demand."[320]

There are many interesting similarities and agreements between the Austrian School and Marx. The fact that both Marx and the Austrian School base themselves on praxeology, human action, is of major import uniting both schools of thought in many intricate and fascinating ways.

The *knowledge problem* that Mises' student, F.A. Hayek, formulated added on to the calculation problem that Mises enumerated. It went further in the direction which complexity theory was to advance in later decades; and Hayek laid the initial foundations for complex systems thinking as far back as the 1930's. In the introduction to the new edition of Hayek's "*The Fortunes of Liberalism*" Peter G. Klein stated Hayek's thought distinctly:

> Hayek ... bases a defense of the market not on human rationality, but on human ignorance! "[T]he whole argument for freedom, or the greater part of the argument for freedom, rests on the fact of our ignorance and not on the fact of our knowledge." Hayek's agents are rule followers, responding to price signals within a system selected by a process of evolution-a spontaneous order, rather than a system deliberately chosen; yet their actions bring unintended benefits for the system as a whole, benefits that could not have been rationally predicted. This is quite strange to the modern economist, for whom evolution and spontaneity play little if any role.[321]

Hayek began as early as the mid 1930's to begin to think of the market and economics as well as all social phenomenon, culture and civilization, not as a given and static condition reacted to by discrete autonomous

---

320   De Soto. *S, EC&E*, 109. Bold mine.
321   F.A. Hayek, *The Fortunes of Liberalism: The Collected Works of F.A. Hayek* (Indianapolis, IL: Liberty Fund, 1992), 6.

rational actors and created by omnipotent rational planners from on high, but as interdependent yet heterogeneous interacting agents who are constantly evolving and bringing about an emergent and spontaneous order that is constantly adapting and changing to, and discovering, new information, just as the cells in complexity theorists computer simulations act. In *The Fatal Conceit*,[322] Hayek states this idea:

> It is important to avoid, right from the start, the notion that stems from what I called the 'fatal conceit': the idea that the ability to acquire skills stems from reason. For it is the other way around: our reason is as much the result of an evolutionary selection process as is our morality. It stems however from a somewhat separate development, so that one should never suppose that our reason is in the higher critical position and that only those moral rules are valid that reason endorses ... Learning how to behave is more the source than the result of insight, reason, and understanding. Man is not born wise, rational and good, but has to be taught to become so. It is not our intellect that created our morals; rather, human interactions governed by our morals make possible the growth of reason and those capabilities associated with it. Man became intelligent because there was tradition –that which lies between instinct and reason–for him to learn. This tradition, in turn, originated not from a capacity rationally to interpret observed facts but from habits of responding.[323]

Hayek then goes on to an almost Marxian social analysis:

> So far as scientific explanation is concerned, it was not what we know as mind that developed civilization, let alone directed its evolution, but rather mind and civilization which developed or evolved concurrently... Shaped by the environment in which individuals grow up,

---

322 F.A. Hayek, *The Fatal Conceit: The Errors of Socialism* (Chicago: The University of Chicago Press, 1988), 76.
323 Ibid., 21.

mind in turn conditions the preservation, development, richness, and variety of traditions on which individuals draw.[324]

In this analysis, we see a restatement of Marx's that, "society makes the man and in return man makes society." In many ways Hayek can be called the grandfather of complexity economics,[325] yet his ideas are based on others intellectual insights and observations going back hundreds of years. Desai sees clearly the revolutionary aspect of Hayek's ideas and his affinity to Marx:

> Hayek was undermining [with the knowledge problem] the entire basis of equilibrium theorizing as it was–and still is–taught in economics, yet his ideas were ignored at the time. An entire generation came to believe that capitalism and socialism were symmetrical; markets and planning were the same thing. The consequences of ignoring risk-taking, property rights, bankruptcies, and innovations were that the achievements of Soviet-type economics were exaggerated as much by their enemies as by their champions. The defenders of capitalism thought the race was in terms of material output, and the models of economics were the best guide in assessing relative success. The idea that an economy is a self-organizing process in which there is a constant search for betterment on the part of millions of individuals, all acting on the basis of local knowledge–an idea that Marx shared with Hayek–was forgotten. The point was not that a socialist planner could not compute all those equations. The point was that even making the most extreme assumptions, it is impossible to centralize knowledge. What is more, it is inefficient–grossly

---

324 Ibid., 22.
325 Struan Jacobs in his paper, "Michael Polyani and Spontaneous Order, 1941-1951," claims that Hayek did not originate the term "spontaneous order" and that since the two intellectuals were conversant with one another, Hayek was most probably influenced and picked up the term from Polyani. http://www.missouriwestern.edu/orgs/polanyi/TAD%20WEB%20ARCHIVE/TAD24-2/TAD24-2-pg14-28-pdf.pdf.

inefficient. Half of Europe had to learn that lesson in the coming half-century, after the end of the debate on socialist calculation.[326]

Complexity theory's response to the socialist calculation problem is in a similar vein and is expressed succinctly by Roger Koppl in his essay, "Policy Implications of Complexity: an Austrian Perspective." He goes over very thoroughly the situation inherent in the various problems of central planning expressed by the Austrian School, but the major and central theme drawn from complexity theory he states thusly:

> The Austrian critique of socialism can be restated as an example of [Brian] Arthur's (1994) 'capturing software' [problem]. The central planning board (or the political process imagined to serve that function) is the 'outside system'. The 'simpler elements' are individuals and groups of individuals such as families and trade unions. There is an 'interactive grammar' that the outside system must learn in order to get the simpler elements to perform as desired. But with central planning and economic policy in general, the simpler elements, persons and groups of persons, are not very simple. They're about as complex as the outside system, a committee of persons. Thus, interactive grammar is very complex.

> The interactive grammar 'allows many combinations of the simple elements'; it must be more complex than the elements programmed by means of it. Indeed, if the grammar is to allow many different final output combinations for the economy as a whole, it must be more complex than the economy as a whole. But the outside system is itself a part of the economy to be programmed with aid of interactive grammar. Thus the grammar must be more complex than the outside system. To do its job, the central planning committee[327] would have to be, in effect, more complex than itself. This is why the

---

326 Meghnad Desai, *Marx's Revenge* (London, UK: Verso, 2004), 198.
327 Or a super Artificial Intelligence as envisioned by the Venus Project.

Austrians make the strange-sounding claim that 'rational economic calculation under socialism is impossible'.

Hayek (1952) produced a similar argument but applied it to the question of the mind explaining itself. I have attempted to adapt this to the context of theorizing, especially in economics and finance (Koppl 1996, 1998). The application to Socialist calculation is straightforward. Long ago, an early complexity theorist made a similar point. 'The men of system', Adam Smith warned, forget that 'in the chessboard of human society, every single piece has a principle of motion of its own, altogether different from that which the legislature might choose to impress upon it'.[328]

Stated concisely, the central organizing committee, whether made up of humans, or a super AI computer as in the imaginings of The Venus Project and its political arm The Zeitgeist Movement, would have to be more complex than the economic system it is trying to govern or the network that it is in fact trying to coordinate and manage, yet it is a part of the self-same network, so in essence it has to be more complex then itself, which is a physical and technological impossibility. Even if you imagined that the Super AI would be like a super-neuron in the brain, thus imbedded and a part of the system it is trying to coordinate, you would still have the same problem. It is why there is no controlling neuron in the brain. The complexity theorist Francis Heylighen, describes the situation in more Hayekian terms:

A fluid regulation of investment and exchange is difficult to achieve in a more traditional, centralized control system. Centralized economies need to plan how much they want to invest in each of the different types of production. (Planning control is based on *feedforward* rather than *feedback*). This leads to the well-known "calculation

---

328   Koppl, Roger, "Policy Implications of Complexity: an Austrian Perspective," in *The Complexity Vision and the Teaching of Economics*, ed. David Colander (Northampton, MA: Edward Algar, 2000), 103.

problem": an enormous amount of information needs to be collected and processed in order to find the optimal allocation of investment over all the different production lines. In the distributed, market system, decisions to shift investment from one product to another are made locally, without knowledge of the global distribution of investment. It is the control loop which will reward (and thus reinforce) good investments, and punish (and thus inhibit) bad investments. Thus, investments are continuously flowing from one place to another while staying only in those places where there is a large enough demand with respect to the supply. This guarantees a relatively balanced distribution of labor and capital, with a minimal need for information processing.[329]

The entire argument against centralized planning can be summed up thusly, "The overly Cartesian and Newtonian mechanistic rationalist and reductionist ideal where everything once known could be calculated down to minutia and then kept in a state of perfectly running equilibrium forever falls apart as it was from the beginning a false ideology fomented on the intellectual scientistic biases of the eighteenth and nineteenth centuries." The paradigm has shifted, and complexity theory has put the slab on top of centralized planning's tomb, which many systems scientists, researchers and the Austrian School of Economics built in the twentieth century. It will be fascinating to see how long it will take for the new paradigm to penetrate sufficiently and bring to an end the old petrified linear biases of the entrenched "orthodoxy" whether economic or ideological. Shaffer describes this new holographic view of the economy:

> By its very nature, a holographic social system diffuses all authority over human action. Centralized power is replaced by decentralized networks, with decision-making residing in autonomous but

---

329 F. Heylighen, "The Economy as a Distributed, Learning Control System," *Communication & Cognition-AI* 13, nos. 2-3, (1997), 9.

interrelated men and women who respond to one another through unstructured feedback systems and processes some have referred to as "emergence." Social relationships are characterized by individuals freely choosing to cooperate with one another for the accomplishment of mutually-desired purposes. Social behavior would be represented by the interconnectedness of independent persons, not the subservient obedience of subjects. The Internet provides a perfect metaphor for such systems, wherein individuals communicate directly with one another.[330]

This view of the freer market economy as a holographic entity is at the heart of complexity theory and complexity economics. One can no longer think of the market as a static system at equilibrium able to be managed by semi-omnipotent planning gods from the top-down coordinating all functions perfectly, as Vladimir Lenin's idea that the economy can be run as simply as the government post office becomes absurd in the face of these modern scientific discoveries. The historical economic failure of the Soviet Union and all communist economies axiomatically consigns this old collectivist paradigm to the tar pit of history as perfect knowledge is a requirement of all command and control systems and perfect knowledge is itself an impossibility, even with a super AI computer imbedded in the system. So the old adage that "the economy is too complex now not to manage and control," shows itself as a farce. The more complex any system becomes the more impossible it becomes to manage and control it from outside of the system. Complex systems evolve their control systems as a way to solve network problems from within.

Complexity theory has now shown the market to be an emergent spontaneous organic living system like any ecological system. It evolves, grows and changes from the bottom-up by the interrelated independent actions of all the individuals who participate in it. Joseph A. Schumpeter describes this evolutionary quality of capitalism succinctly:

---

330 Shaffer, *Boundaries of Order*, 71.

[The] essential point to grasp is that in dealing with capitalism we are dealing with an *evolutionary process*. It may seem strange that anyone can fail to see so obvious a fact which moreover was long ago emphasized by Karl Marx. Yet that fragmentary analysis which yields the bulk of our propositions about the functioning of modern capitalism persistently neglects it ... Capitalism, then, is by nature a form or method of economic change and not only never is but never can be stationary. This evolutionary character of the capitalist process is not merely due to the fact that economic life goes on in a social and natural environment which changes and by its change alters the data of economic action: this fact is important in these changes ... often condition industrial change, but they are not its prime movers. Nor is this evolutionary character due to a quasi-automatic increase in population and capital or to the vagaries of monetary systems of which exactly the same thing holds true. The fundamental impulse that sets and keeps the capitalist engine in motion comes from the new consumers goods, the new methods of production or transportation, the new markets, new forms of industrial organization that capitalist enterprise creates ... Industrial mutation ... incessantly revolutionizes the economic structure from within, incessantly destroying the old one, incessantly creating a new one. This process of creative destruction is the essential fact about capitalism. It is what capitalism consists in and what every capitalist concern has got to live in.[331]

In the end, the Austrian School of economics agrees with Marx's evolutionary vision in seeing the capitalist system as a spontaneously organizing, evolutionary, natural ecological organism. Mises himself makes the following statement which would seem quixotic to many people who are unknowingly misled by disinformation to reflexively discount or despise the Austrian School:

---

331 Schumpeter, *Capitalism*, 82-83. Italics and bold mine.

I fully agree with the Communists and the labor unions, when they say: "What is needed is to raise the standard of living.".... A higher standard of living also brings about a higher standard of culture and civilization.

So I fully agree with the ultimate goal of raising the standard of living everywhere. But I disagree about the measures to be adopted in attaining this goal. What measures will attain this end? Not protection, not government interference, not socialism, and certainly not the violence of the labor unions (euphemistically called collective bargaining, which, in fact, is bargaining *at the point of a gun*).

To attain the end, as I see it, there is only one way! It is a slow method. Some people may say, it is too slow. But there are no short cuts to an earthly paradise. It takes time, and one has to work. But it does not take as much time as people believe, and finally an equalization [of incomes] will come.[332]

The classical liberals saw this equalization of incomes and the higher standard of living coming about through the natural evolution of the capitalist system itself, just as Marx did and as Desai emphasizes in his work. It is the one attribute that they intimately share and where both ideologies can converge in harmony as libertarians and old line Marxists can unite under this common banner and work to achieve a common goal, the elimination of all alienation.

In complexity systems' language, which follows Hayek's thinking, the economic system computes and distributes knowledge and information to all members who make up the spontaneous interrelated network of the market:

---

332 Ludwig von Mises, *Economic Policy: Thoughts for Today and Tomorrow* (Chicago: Regnery/Gateway, Inc. 1979), 89.

In what sense do mental systems compute?" Is still largely un-answered, and remains a subject of confusion and thorny debate among scientists, engineers, and philosophers. However, it is a tre-mendously important question for complex systems science, because a high-level description of information processing in living systems would allow us not only to understand in new and more comprehen-sive ways the mechanisms by which particular systems operate. But also to abstract general principles that transcend the overwhelming details of individual systems.[333]

Complex system[s] … in which simple components act without a cen-tral controller or leader, who or what actually perceives the meaning of situations so as to take appropriate actions? This is essentially the question of what constitutes consciousness or self-awareness and liv-ing systems. To me this is among the most profound mysteries in complex systems and in science in general. Although this mystery has been the subject of many books of science and philosophy, it has not yet been completely explained to anyone's satisfaction.[334]

Brian Arthur states emphatically, "Complexity therefore portrays the economy not as deterministic, predictable and mechanistic; but as process-dependent, organic and always evolving."[335] Socialist ideology stated that "anarchy" in the production system, the market, was its main fault and failure keeping capitalism inefficient, but complexity theory has exploded this old fallacy and shown us that "chaos" is absolutely necessary for an adaptive evolutionary system. Ray Kurzweil states this understanding from complexity theory eloquently:

The other required resource for continued exponential growth of order is the "chaos" of the environment in which the evolutionary

---

333 Melanie Mitchell, *Complexity a Guided Tour* (New York: Oxford University Press, 2009), 172.
334 Ibid., 184.
335 Brian Arthur, "Complexity and the Economy," in *The Complexity Vision and the Teaching of Economics*, ed. David Colander (London, UK: Edward Elder, 2000), 26.

process takes place and which provides the options for further diversity. The chaos provides the variability to permit an evolutionary process to discover more powerful and efficient solutions ... Technological evolution, human ingenuity combined with variable market conditions keeps the process of innovation going.[336]

This finding–that it is the very chaos, the "anarchy" of the market system, which allows it to evolve rapidly and to find solutions that many old time ideologists, right and left, find so threatening. "Anarchy" is not something to be legislated and organized away, as the static minded idealists believe, it is to be embraced and allowed to continue as it is the very *sine qua non* of complex evolutionary systems. As Kevin Kelley states so brilliantly:

As networks have permeated our world, the economy has come to resemble an ecology of organisms, interlinked and co-evolving, constantly in flux, deeply tangled, ever expanding at its edges. As we know from recent ecological studies, no balance exists in nature; rather, as evolution proceeds, there is perpetual disruption as new species displace old, as natural biomes shift in their makeup, and as organisms and environments transform each other. ... This notion of constant flux is familiar to ecologists and those who manage large networks. The sustained vitality of a complex network requires that the net keep provoking itself out of balance.

If the system settles into harmony and equilibrium, it will eventually stagnate and die.

Innovation is disruption; constant innovation is perpetual disruption. This seems to be the goal of a well-made network: to sustain a perpetual disequilibrium. ... Most of the studies of optimal evolution in complex systems confirm this view. The price for progressive

---

336 Kurzweil, The *Singularity*, 44.

change in maximum doses is a dangerous (and thrilling) ride to the edge of disruption.… Sustaining innovation is particularly tricky since it flows out of creative disequilibrium.

To achieve sustainable innovation you need to seek persistent disequilibrium. To seek persistent disequilibrium means that one must chase after disruption without succumbing to it, or retreating from it.[337]

The human brain, ant colonies, the ecosystem, the universe, are all complex interrelated systems that compute and distribute information throughout their diverse networks without the need for a centralized controller. There is no worry of "anarchy" in these systems because they are lacking a central director. It was human hubris from the very beginning, and a lower state of scientific awareness, coupled with a pyramidal theological outlook that led intellectuals and scientists to believe in previous centuries imperialistic reductionist paradigms. Shaffer describes succinctly our unrecognized biased thinking:

Collectivist systems have depended upon the mechanistic, reductionist paradigm represented in Newtonian thinking. A belief that nature is structured in relatively simple patterns capable of being reduced to identifiable and measurable calculations, is essential to hierarchically planned and controlled societies. To a collectivist, the world consists largely of "matter"—human beings included—whose qualities and differentiations are largely confined to chemical or mechanical description, and whose essence is to be servo-mechanisms in some giant, institutional purpose.[338]

This older notion of the *ancien regime's* that the universe is like a huge monarchical clockwork system with God on his throne issuing orders to

---

337 Kelley, *New Rules*, 108-114. Bold mine.
338 Shaffer, *Boundaries*, 251.

the imperium from on high and the ruling monarch or the state as his emissary is exploded with modern systems theory. The emergent, spontaneous, evolving, complex invisible hand has strangled the old empirical mechanistic Cartesian and Newtonian reductionist model. The only *Holy Ghost* there is, is the ghost that arises from the system itself. "Our shock" today as Hayek would say, is our discovery that interventionist socialism in its desire to control everything from the top-down was not actually a progressive ideology, but a regressive conservative ideology that adheres to the old pyramidal paradigm. It was a Romantic desire for a return to the *ancien regime* marching under classical liberal banners and slogans as Murray Rothbard explains:

> Socialism, like liberalism and against conservatism, accepted the industrial system and the liberal *goals* of freedom, reason, mobility, progress, higher living standards for the masses, and an end to theocracy and war; but it tried to achieve these ends by the use of incompatible, conservative means: statism, central planning, communitarianism, etc. Or rather, to be more precise, there were from the beginning two different strands within socialism: one was the right-wing, authoritarian strand, from Saint-Simon down, which glorified statism, hierarchy, and collectivism and which was thus a projection of conservatism trying to accept and dominate the new industrial civilization. The other was the left-wing, relatively libertarian strand, exemplified in their different ways by Marx and Bakunin, revolutionary and far more interested in achieving the libertarian goals of liberalism and socialism; but especially the smashing of the state apparatus to achieve the "withering away of the State" and the "end of the exploitation of man by man." Interestingly enough, the very Marxian phrase, the "Replacement of the government of *men* by the administration of things," can be traced, by a circuitous route, from the great French radical laissez-faire liberals of the early nineteenth century, Charles Comte (no relation to Auguste) and Charles Dunoyer. And so, too, may the concept of the "class struggle"; except

that for Dunoyer and Comte the inherently antithetical classes were not businessmen versus workers, but the producers in society (including free businessmen, workers, peasants, etc.) versus the exploiting classes constituting, and privileged by, the State apparatus.[339]

The original classical liberal theory of class conflict was thus conceived as a war between the state and its privileged cronies, and the entrepreneur and the workers united against their theft. A much more coherent and systematic understanding of the forces at work in society as it recognized that oppression came from a coercive system and not from one class of society against another. The oppressive class belonged to the system and was privileged by it by having favors granted to it by political power that other members of society were not privy to. It was this old failed Mercantilist system that was the problem as it created the class conflict to begin with. Its abolishment would abolish all classes, which is something freer market capitalism does as it evolves.

For a new effective social movement to arise in the twentieth century it must first free itself from the old failed social and economic paradigms, right and left, and correct the inner contradictions in its ideology, and update itself to modern scientific discoveries. It must recapture the Promethean ideal of Marx who shared this ideal with the classical liberals and rise like a phoenix from its own funeral pyre before its adherence to old failed paradigms (religiously clung to in an unshakable fundamentalist faith) consigns humanity to a global gulag filled with privation, misery, oppression and total stagnation sustained by redistributing ever dwindling resources artificially constrained by a QWERTY eco-collectivism. If the idea of the left today is that in order for socialism to win, it must consign all change and evolution, especially technological evolution, to oblivion, it must do so by going against the very complex laws of the universe and by doing this it has totally abandoned dialectics, the very foundation of Marx's *scientific socialism.* Knowingly or

---

339 Murray Rothbard, *Egalitarianism as a Revolt Against Nature* (Auburn, AL: Ludwig von Mises Institute Press, 2000), 28.

unknowingly, if the left does this it has accepted right-wing conservative desires and ideals formed in the early nineteenth century. Once the inner contradictions and unscientific errors are removed, corrected and updated with complexity theory, a convergence of ideologies into one effective and world revolutionizing movement is finally possible. The two hundred year old Punch and Judy show separating socialists from libertarians, classical liberals from progressives and conservatives, and environmentalists from techno-optimists can finally come to an end. In a holographic universe, holographic action can lead to effective harmonious results.

Appendix B

Who Won the Socialism Calculation Debate?

"It turns out of course that [Ludwig von] Mises was right."

-HEILBRONER

While modern ideological myth has Oskar Lange winning the *socialist calculation* debate as de Soto mentions in his book, yet the facts are diametrically opposed to this pretension. Even the new left writer David Ramsay Steele in his *From Marx to Mises* destroys the Lange winning myth as well as the Langian system as he states:

> Problems… arise because Lange's is a purely 'static' system. His essay is heavily influenced by the brilliant static analysis of Walras. In economics, 'statics' refers to imaginary scenarios in which 'the data' (preferences, knowledge, resources) do not change. Thus, statics is illustrative and not intended to be necessarily true to life. Statics also generally implies that delay is costless: as long as equilibrium is reached, it doesn't matter how long it takes. This goes along with the freezing of the data. When 'dynamics' is introduced, we confront the fact that equilibrium is constantly moving and the path to equilibrium affects future equilibria. Statics is a worthy and useful

attempt to simplify the analysis by extracting from this problem. But turning to dynamics, it is immediately obvious that rapid movement towards approximate equilibrium is vital, whereas ultimate arrival at precise equilibrium is of no importance.[340]

The dynamic issue brought up by Hayek was never rebutted by Lange as Steele mentions later on the same page,

> In 1940 Lange wrote a letter to Hayek, responding to Hayek's criticisms. Lange states that Hayek has moved "the weight of the argument from pure static aspects to the dynamic ones", concedes that Hayek has raised problems yet to be solved, and asserts that Lange will write a reply to Hayek's paper "sometime in the fall" ... Lange's reply never appeared, though he lived until 1965. [341]

Lange never answered Hayek as there is no solution to the economic calculation and knowledge problem brought up by real world dynamic systems. As complexity theory has now fully proven it is impossible to manage a nonlinear dynamic system that is always in the process of creating novelty and which never comes to, nor can ever come to, equilibrium. As Kevin Kelly reminds us:

> As networks have permeated our world, the economy has come to resemble an ecology of organisms, interlinked and co-evolving, constantly in flux, deeply tangled, ever expanding at its edges. As we know from recent ecological studies, no balance exists in nature; rather, as evolution proceeds, there is perpetual disruption as new species displace old, as natural biomes shift in their makeup, and as organisms and environments transform each other.... This dynamic state might be thought of as "compounded rebirth." And its genesis hovers on the edge of chaos.... When flux is inhibited, slow death

---

340   David Ramsay Steele, *From Marx to Mises: Post-Capitalist Society and the Challenge of Economic Calculation* (La Salle, IL: Open Court Publishing Co., 1992), 166.
341   Ibid, 167.

takes over.… This notion of constant flux is familiar to ecologists and those who manage large networks. The sustained vitality of a complex network requires that the net keep provoking itself out of balance. If the system settles into harmony and equilibrium, it will eventually stagnate and die. Innovation is disruption; constant innovation is perpetual disruption. A few economists studying the new economy (among them Paul Romer and Brian Arthur) have come to similar conclusions. Their work suggests that robust growth sustains itself by poising on the edge of constant chaos. "If I have had a constant purpose it is to show that transformation, change, and messiness are natural in the economy," writes Arthur.… Most of the studies of optimal evolution in complex systems confirm this view. The price for progressive change in maximum doses is a dangerous (and thrilling) ride to the edge of disruption.… Sustaining innovation is particularly tricky since it flows out of creative disequilibrium. To achieve sustainable innovation you need to seek persistent disequilibrium. To seek persistent disequilibrium means that one must chase after disruption without succumbing to it, or retreating from it.[342]

Looking at all of the ideological designs for a socialized world, especially from the more extreme environmentalist contingent, one sees readily that Mises actually won the socialist calculation argument. When you realize that Mises statement about socialism not being able to calculate was not that socialism was impossible, but rather that socialism could not do other than manage a: non-industrial, static, steady-state, non-dynamic economic system at equilibrium, then everything becomes readily clear. Matt Ridley states these extreme environmentalist views concisely:

Many of today's extreme environmentalists not only insist that the world has reached a 'turning point'-quite unaware that their

---

342 Kevin Kelly, *New Rules*, 109,110,114.

predecessors have made the same claim for 200 years about many different issues-but also insist that the only sustainable solution is to retreat, to cease economic growth and enter progressive economic recession. What else can they mean by demanding a campaign to 'de-develop the United States', in the words of President Obama's science advisor John Holdren; or 'isn't the only hope for the planet that the industrialized civilizations collapse? Isn't it our responsibility to bring that about?', in the words of Maurice Strong, first Executive Director of the United Nations Environment Program (UNEP); or that what is needed is 'an ordered and structured downsizing of the global economy' in the words of the journalist George Monbiot? This retreat must be achieved, says Monbiot, by 'political restraint'. This means not just that growing your company's sales would be a crime, but failing to shrink them; not just that traveling further than your ration of miles would be an offense, but failing to travel fewer miles each year; not just that inventing a new gadget would be illegal, but failing to abandon existing technologies; not just that growing more food per acre would be a felony, but failing to grow less-because these are the things that constitute growth ... Here's the rub: this future sounds awfully like the feudal past.[343]

This is an open declaration to Ludwig von Mises, F.A. Hayek, Hans de Soto and the entire Austrian School of Economics that they won the socialist calculation debate hands down as the environmental neo-socialist contingent has adopted the very static, non-dynamic, steady state, economic system as their model. They are actively espousing putting into place the very system, and only system, that Mises said was the one that socialism could and would be able to manage as he said, as quoted by Rothbard, "That socialist central planning simply cannot operate an advanced industrial economy."[344] So the goal of the radical eco crowd

---

343 Ridely, *The Rational*, 311.
344 Murray Rothbard, *The Betrayal of the American Right* (Auburn, AL: Ludwig von Mises Institute Press, 2007), 183.

and todays green neo-communists is to actually create a system which would bring an end to an advanced industrial economy, to de-industrialize the developed nations, so that finally socialism could work. The entire green neo-left ideology of today's action plan is to firmly retreat from evolutionary disequilibrium and to hide in the Never Never Land of neo-classical economics' equilibrium fallacies.

So in order to have socialism then, the industrial revolution and scientific and technological advancement must be contained, rolled back and eventually eliminated, which is the stated goal of the extreme environmentalists. Axiomatically then the Misesean solution was the one chosen by the neo-left. Only those who have not studied and followed the entire socialist calculation argument in depth could miss this glaring fact in all of the eco-propaganda of today. That it violates Karl Marx's evolutionary insight that capitalism must fully evolve to its omega point is missed by far too many. So one comes to comprehend that quite possibly the propagandists of the world eco-left are actually trying to create a self-fulfilling QWERTY prophesy, which is based upon Mises' incredible insight, specifically designed to create a static economic system cobbled together under the pleasant sounding environmental ideals of "sustainability" and "the precautionary principle" and in complete rejection of Karl Marx's philosophy. However, complexity theory and its amazing discoveries uphold Mises and Hayek's theories, as the complexity theorist George Cowan relates:

> The issue that grabs him [Cowan] the hardest, he says, is adaptation-or, more precisely, adaptation under conditions of constant change and unpredictability. Certainly he considers it one of the central issues in the elusive quest for global sustainability. And not incidentally, he finds it to be an issue that's constantly slighted in all this talk about "transitions" to a sustainable world. "Somehow," he says," the agendas been put into the form of talking about a set of transitions from state A, the present, to a state B that's sustainable. The problem is that there is no such state. You have to assume that the transitions

are going to continue forever and ever and ever. You have to talk about the systems that remain continuously dynamic, and that are embedded in environments that themselves are continuously dynamic. "Stability, as John Holland says, is death; somehow, the world has to adapt itself to a condition of perpetual novelty, at the edge of chaos... So if anything were getting back to Heraclitus: 'Everything moves.' A term like 'sustainable' doesn't really capture that."[345]

The desperate need to cling to neo-Malthusian ideas and to fight anyone who impugns those beliefs with Cornucopian facts thus becomes readily apparent, as any evidence that goes against neo-Malthusian notions makes the need for the creation of a static, steady-state, sustained, command and control economic system limited by a draconian precautionary principle irrelevant. One then does not have to stop the world and count every resource in order to begin an efficient production system as being carried out by the U.N.'s Agenda 21 program or envisioned by the Venus Project and The Zeitgeist Movement. Spontaneous complex evolutionary forces are already moving us toward an increasingly highly efficient production system driven by technology using prices as a means of efficient measurement.

Neo-Malthusian ideas support the need for control and rationing if the world and humanity is to survive in a finite universe dominated only by the law of diminishing returns. However, the evolution of the Technium and its burgeoning abundance under the laws of increasing and exponential returns destroys this pessimistic propaganda and old petrified static thinking and makes it totally unnecessary as "that which is getting more and more abundant does not need to be counted, rationed, and efficiently distributed, and that which is politically and artificially rationed will never be free to become more abundant." Marx stated that the entire capitalist system had to reach its full evolution before the revolution could or would come and the Deep Greens today are trying to intervene and create a static Soviet and fascist style economic

---

345 Waldrop, *Complexity*, 356.

system (Agenda 21), which will artificially end capitalism's full and complete evolution. Matt Ridley unequivocally states the problem with this outdated steady state ideal:

> The dissemination of useful knowledge causes that useful knowledge to breed more useful knowledge. Nobody predicted this. The pioneers of political economy expected eventual stagnation. Adam Smith, David Ricardo and Robert Malthus all foresaw that diminishing returns would eventually set in, that the improvement of living standards that they were seeing would Peter out. 'Discovery, and useful application of machinery, always leads to the increase of the net produce of the country, although it may not, and will not, after an inconsiderable interval, increase the value of that net produce,' said Ricardo: all tends toward what he called a 'stationary state'. Even John Stuart Mill, conceding that returns were showing no signs of diminishing in the 1840s, put it down to a miracle, innovation, he said, was an external factor, a cause but not an effect of economic growth, an inexplicable slice of luck. And Mill's optimism was not shared by his successors. As discovery began to slow, so competition would drive the profits of enterprise out of the increasingly perfect market until all that was left was rent and monopoly. With Smith's invisible hand guiding infinite market participants possessed of perfect information to profitless equilibria and vanishing returns, neo-classical economics gloomily forecast the end of growth.

> It was a description of an entirely fictional world. The concept of a steady final state, applied to a dynamic system like the economy, is as wrong as any philosophical abstraction can be. It is Pareto piffle. As the economist Eamonn Butler puts it, the 'perfect market is not just an abstraction; it's plain daft ... Whenever you see the word equilibrium in a textbook, blot it out.' It is wrong because it assumes perfect competition, perfect knowledge and perfect rationality, none of which do or can exist. It is the planned economy, not the market, that requires perfect knowledge.

The possibility of new knowledge makes the steady-state impossible. Somewhere somebody will have a new idea and that idea will enable him to invent a new combination of atoms both to create and exploit imperfections in the market. As Frederick Hayek argued, knowledge is dispersed throughout society, because each person has a special perspective. Knowledge can never be gathered together in one place. It is collective, not individual. ... There is no equilibrium in nature; there is only constant dynamism. As Heraclitus put it, 'nothing endures but change.'[346]

Classical economics and its steady state equilibrium bias and its penchant for finite immiseration thinking are pushing the entire world to the brink of a self-fulfilling economic and societal disaster.

Confusedly, today's neo-Marxists are in actuality anti-Marxists. Marx and Engels despised Malthus and refuted his theories and rightly so. The entire research of the techno-optimists and complexity theorists upholds and proves Marx's and Engles' contention against Malthus correct. Malthus and Malthusianism is the enemy of socialism and all progressive thought and is a defense of the ideology of the left's enemies. As Ronald Meek's quotes Marx,

"The hatred of the English working class against Malthus," wrote Marx, "... Is therefore entirely justified. The people were right here in sensing instinctively that they were confronted not with a *man of science* but with a *bought advocate*, a pleader on behalf of their enemies, a shameless sycophant of the ruling classes." It was for this reason that Marx and Engels spent so much time and energy in attacking Malthus's doctrines. [347]

Later on Meek's unequivocally declares,

---

346   Matt Ridley, The Rational Optimist, 249.
347   Ronald L. Meeks, ed. *Marx and Engels on the Population Bomb*, (Berkeley, CA: Ramparts Press, 1971), 16.

The theories of Malthus, now as always, are serving as weapons in the hands of people who, whether they are aware of it or not, are hindering the progress of mankind towards a fuller more abundant life. If the social struggles of the early 19th century were essentially summed up in the controversy between Malthus and Ricardo, those of our own times are perhaps not unfairly summed up in that between Malthusian's and Marxists. [348]

And at the end of his book he definitively excoriates Malthus,

Malthus's book *On Population* was a tract against the French revolution in the contemporary ideas of reform in England (Godwin, etc.). It was an apology for the poverty of the working classes. The *theory* was a plagiarism of Townsend, etc.

His *Essay on Rent* was a tract on behalf of the landlords against industrial capital. The theory was a plagiarism of Anderson.

His *Principles of Political Economy* was a tract in the interests of the capitalists against the workers and the interested of the aristocracy, the Church, and the "tax devourers" (*Steuerfresser*), etc., against the capitalists. The theory was a plagiarism of Adam Smith. Where it was Malthus's own invention, it was pitiably poor. [349]

The physicist and futurist Robert Zubrin in his book *The Merchants of Despair* states in the chapter *The Betrayal of the Left* the abandonment of the old left's principles by the neo-left:

It was thus very disturbing to many American leftists when people started showing up at their meetings in the late 1960s insisting that they take up the cause of population control. This is a complete

---

348   Ibid., 46.
349   Ibid., 188.

break from the lefts traditions and commitments. Since the days of Henry George and Frederick Engels, American leftists had always been vehemently opposed to Malthusianism, which they correctly understood as a reactionary racist doctrine conceived for the purpose of denying the just aspirations of working people. But now, descending upon the meetings of the Students for a Democratic Society ... came the acolytes of Paul Ehrlich. Instead of the *Grapes of Wrath*, they carried copies of *The Population Bomb*. Instead of voting rights for minorities, they wanted to give them abortions. Instead of "Stop the War," their buttons read "Stop at Two"; instead of "Power to the People," their slogan was "People Pollute."

At first they met resistance. The Marxists rushed reprints of their founding fathers' anti-Malthusian tracks back into publication. The Black Panther Party expressed itself rather more plainly, saying, "What pollutes our air is not industrial smog but exclusion from the industrial benefits of racist, imperialist Amerika" the Christian radical Richard Neuhaus, pastor of the Lutheran Church of St. John the evangelist in Brooklyn and founder of National Clergy and Laymen Concerned About Vietnam, wrote an entire book blasting Ehrlich and the ecology movement for their flagrant anti-humanism. Entitled *In Defense of People: Ecology and the Seduction of Radicalism*, the book makes poignant reading today, recalling as it does the waning moments of the era when the left stood up for human beings.[350]

Robert Zubrin's book is required reading today for those people who have been suffocating in the analithic ideological smog of Neo-Malthusianism for over four decades and wish to finally free themselves from the status quo of revisionist neo-left ideology.

Marx and the classical liberal's defense against that apologist of Tory privilege Malthus, have now been proven correct by Simon et al.

---

350 Robert Zubrin, *Merchants of Despair: Radical Environmentalists, Criminal Pseudo-Scientists, and the Fatal Cult of Antihumanism*, (New York, NY: New Atlantis Books, 2012), 126.

and yet the world's green propaganda machine is geared up to fight those very ideas that Marx and the older Marxists upheld and championed. The fact that libertarians have mainly become the promulgators and defenders of this cornucopian science is another aspect of the farce that politically rigid, reactionary neo-left ideologies foster, which brings us to the central paradox of today: To be faithful to irrational postmodern ideology progressives have to deny Marx and science, but to take up and champion Marx and science and become truly progressive requires one to deny todays irrational postmodern ideology. Will true progressives have the courage to break out of the "conservative fundamentalism" they have unwittingly fallen into and take up the banner and become true progressives championing the full evolution of science and technology and come to the aide of the Technium fighting to remove all blockages and roadblocks on the road to its full evolution? That is the pertinent unanswerable question. George Reisman stated an incredible insight under the title, *Why There Are No Limits to Progress in a Free Economy*:

> The picture I have painted of a free economy is one of continuous progress and improvement. So it has been in the United States over the last two hundred years, during most of which time we had a substantially free economy. As the free economy has come to be steadily undermined and the transition to a form of socialism drawn even closer, however, the foundations of economic progress have been eroded. For reasons that should become progressively clearer from now on, a controlled or socialist economy cannot have economic progress. **I believe that advocates of socialism know this, or at least that they sense it, and that, as a result, they have launched a widespread campaign to try to deny the very possibility of continuous economic progress. The nature of their attempt is summed up in the phrase space "The Limits to Growth." The motivation of the supporters of that phrase, I believe, is to be able to blame the end**

of economic progress not on the end of capitalism, but on the fundamental nature of the world.[351]

These words were written in 1979, just at the beginning of the environmental movement and just after the Club of Rome came out with their widely refuted study *The Limits to Growth*. In the thirty plus years that have since passed he couldn't have been more prescient. Chaos and complexity theory's discovery that there are no-limits to knowledge and thus no actual limits to growth decimates the linear prognostications found within the *Limits to Growth* and its thinking based upon classical economy's failed equilibrium theories.

Today's activists seek to hide their artificially created resource shortages under the blanket of neo-Malthusian determinism and the law of decreasing returns. To accomplish this, they have the implicit help of the media and fellow travelers who throw down the Orwellian memory hole any recollection of the previous interventions and the unintended consequences that have led to today's advancing artificial resource shortages created through inflation, legislation, regulation and activism. To save the world from the latest eco-calamity du jour, eco-stasists must create the only system that revisionist neo-communism can manage, a command and control, top-down, static despotism. It is the only solution ever proffered by pundits like Noam Chomsky and Naomi Klein, and the cornucopians threaten that propaganda down to its very core by proving Marx et al. evolutionary insights correct. That such a system contradicts both classical liberalism and democratic socialist's ideals rarely seems to be recognized or appreciated. If in order to save the Earth we have to enslave humanity and alienate everyone to a global state, we have unwittingly made a Faustian bargain with the Devil, which in the end will save neither the earth nor humanity. One has only to look at the poverty, devastation and ecological disaster of the Soviet Union and Eastern Europe after the fall of the iron curtain in 1989 and Detroit City today to see

---

351 Reisman, *Economy*, 15. Bold mine.

what lies in store for us all in the future if this reactionary static ideal is ever realized.

Strangely, this entire battle at its heart is not an argument between conservative or libertarian "deniers" and liberal progressive "acceptors," with the conservatives always being portrayed as against science and the left as champions of science. It is actually a battle between two different strains within Marxism itself, the postmodern one that has thrown out almost all logic and science and is heavily into interventionism and the old one that still clings to science and dialectical ideas if only by a thread. Ludwig von Mises made this point decades ago about the conflict between those who were advocating a third-way economic system between socialism and capitalism and the communists who opposed them as bourgeois revisionists:

> What we must realize is that the antagonism between the interventionists and the communists is a manifestation of the conflict between the two doctrines of the early Marxism and of the late Marxism. It is a conflict between the Marx of 1848, the author of the *Communist Manifesto*, and the Marx of 1867, the author of *Das Capital*. And it is paradoxical indeed that the document in which Marx endorsed the policies of the present-day self-styled anti-communists [the interventionists] is called the *Communist Manifesto*.[352]

That it took the actions of "bourgeois" economists and scientists to rediscover and prove the evolutionary insights of Marx correct is a travesty, that the vast majority of the world's left today fights against them so vehemently is the tragedy, that ignorance and propaganda hides all of these facts from too many people's consciousness is the farce. There is a fundamental antagonism that goes beyond even the doctrines of the early Marx versus the older Marx, and it is foundational to the antagonism in the world today and that conflict is between the ideologies

---

352 Ludwig von Mises, *Middle of the Road Policy Leads to Socialism* (Auburn, AL: Ludwig von Mises Institute Press, 1988), 62.

of *Dynamism* and *Stasis.* Virginia Postrel in her work *The Future and Its Enemies,* states this profound divide succinctly:

> How we feel about the evolving future tells us who we are as individuals and as a civilization: Do we search for stasis-a regulated, engineered world? Or do we embrace dynamism-a world of constant creation, discovery, and competition? Do we value stability and control, or evolution and learning? Do we declare with Appello that "we're scared of the future" and join Adams in decrying technology as "a killing thing"? Or do we see technology as an expression of human creativity and the future as inviting? Do we think that progress requires a central blueprint, or do we see it as a decentralized, evolutionary process? ... Do we crave predictability, or relish surprise? These two poles, stasis and dynamism, increasingly define our political, intellectual, and cultural landscape. [353]

Postrel goes on to describe our present existential dilemma:

> The future we face at the dawn of the twenty-first century is, like all futures left to themselves, "emergent, complex messiness." It's "messiness" lies not in disorder, but in an order that is unpredictable, spontaneous, and ever shifting, a pattern created by millions of uncoordinated, independent decisions. That pattern contains not just a few high-tech gizmos, but all the variegated aspects of life. As people create and sell products or services, adopt new fashions of speech or dress, form families and choose hometowns, make medical decisions and seek spiritual insights, investigate the universe and invent new forms of art, these actions shape the future no one can see, a future that is dynamic and inherently unstable ... Ours is a magnificently creative era. But that creativity produces change, and that change attracts enemies, philosophical as well as self-interested. [354]

353 Postrel, *The Future,* xiv.
354 Ibid., xv.

We are at a crossroads as a culture between choosing between Up or Down, between extropy and entropy, the law of exponential returns or of clinging to the old linear law of diminishing returns. That the post-modern neo-left has chosen stasis and entropy and has become nearly as antiscientific, antitechnology and anti-evolutionary as the most reactionary and revisionist right wing fundamentalist Christian who longs for a return to the Garden of Eden and the static teaching of the Bible is disconcerting. Are we at war between the older simian parts of our brains and its longing for the Neolithic certainties of tribe, clan, status and stasis and the new evolving parts of our brain which crave novelty, spontaneity, and constant unending change? Peter Diamandis thinks we are as he feels that all of this fear-based ecological propaganda is coming from our amygdala's desire for certainty and stasis as a way to end fear. Ideologically today we stand like a freed Auschwitz victim on the threshold of our prison barracks blinking in the harsh sunlight of a new era, with the Technium as our liberator. Behind us lies the old dark constrained past with its privations, poverty and suffering, forced upon us by a pretechnological past, while before us lies an uncertain road to total freedom, liberty, abundance and a new complex world. Let us hope that we do not do what many of the Auschwitz victims did when the Allies first freed them and return to the familiarity of our dark cells. Afraid of the new light, liberty and freedom which blinds us now as our eyes and minds have not yet become accustomed to the light of a new dawning exponential paradigm. Ludwig von Mises at the end of his work *The Anti-Capitalist Mentality* made a profound insight,

> In the universe there is never and nowhere stability and immobility. Change and transformation are essential features of life. Each state of affairs is transient; each age is an age of transition. In human life there is never calm and repose. Life is a process, not a perseverance in a status quo. Yet the human mind has always been deluded by the image of an unchangeable existence. The avowed aim of all utopian movements is to put an end to history and to establish a final and

permanent calm. The psychological reasons for this tendency are obvious. Every change alters the external conditions of life and well-being and forces people to adjust themselves anew to the modification of their environments. It hurts vested interests and threatens traditional ways of production and consumption. It annoys all those who are intellectually inert and shrink from revising their modes of thinking. Conservatism is contrary to the very nature of human acting. But it has always been the cherished program of the many, of the inert who dully resist every attempt to improve their own conditions which the minority of the alert initiate. In employing the term reactionary one mostly refers only to the aristocrats and priests who called their parties conservative. Yet the outstanding examples of the reactionary spirit were provided by other groups: by the guilds of artisans blocking entrance into their field to newcomers; by the farmers asking for tariff protection, subsidies and "parity prices"; by the wage earners hostile to technological improvements and fostering featherbedding and similar practices. ... The powers that be do not like new ideas, new ways of thought and new styles of art. They are opposed to any kind of innovation. Their supremacy would result in strict regimentation; it would bring about stagnation and decay.[355]

Which is a sentiment that any progressive, socialist, or leftist could second quite easily today. We have friends in many surprising places that we once thought of as our enemies and we have enemies that have sneaked into our tent, wear our clothes and mimic our desires, who bamboozle us with millions of dollars in donations and write for us our propaganda memes that we march to, but who are actually our inherent enemies diverting us to supporting the very corporations and polices that we once vehemently fought against. Ideological blindness and simple faith is no longer suitable for our cause. Our next revolution must be within our own ranks, we have to throw off the mantle that the many establishment Foundations have smothered us in. Stasis and a steady state system was

---

355 Ludwig von Mises, *The Anti-Capitalist Mentality*, (Grove City, PA: Libertarian Press, 1972), 84.

never a Left wing ideal, today with the help of complexity theory we need to rediscover dialectical thinking. We must escape the blind alley that old false ideas have trapped us in. The Techno-Optimists have the solution and have solved the old Marxian problem and uncertainty. Our era is before us, and we can only rise to the heights by breaking the anchor chains that continue to bind us to a failed Malthusian static steady state ideology and the earth. We stand at the edge of Early Futurity, it is time we become the midwives of history and help give birth to the Messianic age about to break the water of the capitalist womb that still contains it. The economic event horizon is coming into view over the next rise; we can feel its inextricable gravitational pull propelling us forward at greater and greater speed. Our historical and world changing mission is to grease capitalism's skids so that it naturally slides to this transcendence point, the omega point. It is time we finally became true Evolutionaries and fulfill or historical imperative.

Appendix C
What Problem Was Keynes Trying to Solve?

There is no subtler, no surer means of overturning the existing basis of society than to debauch the currency. The process engages all the hidden forces of economic law on the side of destruction, and does it in a manner which not one man in a million is able to diagnose. -J. M. KEYNES

"What problem was John Maynard Keynes trying to solve?" This is a much more interesting question that rises above the din of the battle between economic schools focused on where Keynes and his theory went wrong. What was Keynes actually trying to do when he wrote his magnum opus the *General Theory*? When researched this becomes an exciting detective story that opens up a great vista and gives comprehension to a subject that has been mired in murkiness, misdirection and ad hominem attacks for almost a century. The amazing thing that is realized after one does the honest in depth research is that Keynes is trying to solve the crisis in Marxism/socialism, and the monetary cranks and utopians on how to realize abundance. To do this without openly showing that he was taking up the socialist problem of realizing utopia, Keynes decided to go all the way back to David Ricardo, Malthus and the mercantilist and monetary cranks of the 16th through the 19th centuries, as Hunter Lewis states:

British economist John Maynard Keynes's principal book, *The General Theory of Employment, Interest, and Money*, occupies the same place in progressivism that Karl Marx's *Capital* occupies in communism. One is the "sacred text," obscure enough to require "priestly" interlocutors, the other the actual social system, although it could be argued that Keynes's system may be more accurately described as crony capitalism. ... Keynes's own explicit admission in *The General Theory* that he was reviving the thinking of the mercantilists, earlier economists from the 16th and 17th centuries who were unabashed apologists for the crony capitalism of their day.[356]

Keynes then brought all of the Mercantilist theories in through the back door disguised under a new lexicon in his work which he quite obviously and hubristically named after Einstein's work, *The General Theory*.

The main proposition that underlies all of his thinking is the older Marxian idea that the way to the revolution/utopia is the one that I have mentioned many times throughout this work. That the greater and more efficient that production becomes, the lower prices and profits will fall until the capitalists and workers are all eventually immiserated, the rentier and the speculator is eliminated and utopia finally dawns. *The law of immiseration* is central and foundational to his ideas and it is this law and how to obtain its full effects that he was pursuing in his works. Keynes is trying to achieve the immiseration goal though not through the evolution of the productive material forces as Marx theorized, he is instead trying to do it through artificially dropping the interest rate to zero through inflating the money supply, as he accepted uncritically the proposition of the monetary cranks of earlier centuries that there is not enough money in the economy to buy everything that is produced and it is this shortage of money that causes prices to increase, and the need to pay interest that keeps utopia from being realized. This is also a widely held fallacious belief today among many on the neo-left and in economics departments in colleges and universities worldwide as well.

---

356 Hunter Lewis, *Free Prices Now: Fixing the Economy by Abolishing the FED* (Edinburg, VA: AC2 Books, 2013), 200.

This is the foundational idea underlying all of Keynes thought. The problem is that inflating the money supply does not make money more abundant, it makes money scarcer as the inflation continues. As you constantly expand the money supply and bank credit the value of the currency consistently falls so the effect is that as the value of savings and purchasing power continually shrinks it takes more and more currency to buy the same amount of goods you once did. It is as if the amount of money needed to buy any good in the economy is vanishing. If one had $10,000 in savings before the inflation and there was only a light inflation of 2% a year, in a decade your and everyone else's savings would fall by more than 20%. At the same time the prices throughout the economy would be rising giving a doubling effect to the currency's value loss, your real wage and your savings are shrinking while prices continue to increase. As inflation gallops onward the money supply actually is falling in value and thus a shrinking effect of the money supply is realized, you now have a shortage of money. Inflation puts the realization of utopia off and completely derails the goals of the older Marxist's and all utopians. It is as if the ladder you are using to try to climb to the stars is dissolving under you at an ever increasing rate of speed. As F.A. Hayek put it:

> Let us simply note, then, that inflation makes it more and more impossible for people of moderate means to provide for their old age themselves; that it discourages saving and encourages running into debt; and that, by destroying the middle class, it creates a dangerous gap between the completely propertyless and the wealthy that is so characteristic of societies which have gone through prolonged inflations and which is the source of so much tension in those societies.[357]

The crisis in Marxism, of why the revolution didn't come in 1914, was the pivotal foundational issue that continues to drive all of our economic, political and ideological beliefs today and it was paramount in many socialist's minds in the early twentieth century. The central problem

---

[357] F. A. Hayek, *The Constitution of Liberty* (Chicago, Illinois: the University of Chicago Press, 1960), 338.

that needed to be addressed and solved was how to eliminate all scarcity in the economic system and bring about an abundance of goods so that communism could come. This was the key pivotal issue that made, or broke, Marxism and socialism in general. How to achieve this ideal goal was the burning passion of socialist intellectuals and economists of the time-and Keynes as a Fabian socialist, was trying to solve this foundational issue in a way that would not be glaringly obvious to non-socialists. He was actually bringing neo-Marxism in through the back door and trying to accomplish the goals of the earlier Marx as related in the *Communist Manifesto*. A shocking declaration, but one shared by the American economist Martin Bronfenbrenner as related by W.H. Hutt:

> In what is probably the most effective recent defense of Keynesianism, Bronfenbrenner has argued that the great virtue of the doctrine has been that, through its influence upon policy-through the consequent secular inflation-the "peaceful acceptance" of Marxian aims has been secured. Where the drastic measures which Marx himself contemplated would have failed, Keynesian methods have quietly succeeded. "Secular inflation" has, in fact, proved to be the "principal weapon for extortion of surplus value"... Bronfenbrenner describes inflation as a "social mollifier" which permits the politically dominant groups... To increase their share of the real national income "without decreasing the money income of anyone else, and therefore without arousing the volume and vehemence of opposition which might be expected." This triumph of Marxian aims by more subtle methods than Marx's own, this gradual process which we are currently witnessing of the euthanasia of the politically weak classes is, according to Bronfenbrenner, to be preferred to what he apparently regards as the inevitable alternative, expropriation on Orthodox Marxian lines.[358]

---

358 W. H. Hutt, *Keynesianism: Retrospect and Prospect* (Chicago, IL: Henry Regnery Co, 1963), 48.

It was an ingenious sleight of hand trick to go back to all the common sources that influenced and were used by Marx and then bring them back in using a new jargon to obfuscate what you were actually doing, trying to solve the socialist abundance conundrum. Yet Keynes solution was fallacious and has caused all of the economic problems we have today: the slowing growth rates of the Western economies, a greater disparity between the rich and the poor, a shrinking middle class, rising prices, a lower savings rate, sluggish productivity, short term thinking etc. Let us take the slowing of the economic growth rate which so many now say we have to get used to, that it is just a given of today's capitalist system. As Hunter Lewis mentions so clearly:

> There is a diminishing return to taking on debt.

> In the United States, we have operated on Keynesian principles since World War II. The government has printed money. Debt levels have grown. We have not only gotten inflations and bubbles. We have also gotten less and less growth for each increment of debt.

> During the decade 1950-1959, we added $338 billion in debt, and we got 73¢ in economic growth (increase in gross domestic product) for each $1 in new debt. For the decade 1990-1999, we added $12.5 trillion in debt, but only got 31¢ of growth per dollar of debt. For the 7 plus years 2000-2008 (1st quarter), we added $24.3 trillion in debt, but only got 19¢ in growth for every dollar of debt. It thus required more and more debt to generate further growth.

> Eventually the return on debt becomes negative. [359]

Thomas Woods in his book *Rollback* also comments on the law of diminishing returns in government assistance programs:

---

359 Hunter Lewis, *Where Keynes Went Wrong: and Why World Governments Keep Creating Inflation, Bubbles, and Busts* (Mt. Jackson, VA: Axios Press, 2009), 105. I highly recommend this work.

At least two thirds of the money assigned to government welfare budgets is eaten up by bureaucracy. Taken by itself, this would mean it would take three dollars in taxes for one dollar to reach the poor. But we must add to this the well-founded estimate of James Payne that the combined public and private costs of taxation amount to 65 cents of every dollar taxed. When we include this factor, we find the cost of government delivery of one dollar to the poor to be five dollars. So a private system would not need to duplicate the entire government welfare budget out of private funds.[360]

It would take $5 in taxes taken from productivity to deliver $1 to a welfare recipient! This same process is also seen in corporate subsidies. The law of diminishing returns in action! There is only a negative multiplier at play where government benefits are concerned and as we take on more and more public debt that multiplier is only becoming increasingly negative.

Today neo-Keynesians like Paul Krugman say that we have to get used to the anemic and lower growth rate of our economies given the nature of the world and its finite resources. "It is just natural and bound to happen that capitalism would begin to Peter out!" Zero growth enthusiasts also parrot this line, barking on cue like Pavlov's dogs, yet it is nothing but a protective propaganda meme to keep everyone from realizing that it is the very inflationary economic monetary policies of our government and economic elites like Krugman that is causing the slowing growth rate and its ever increasing poverty and disparity. People who desire and want utopia keep spreading Keynesian and the prior century's fallacious monetary ideas to their own detriment. Even the idea of a universal basic income (UBI) is right out of Keynesian economics which are all designed to bolster and shore up the failing welfare state. Lewis mentions this situation as follows:

---

360 Thomas E. Woods, Jr., *Rollback: Repealing Big Government Before the Coming Collapse*, (New York, NY: Regnery Press, 2011), 129.

Can scarcity be abolished through the Keynesian program of driving down interest rates?

To try to answer this question, consider two variant views on human poverty:

A. Billions of human beings live in poverty because food, clothing, shelter, and amenities are still scarce, which makes them expensive. In order for the entire human race to escape poverty, we need to work hard, save, and invest in order to produce more and better goods more cheaply.

B. The problem is not that goods are scarce. Is that money is scarce. Government should distribute more cash so that everyone has enough.

Most people will readily see that B is a fallacy. It will not work. Even if we gave every poor person $1 million a year, it would not help them, as there would be more money in the world, there would be no more food, clothing, shelter, and amenities. The only result from a flood of new money would be soaring prices. People who had been poor on $300 a year would now be poor on $1 million a year. [361]

Now let us consider a third alternative:

C. The problem is not that the goods are scarce. It is that lendable money is scarce. If government will provide unlimited funds to

---

[361] As you can see, B is the UBI/GBI solution to poverty. It is the same inflationary monetary fallacies that undergird this idea of trying to eliminate poverty through redistribution of money, which will result in governments increasing the money supply to provide the funds necessary for each person to have a minimum basic income. Monetary cranks of early centuries put forward these ideas, which Keynes adopted. Only a Universal Productivity Fund (UPF) can accomplish through the productive evolutionary means, what the UBIers want to do through the inflationary devolutionary means.

borrow, we can invest those funds in new factories and businesses and, within a generation, nothing will be scarce.

C is Keynes's solution, and unfortunately it is just as much of a fallacy as B. Printing money and lending it to people will have the same result as printing money and giving it to people. It will either make existing goods and services cost more, in which case we will call it inflation. Or it will make assets cost more, in which case we will call it a bubble. Either way, it is really inflation.[362]

So you can readily see that both B and C are solutions based on the childish fairy tale notion of *Rumpelstiltskin Economics*, that one can spin fiat paper into gold. Yet the more you spin the less it is worth until such time as the value completely collapses along with the economic structure and society itself. Bringing capitalism down now through inflation doesn't pave the way for socialism to arise; it only paves the way for poverty to spread and want and misery to become universal again. The devastation it causes makes inventing a new world from the ground up impossible.

The economic author Henry Hazlitt was a determined foe and critic of Keynesianism and wrote many books and articles against the "new economics." His best known works were: *The Failure of the New Economics* and *The Critics of Keynesian Economics*, which he edited. What these works and other works criticizing Keynesianism provides to the honest researcher is the firm understanding that Keynes was an admitted Fabian socialist and that he was trying to solve the "economic issues of capitalism" by monetary and fiscal means for Fabian socialist ends. In fact when reading his *General Theory* the underlying theme of his idea becomes apparent as Hazlitt details:

---

362 Ibid, 103.

N.B. a third alternative D is to eliminate monetary prices, an idea common among the Resource Based Economy enthusiasts. It is thought that without monetary prices holding back production and resource development, everything would be free. This is another fallacious idea based on old monetary crank theories and only those who are completely ignorant in economics propose such a false and naïve solution.

The central problem with which economics deals, the problem with which mankind has been struggling since the beginning of time, is the problem of scarcity, and this problem is assumed away in a few blithe words [by Keynes]. It is *"comparatively easy to make capital-goods so abundant that the marginal efficiency of capital is zero."*

Did Keynes stop to think for a moment what this would imply? It would imply that capital goods were so abundant that they had no exchange value! And if they had no value, they would be as free as air or (most) water or other goods without scarcity. It would be worth nobody's while to keep such capital goods in repair (unless it cost nothing, not even anybody's labor, to keep them in repair). There would be no problem even of replacement. For as soon as there were a problem of replacement, it would mean that capital goods once more had a value and cost something to produce: therefore, presumably, capital goods would cost nothing to produce.

Moreover, if the marginal efficiency of capital were zero, it would also mean that no *consumer goods* would have any scarcity, price, or exchange value. For as long as any consumer goods anywhere failed to reach the point of satiation, and had a price or a value, then capital to help produce these consumer goods would have *some* marginal yield above zero.

A marginal efficiency of zero for capital would mean, in brief, such an abundance of *everything* that neither capital goods nor consumers goods would have any scarcity, any price, or any exchange value. In such circumstances the rate of interest, of course, would also fall to zero—not only because the rate of interest and the marginal yield of capital tend toward equality.

The capitalist system, in fact—which is the system of free, private, competitive enterprise—has been doing more to reduce production costs, and to relieve scarcity, than any system in history. It is because America has come nearer to adopting a full free private enterprise system that it has done more to relieve scarcity than any other nation in history.[363] But as human wants are insatiable, and as both consumer and capital goods will always, to repeat, cost *something* to produce, **the day when capital will cease to have any yield at all, and when consumer goods cease to have a price, and when no scarcity of any kind exists, is still far, far off.** All talk of making capital so plentiful as to reduce its marginal efficiency to zero "within a single generation" [364] is the purest moonshine.

No doubt Keynes's "system" owes part of its popularity to the impression that he has at last provided not only that Economics of Abundance, of which the Utopians have been dreaming from time immemorial, but has combined with it a Conspiracy Theory according to which the Moneylenders keep everything scarce in order that they may continue to receive Interest. [365]

This is the central theme of today's neo-left. Every book you read and every blog you scan has the idea of the last sentence of this passage that "Moneylenders keep everything scarce in order that they may continue to receive Interest."[366] This shows a complete and total failure on behalf of far too many people to recognize that inflating the money supply and bank credit is what actually continues to keep everything scarce. As Hazlitt cogently states about Keynes, "it is already clear that Keynes is determined, with no matter what argument or assertion, to exculpate excessively high wage-rates from all blame for unemployment and to pin that blame on to the demand of lenders for the payment of interest

---

363 This is Marx's insight as well, it underlies the law of immiseration.
364 Note: Bold mine. Hazlitt implicitly implies here that this event will happen in the future, but it won't be brought about by increasing inflation, it can only be brought about by increasing real savings and production based upon real savings as only that feeds the law of increasing/exponential returns.
365 Harry Hazlitt, *The Failure of the New Economics* [1959] (Auburn, Al: The Ludwig von Mises Institute, 2007), 232-233. Bold mine.
366 Ibid., 232.

on their loans."[367] Today the neo-left along with the entire economic establishment does the exact same thing. The paying of interest, and not inflation, is the great bugaboo with disastrous ideological results as the neo-left is now helping to debauch and defraud the worker's real wage rate. The other fascinating thing is that Keynes himself when talking about previous century's lack of development in his essay *Economic Possibilities for Our Grandchildren*, states that "This slow rate of progress, or lack of progress, was due to two reasons-to the remarkable absence of important technical improvements and to the failure of capital to accumulate."[368] So he understood that capital formation was paramount to creating a future world of abundance, yet he seems to have no clue that inflation actually consumes capital formation.

To continue: interest is paid on the lending of money and is linked to the time preference of individuals in society and the real savings rate in the economy. Inflating the money supply in order to lower the interest rate has only a limited effect as the real rate of interest in the economy will always reassert itself causing real interest rates to rise. Once this disparity between the real rate of interest and the artificially lowered interest rate becomes apparent calamity is not far behind, the economic crisis, the bust soon begins. The booms caused by inflating the currency always end in busts that erase the productive gains made during the boom. Thus the Keynesian and monetarist theories create an economic *Sisyphus Syndrome* where the boulder of production that we roll up the hill with the help of an inflating cushion of currency eventually comes crashing down to the bottom again once the inflation loses its momentum. Inflation gives the appearance of increasing wealth and growth, while the house of cards it stands upon buckles under the strain of its increasing weight. Eventually it all tumbles down leaving us right back to where we were before the boom. The only people who this cycle makes better off are the rich bankers and well connected cronies who get the

---

367   Ibid, 244. A statement found throughout the works of such utopian groups as the Venus Project and the Zeitgeist Movement.
368   John M. Keynes, "Economic Possibilities for Our Grandchildren," *Essays in Persuasion*, (New York: W.W. Norton & Co., 1963) 358-373.

new money first and are invested in assets whose value increase with the prices.

Inflation covers over and disguises the natural rate of deflation in the growing highly more productive economy. As I mentioned in earlier chapters, greater productivity actually lowers the prices of all goods and services in the economy. As science and technology has been applied to production at an ever increasing rate this natural rate of deflation has been growing steadily. In the late 19th century it ran about 1.2% a year, today it runs about 3% to 4% a year. Hunter Lewis describes this process:

> Consumer prices should steadily fall. This should specially help poor people, who will be able to buy more with their limited incomes. But everyone should benefit from being able to buy more with less. If prices should fall by, say, 3% a year, but in fact rise by 3%, what is happening? The explanation is that government is creating (and injecting into the economy) enough new money to raise prices 6%, of course, this is masked. It appears that prices are only rising 3%, when they are actually rising 6%.[369]

This is a phenomenon that has been happening since the 1920s and has especially picked up from the 1970s onward with increasing computerization and technological advancement. So Ray Kurzweil in his work the *Singularity is Near* gets this incorrect. As he states that "inflation is being over reported," his possible lack of economic understanding actually makes him miss the fact that inflation has been and is purposely being underreported. If prices are going up 2% a year due to inflation and the technological deflation rate is 4% a year, then the actual inflation rate is the difference between +2% and -4%, or 6%. Since the web site Shadow Statistics reports that the actual inflation rate of the U.S. is closer to 6% a year presently, then the actual and real inflation rate is +6% subtracting -4% or 10% per annum. Inflation is thus being horribly underreported! The new Federal Reserve policy, changing from trying

---

369 Lewis, *Where Keynes Went Wrong*, 95.

to stabilize prices to having a 2% a year inflation rate, is being done to try to combat this natural deflation rate of the economy brought about by the law of increasing returns. The great fear of the central bankers, big government bureaucrats and the entire crony capitalist regime is deflation, as deflation redistributes wealth from the rich to the poor and thus closes the disparity gap. Jörg Hülsmann insightfully mentions the benefits of deflation in his book *Deflation & Liberty*:

> Deflation is not a mere redistribution game that benefits some individuals and groups at the expense of other individuals and groups. Rather, deflation appears as a great harbinger of liberty. It stops inflation and destroys the institutions that produce inflation. It abolishes the advantage that inflation-based debt finance enjoys, at the margin, over savings-based equity finance. And it therefore decentralizes financial decision-making and makes banks, firms, and individuals more prudent and self-reliant than they would have been under inflation. Most importantly, deflation eradicates the re-channeling of incomes that result from the monopoly privileges of central banks. It thus destroys the economic basis of the false elites and obliges them to become true elites rather quickly, or abdicate and make way for new entrepreneurs and other social leaders…deflation was foremost a political problem…deflation brings down the politico economic establishment, which thrives on inflation and debts, and that it therefore brings about some circulation of the elites… Deflation puts a brake—at the very least a temporary brake—on the further concentration and consolidation of power in the hands of the federal government and in particular in the executive branch. It dampens the growth of the welfare state, if it does not lead to its outright implosion. In short, deflation is at least potentially a great liberating force. It not only brings the inflated monetary system back to rock bottom, it brings the entire society back in touch with the real world, because it destroys the economic basis of the social engineers, spin doctors, and brain washers. In light of these considerations, deflation is not merely one fundamental policy option next

to the fundamental alternative of re-inflation. Rather, if our purpose is to maintain and—where necessary—to restore, a free society, then deflation is the only acceptable monetary policy.[370]

We engage the law of diminishing returns by using inflation and bank credit expansion while derailing and destroying the law of increasing returns which can and would carry us naturally to utopia as the capitalist system evolves toward exponentialism and its own transcendence. Imagine what would happen if the natural deflation rate brought about by the evolution of the Technium kept increasing, from the roughly 3% a year today, to 10% or even 20% in the near future under nanotechnology and the rise of the Hyper-Net. With a non-inflationary currency like Bitcoin, both the value of the currency and the savings in the economy would begin to grow first linearly and then exponentially. The greater the accumulation of savings and capital the lower the real rate of interest becomes and the more production increases driving prices lower, which in turn increases the savings rate and real wages, thus increasing the purchasing power of the currency allowing more savings. The law of increasing returns sets in and the rate of science and technological discoveries applied to production increases, sending prices down further, expanding resources and naturally lowering interest rates yet again. This synergistic effect once it fully kicks in causes a positive feedback loop which would bring us to the utopia we all desire: socialists, communists, communitarians Singularitans, Transhumanist's, Zeitgeisters, Libertarians, Anarchists, Trekkers et al. We must abandon Keynes and all of his fallacious theories, including the monetary theories of the Chicago school of economics, as they have kept us from moving forward to our real goal which is the transcendence of the present system through its full evolution, as Karl Marx[371] himself theorized, and that

---

370 Jörg Hülsmann, *Deflation & Liberty* (Auburn, Alabama: Ludwig von Mises Institute, 2008), 40.

371 See Meghnad Desai's *Marx's Revenge* for a full dissertation on Marx's idea of the necessity for the full evolution of the capitalist system before socialism can dawn done by a Marxian economist of high standing.

cannot be accomplished using inflationary and redistributive means, it can only be done using the deflationary forces of the productive means and the productive means has to be based on real savings and capital accumulation. Strangely even Keynes saw this effect of compound interest coupled with technological advancement:

> The modern age opened; I think, with the accumulation of capital which began in the sixteenth...century. For I trace the beginnings of British foreign investment to the treasure which Drake stole from Spain in 1580. In that year he returned to England bringing with him the prodigious spoils of the *Golden Hind.* Queen Elizabeth was a considerable shareholder in the syndicate which had financed the expedition. Out of her share she paid off the whole of England's foreign debt, balanced her Budget, and found herself with about £40,000 in hand. This she invested in the Levant Company –which prospered. Out of the profits of the Levant Company, the East India Company was founded; and the profits of this great enterprise were the foundation of England's subsequent foreign investment. Now it happens that £40,000 accumulating at 3f per cent compound interest approximately corresponds to the actual volume of England's foreign investments at various dates, and would actually amount today to the total of £4,000,000,000 which I have already quoted as being what our foreign investments now are. Thus, every £1 which Drake brought home in 1580 has now become £100,000. Such is the power of compound interest!... If capital increases, say, 2 per cent per annum, the capital equipment of the world will have increased by a half in twenty years, and seven and a half times in a hundred years... At the same time technical improvements in manufacture and transport have been proceeding at a greater rate in the last ten years than ever before in history. In the United States factory output per head was 40 per cent greater in 1925 than in 1919. [372]

---

372 John Keynes, *Economic Possibilities.*

It is one of those strange vagaries of history that someone like Keynes, who had all the pieces of the puzzle in front of them, yet solved the puzzle using smuggled in pieces from an entirely different box, all to uphold their fallacious ideological view point. Our world today would be incredibly wealthy with poverty eliminated decades ago if Keynes had followed his train of thinking above and intuited the "utopian" vision within classical liberalism.

The historical refrain of the economic hacks and pundits of the establishment cried that "savings poison the economy," and Keynes bought it. Savings poisons the economy all right; it poisons the imperialist crony capitalist system which saves itself by using inflation and credit expansion to keep prices and profits artificially higher! It derails the *law of the ever falling rate of profit* [and prices] discovered by the classical liberal and classical economists of the19th century and championed by Karl Marx. Stuffing the present neo-Mercantilist economy's throat with real natural savings and capital accumulation would make the cronies and banksters choke and suffocate and speed up the process of transcending the present system as savings is the super charged amniotic fluid that the messianic system now lying in the womb of the present capitalist economic system needs in order to fully develop. Our pregnant mother needs prenatal megavitamins in high doses for she has been starved on purpose over the last 100+ years. Marx wanted socialists to be midwives, not abortionists, and it is time we took up that sacred duty and helped bring the new economic system into the world, strong and healthy. If we want to achieve a utopia for all humanity, there is no other path we can take but the evolutionary path of the full development of the "productive material forces," the Technium. The economic event horizon of the singularity before us shows us the way we need to travel, what is holding us back from achieving this event horizon is our clinging to these outworn and refuted inflationary monetary fallacies of Malthus ala Keynes and the 16th through the 19th century monetary cranks. The sooner we abandon them for good, the faster we can accelerate to the transcendence point, the Omega Point, of the system we have today and its continual creation of artificial scarcity on behalf of a government run and controlled well-connected oligopoly.

Appendix D

Index of Economic Figures, 210 years of declining prices

My Book only contains a small sampling of the facts and figures available that are indicative of the economic singularity that we are presently accelerating toward. Peter Diamandis' book *Abundance*, Matt Ridley's *The Rational Optimist*, the works of Indur Goklany, Julian Simon, Ramez Naam, Hans Rosling and many others, are full of the incredible truth that Abundance is Our Future and that the natural deflation caused by the Technium is the only real mechanism for our getting to utopia from here. The amount of evidence and documentation for the Techno-optimist position is extensive. I could site hundreds of graphs and figures which I have uncovered over years of research, but due to cost constraints in publishing this work and the fact that most of these figures can be found in the works of the Techno-optimists already mentioned above and in their TED videos, I have decided to place most of these figures on my web site at www.TheSingularityandSocialism.com.

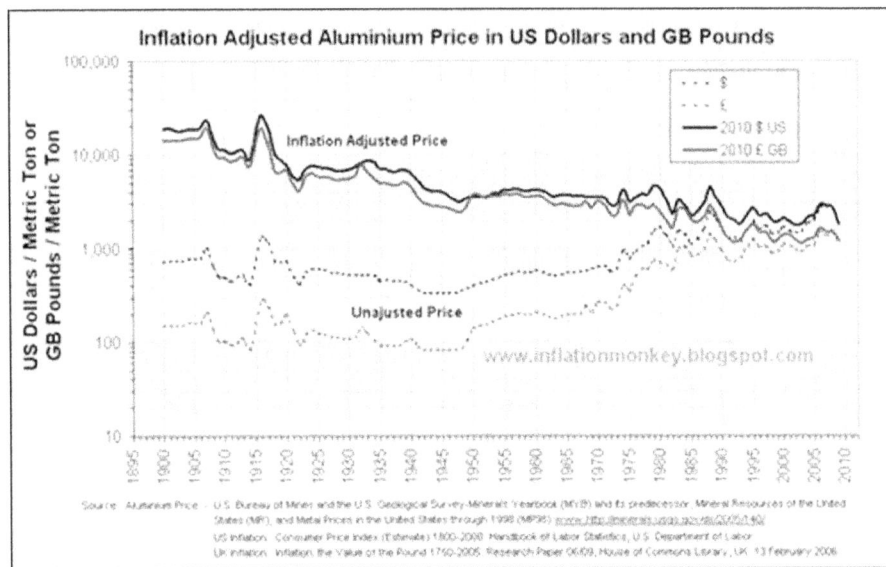

16 Inflation Adjusted Aluminum Prices[373]

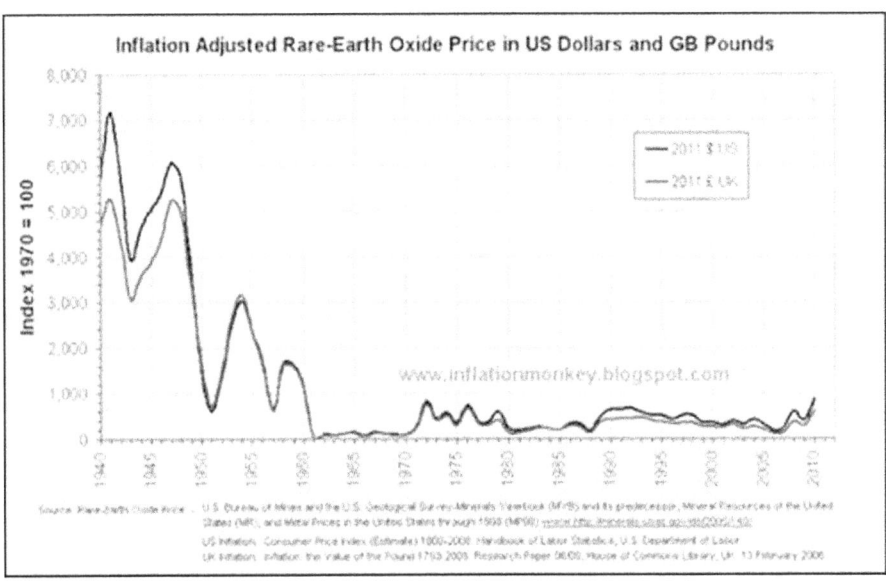

17 Inflation Adjusted Rare Earth Prices[374]

---

373 "Inflation Adjusted Aluminium Price in US Dollars and GB Pounds," *Inflation Monkey* (Blog), www.InflationMonkeyBlogSpot.com
374 "Inflation Adjusted Rare-Earth Price in US Dollars and GB Pounds," *Inflation Monkey* (blog), www.InflationMonkeyBlogSpot.com.

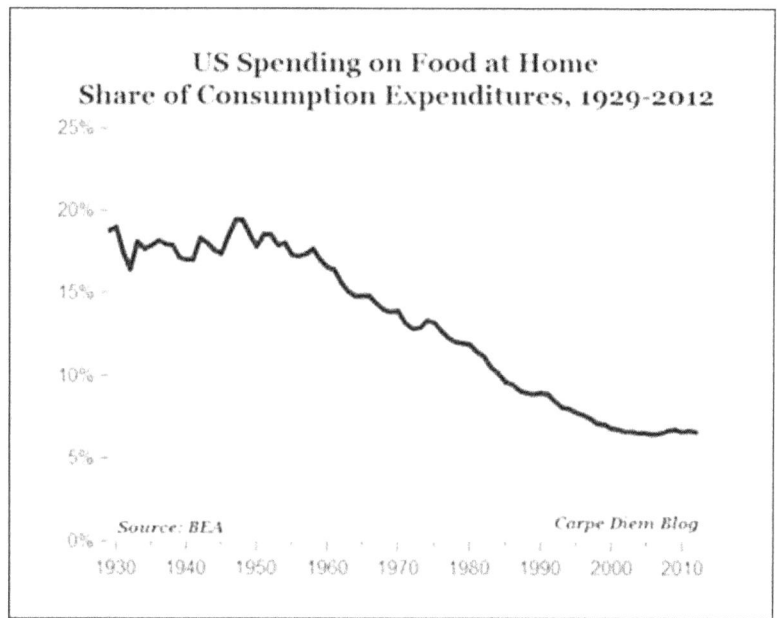

18 Inflation Adjusted US Food Prices[375]

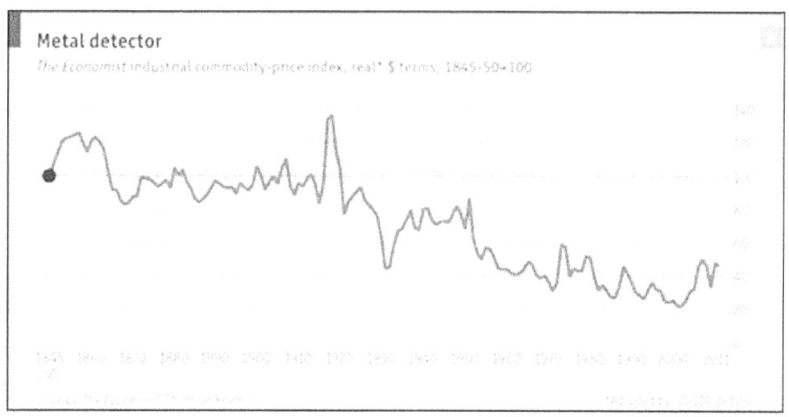

19 Inflation Adjusted Metal Prices 1845-2011[376]

---

375   Mark J. Perry, "When it comes to spending on food as share of total consumer expenditures, Americans have the most affordable food on the planet, and it's gotten better over time," *American Enterprise Institute*, (Blog), http://www.aei.org/publication/when-it-comes-to-spending-on-food-as-share-of-total-consumer-expenditures-americans-have-the-most-affordable-food-on-the-planet-and-its-gotten-better-over-time/
376   R.A. "Hitting Our Limits?" *The Economist* (Blog) Oct 14, 2011, http://www.economist.com/blogs/freeexchange/2011/10/resource-prices.

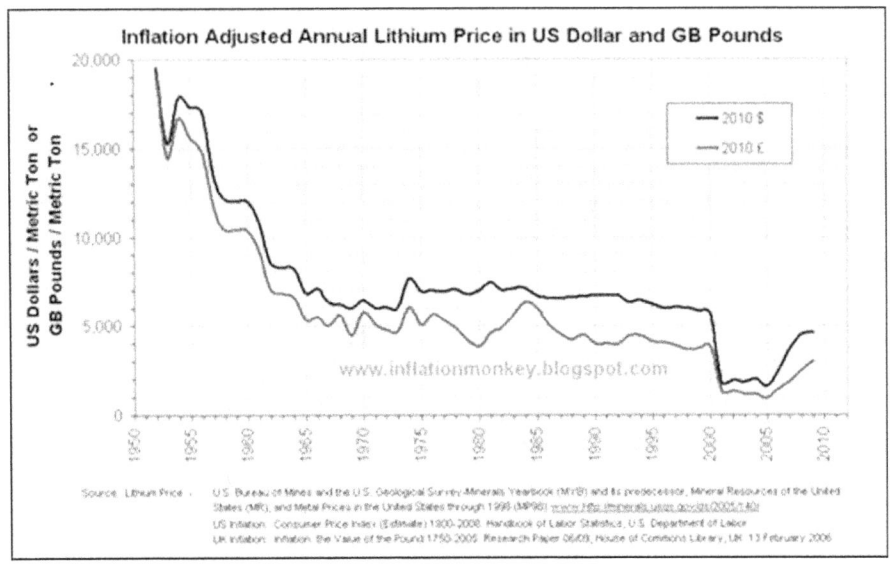

20 Inflation Adjusted Annual Lithium Prices[377]

---

377 "Inflation adjusted Annual Lithium Price in US Dollars and GB Pounds," *Inflation Monkey* (Blog), www.inflationmonkey.blogspot.com.

Bibliography

Anderson, Chris. *FREE: How Today's Smartest Businesses Profit by Giving Something for Nothing.* New York: Hyperion Books, 2009.

Andriopolous, Stefan. "The Invisible Hand: Supernatural Agency in Political Economy and the Gothic Novel." *ELH*, Vol. 66. No. 3 (Fall 1999): 739-758.

Arthur, Brian. "Complexity and the Economy." In *The Complexity Vision and the Teaching of Economics,* edited by David Colander, 19-28. Cheltenham, UK: Edward Elder, 2000.

Arthur, Brian, Steven N. Durlauf, David A. Lane ed., *The Economy as an Evolving System II,* Boulder, CO: Westview Press, 1997.

Ayau, Manuel F. *Not a Zero Sum Game, the Paradox of Exchange.* Guatemala: Universidad Francisco Marroquin, 2007.

Barry, Norman. "The Tradition of Spontaneous Order" *Library of Economics and Liberty.* 1982, (Retrieved November 6, 2012): B.4. http://www.econlib.org/library/Essays/LtrLbrty/bryTSO1.html.

Beckworth, David, ed., *Boom and Bust Banking: The Causes of the Great Recession.* Oakland, CA: The Independent Institute, 2012.

Brutzkus, Boris. *Economic Planning in Soviet Russia*. Westport, CN: Hyperion Press Inc., reprint ed., 1993.

Burke, James. *The Day The Universe Changed*. Film. Produced by Richard Reisz. 1985: United Kingdom: BBC: RKO Pictures. TV.

Chardin, Pierre Teilhard de. *The Future of Man*. [1959] New York: Image Books/Doubleday, 2004.

-. *The Phenomenon of Man*. [1955] New York: Harper Perennial, 2008.

Colander, David, ed. *The Complexity Vision and the Teaching of Economics*. Cheltenham, UK: Edward Elgar, 2000.

D'Amato, Paul. *The Meaning of Marxism*. Chicago: Haymarket Books, 2006.

Desol, Chantal. *The Unlearned Lessons of the Twentieth Century: Essays on Late Modernity*. Wilmington, DE: ISI Books, 2006.

-. *Icarus Fallen: The Search for Meaning in an Uncertain World*. Wilmington, DE: ISI Books, 2003.

De Soto, Jesus Huerta. *Socialism, Economic Calculation and Entrepreneurship*. Cheltenham, UK: MPG Books Group, 2010.

Desai, Meghnad, *Marx's Revenge: The Resurgence of Capitalism and the Death of Statist Socialism*. London: Verso, 2004.

Diamandis, Peter and Steven Kotler. *Abundance: the Future is Better than You Think*. New York: Free Press, 2012.

-. *Abundance is Our Future*. TED.com video. 16.14 min. 2012. http://www.ted.com/talks/lang/en/peter_diamandis_abundance_is_our_future.html.

Fichte, Johann G. "What is a People in the Higher Meaning of the Word, and What is Love of Fatherland," in *European Romanticism: A Brief History with Documents*, edited by Warren Breckman, 113-122 (New York: Bedford/St Martin's, 2008),

Fuller, R. Buckminster. *Utopia or Oblivion: the Prospects for Humanity*, edited by Jaime Snyder. [1969] New York: Lars Müller Publishers, 2008.

Gevers, Johann. "The Four Pillars of a Decentralized Society," *Youtube:TEDxZug*, July 7, 2014, 16.12 minutes, https://www.youtube.com/watch?v=8oeiOeDq_Nc.

Goklany, Indur M. "Economic Growth and the State of Humanity." *PERC Policy Series*, PS-21, Bozeman, MT: PERC, (April 2001): 1-28. http://www.perc.org/articles/article185.php.

-. *The Improving State of the World: Why We're Living Longer, Healthier, More Comfortable Lives on a Cleaner Planet.* Washington, DC: Cato Institute Press, 2007.

Gorbis, Marina, *The Nature of the Future.* New York, NY: Free Press, 2013.

Goudge, T.A. "Salvaging the 'Noosphere'" *Mind, New Series.* Vol. 71, No. 284 (Oct. 1962): 543-544. http://www.jstor.org/stable/2251897.

Hayek, F.A., ed. *Capitalism and the Historians.* Chicago: The University of Chicago Press, 1954.

-. *The Constitution of Liberty.* Chicago: The University of Chicago Press, 1960.

-. Economics and Knowledge, *Economica IV* (new ser., 1937), 33-54.

-. *The Fatal Conceit: The Errors of Socialism.* Chicago: The University of Chicago Press, 1988.

-. *The Fortunes of Liberalism:* The Collected Works of F.A. Hayek. Indianapolis, IN: Liberty Fund, 1992.

Heylighen, Francis. "Conceptions of a Global Brain: an Historical Review" *Technological Forecasting and Social Change.* (n.d.): 1-14. http://www.academia.edu/1823746/ Conceptions_of_a_Global_Brain_an_historical_review.

-. (1997): "The Economy as a Distributed, Learning Control System" *Communication & Cognition-AI* 13, nos. 2-3 (1997): 207-224.

-. "The Global Superorganism: an evolutionary-cybernetic model of the emerging network society." *Journal of Social and Evolutionary Systems.* (n.d.): 1-37, http://pespmc1.vub.ac.be/Papers/Superorganism.pdf

Hoppe, Hans-Hermann, *A Theory of Socialism and Capitalism.* Auburn, Alabama: Ludwig von Mises Institute, 2010.

Hülsmann, Jörg Guido. *Deflation & Liberty.* Auburn, AL: Ludwig von Mises Institute Press, 2008.

Hutt, W.H., *Keynesianism: Retrospect and Prospect.* Chicago, IL: Henry Regnery Co, 1963.

Johnson, Steve. *Where Good Ideas Come From: The Natural History of Innovation.* New York: Riverhead Books, 2010.

Kapadaia, Reshma, Alyssa Abkowitz, Ian Salisbury and Missy Sullivan. "The Return of Fossil Fuels." *Smart Money Magazine.* August 2012: 52-57.

Karlgaard, Rich. "Americas Missing Wealth," *Forbes*, October 20, 2014. http://www.forbes.com/sites/richkarlgaard/2014/09/30/americas-missing-wealth.

Kelly, Kevin. "The Cosmic Genesis of Technology." *The Technium* (blog). January 2009, http://www.kk.org/thetechnium/archives/2009/01/the_cosmic_gene.php

-. *How Technology Evolves*. TED.com video. 19.58 min. 2005. http://www.ted.com/talks/lang/en/kevin_kelly_on_how_technology_evolves.html

-. New Rules for the New Economy: 10 Radical Strategies for a Connected World. New York: Penguin Books, 1999.

-. "Technology Wants to Be Free." *The Technium* (blog). November 14, 2007. http://www.kk.org/thetechnium/archives/2007/11/technology_want.php.

-. *What Technology Wants*. New York: Viking, 2010.

Kelly, Kel. *The Case for Legalizing Capitalism*. Auburn, AL: Ludwig von Mises Institute Press, 2010.

Keynes, John M. *The General Theory of Employment, Interest and Money*. London, UK: Macmillan, 1939.

Robert Klassen, *Economic Government*. Lincoln, NB, Writers Club Press, 2001.

Kolakowski, Leszek. *Main Currents of Marxism*. [1978] New York, NY: Norton Press, 2005.

Koppl, Roger. "*Policy Implications of Complexity: an Austrian Perspective.*" *In* *The Complexity Vision and the Teaching of Economics,* edited by David Colander, *97-117. Northampton, MA: Edward Algar, 2000.*

Kuehnelt-Leddihn, Erik von. *Leftism Revisited: From de Sade to Marx to Hitler and Pol Pot.* Washington, DC: Regnery Gateway, 1990.

Kurzweil, Ray. *The Accelerating Power of Technology.* TED.com video, 23 min. 2005, http://www.ted.com/talks/lang/en/ray_kurzweil_on_ how_technology_will_transform_us.html

-. "The Law of Increasing Returns." *Accelerating Intelligence.* (blog), March 7, 2001. http://www.kurzweilai.net/the-law-of-accelerat-ing-returns.

-. "Kurzweil's Law." *Kurzweil Accelerating Intelligence.* (blog), January 12, 2004. http://www.kurzweilai.net/kurzweils-law-aka-the-law-of-ac-celerating-returns.

-. *The Singularity is Near.* New York: Penguin Books, 2005.

Lenin, Vladimir I. "Imperialism, The Highest Stage of Capitalism." In *The Essential Works of Lenin: What is to Be Done?" and Other Writings,* edited by Henry M. Christman, 177-270. New York: Dover Publications, Inc., 1987.

Lewis, Hunter. *Where Keynes Went Wrong: And Why World Governments Keep Creating Inflation, Bubbles, and Busts.* Mt. Jackson, VA: Axios Press, 2009.

-. *Free Prices Now: Fixing the Economy by Abolishing the FED.* Edinburg, VA: AC²Books, 2013.

Lomborg, Bjorn. *The Skeptical Environmentalist: Measuring the Real State of the World.* New York: Cambridge University Press, 2001.

Magee, Glenn Alexander. *Hegel and the Hermetic Tradition.* London, UK: Cornell University Press, 2001.

Marx, Karl. *Capital, A Critique of Political Economy.* Edited by Frederick Kautsky, Chicago: Charles H. Kerr & Co., 1909. http://oll.liberty-fund.org/title/965

-. *The Communist Manifesto.* Edited by Frederic L. Bender. New York: W. W. Norton & Company, Inc., 1988.

Matt, Daniel C. *The Essential Kabbalah: The Heart of Jewish Mysticism.* New York: Harper Collins, 1996.

Meeks, Ronald L., ed. *Marx and Engels on the Population Bomb.* Berkeley, CA: Ramparts Press, 1971.

Miranda, Jose. *Marx Against the Marxists.* New York: Orbis Books, 1986.

Mises, Ludwig von. *The Clash of Group Interests.* [1945] Auburn, AL: Ludwig von Mises Institute Press, 2011.

-. *Critique of Interventionism.* [1929] New York: The Foundation for Economic Education, 1996.

-. *Economic Calculation in the Socialist Commonwealth.* [1920] Auburn, AL: Praxeology Press 1990

-. *Economic Policy: Thoughts for Today and Tomorrow.* Chicago: Regnery/Gateway, Inc. 1979.

-. *The Free Market and Its Enemies: Pseudo-Science, Socialism, and Inflation.* New York: Foundation for Economic Education, 2004.

-. *Human Action: A Treatise on Economics.* [1949] San Francisco: Fox & Wilkes, 1996.

-. *Marxism Unmasked: From Delusion to Destruction.* New York: Foundation for Economic Education, 2006.

-. *Middle of the Road Policy Leads to Socialism.* Auburn, AL: Ludwig von Mises Institute Press, 1988.

-. *Planning for Freedom.* [1952] Grove City, PA: Libertarian Press, 1980,

-. *Socialism: An Economic and Sociological Analysis.* [1922] Indianapolis, IN: Liberty Fund Inc., 1981.

Mitchell, Melanie. *Complexity a Guided Tour.* New York: Oxford University Press, 2009.

Molyneux, John, *What is the Real Marxist Tradition.* Chicago, Haymarket Books, 2003.

Popper, Karl R. *The Open Society and Its Enemies: Hegel and Marx Vol. 2.* Princeton, NJ.: Princeton University Press, 1962.

Postrell, Virginia. *The Future and Its Enemies.* New York: The Free Press, 1998.

Raico, Ralph. "The Rise, Fall, and Renaissance of Classical Liberalism." *Ludwig von Mises Institute,* (blog). August 23, 2010. http://mises. org/daily/4600.

Read, Leonard E. *I Pencil: My Family Tree as Told to Leonard E. Read.* New York: Foundation for Economic Education, 1958.

Reisman, George. *The Government Against the Economy.* Ottawa, Canada: Jameson Books, 1979.

Revel, Jean-Francois. *The Totalitarian Temptation.* New York, NY: Penguin Books, 1978.

-. *Without Marx or Jesus: The New American Revolution Has Begun.* New York, NY: Doubleday & Co, 1970.

-. *The Last Exit to Utopia: The Survival of Sovietism in a Post-Soviet Era.* New York, NY: Encounter Books, 2009.

Reynolds, Glenn. *An Army of Davids: How Markets and Technology Empower Ordinary People to Beat Big Media, Big Government and Other Goliaths.* Nashville, TN: Nelson Current, 2006.

Ridley, Matt. *The Rational Optimist: How Prosperity Evolves.* New York: Harper Perennial, 2010.

-. *When Ideas Have Sex.* TED.com video. 16.27 min. 2010. http://www.ted.com/talks/lang/en/matt_ridley_when_ideas_have_sex.html.

Rockwell, Llewellyn H. *The Left, The Right, & The State.* Auburn, AL: Ludwig von Mises Institute Press, 2008.

Rothbard, Murray. *The Betrayal of the American Right.* Auburn, AL: Ludwig von Mises Institute Press, 2007.

-. *Economic Controversies.* Auburn, AL: Ludwig von Mises Institute Press, 2011.

-. *Economic Thought before Adam Smith, Vol. I.* Auburn, AL: Edward Elgar Publishing, 2006.

-.*Classical Economics: An Austrian Perspective on the History of Economic Thought, Vol II.*, Auburn, AL: Edward Elgar Publishing, 2006.

-. *Egalitarianism as a Revolt Against Nature.* Auburn, AL: Ludwig von Mises Institute Press, 2000.

-. "Karl Marx: Communist as Religious Eschatologist." *The Review of Austrian Economics*, Vol. 4, (1990): 123-179.

Schiff, Peter. *Why an Economy Grows and Why it Crashes.* Hoboken, NJ: Wiley & Sons Inc., 2010.

-. The Real Crash: How to Save Yourself and Your Country. New York, NY: St. Martin's Press, 2012.

Schumpeter, Joseph A. *Capitalism, Socialism and Democracy.* [1942] New York: Harper Perennial, 2008.

Servan-Schreiber, Jean Jacques. *The Radical Alternative.* New York: W.W. Norton & Co. Inc., 1971.

Shafarevich, Igor. *The Socialist Phenomenon.* New York: Harper & Row, 1980.

Shaffer, Butler. *Boundaries of Order: Private Property as a Social System.* Auburn, AL: Ludwig von Mises Institute Press, 2009.

Simon, Julian L., ed. *The State of Humanity.* Malden, MA: Blackwell Publishers, 1997.

-. *The Ultimate Resource*. Princeton, NJ: Princeton University Press, 1981.

-. *The Ultimate Resource II*, Princeton, NJ: Princeton University Press, 1996.

Skousen, Mark. *The Structure of Production*. New York, NY: New York University Press, 1990.

Smith, Adam. *The Wealth of Nations: An Inquiry into the Nature and Causes of*. [1776] Washington, DC: Regnery Publishing, 1998.

Smith, Craig R. and Lowell Ponte, The Great Debasement: The 100 Year Dying of the Dollar and How to Get America's Money Back. Phoenix, AZ: Idea Factory Press, 2012.

Sokal, Alan and Jean Bricmont, *Fashionable Nonsense: Postmodern Intellectual's Abuse of Science*. New York, NY: Picador, 1998.

Steele, David Ramsay, *From Marx to Mises: Post-Capitalist Society and the Challenge of Economic Calculation*. La Salle, IL: Open Court Publishing Co., 1992.

Surette, Leon. *The Birth of Modernism: Ezra Pound, T.S. Eliot, W.B. Yeats and the Occult*. London, UK: McGill-Queens University press, 1994.

Tamedly, Elisabeth L. *Socialism and International Economic Order*. Auburn, AL: Ludwig von Mises Institute Press, 2007.

Thierer, Adam D. "How Free Computers are Filling the Digital Divide." *Backgrounder on Internet and Technology #1361, The Heritage Foundation*, (April 20, 2000). http://www.heritage.org/research/reports/2000/04/how-free-computers-are-filling-the-digital-divide

Thwaites, Thomas. *How I built a Toaster-from scratch*. Ted.com Video. 10.52 min. 2010, http://www.ted.com/talks/thomas_thwaites_how_i_built_a_toaster_from_scratch.html.

Tucker, Jeffery, *It's a Jetsons World: Private Miracles and Public Crimes*. Auburn, Al: Mises Institute, 2011.

Tucker, Robert C. *Philosophy & Myth in Karl Marx*, 3rd edition. [1961] New Brunswick, NJ: Transaction Publishers, 2001.

Ullman-Margalit, Edna. "The Invisible Hand and the Cunning of Reason." *Social Research*, Vol. 64, No. 2 (Summer 1979): 181-198.

Voeglin, Eric. *Science, Politics and Gnosticism*. [1968] Wilmington, DE: ISI books, 2004.

Waldrop, M. Mitchell. *Complexity: The Emerging Science at the Edge of Chaos*. New York: Simon & Schuster, 1992.

Watson, George. *The Lost Literature of Socialism*. Cambridge, UK: The Lutterworth Press, 1998.

Young, George M. *The Russian Cosmists: The Esoteric Futurism of Nikolai Federov and His Followers*. Oxford: Oxford University Press, 2012.

About The Author

C. **James Townsend** holds an M.A. in Liberal Arts from California State University Sacramento and a B.A. in Integrated Studies and a minor in physics from the same institution. He is seeking to obtain his Doctorate in Future Studies in the near future. His interests include: physics, Complexity Theory, political and economic philosophy, Marxism, Techno-Optimism, comparative mystical religions-Gnosticism, Taoism, Zen Buddhism, the Russian Cosmists, Transhumanism and Future Studies. His physical interests include Cheng Man Ching style Tai Chi Chuan and Aikido.

The *Singularity and Socialism* is his first published work and he is presently working on a companion book that takes up the ramifications of the coming economic singularity and the financial instruments that will need to be invented in order to stave off the coming inevitable collapse of the welfare-warfare state and burgeoning technological unemployment.